Kevin Hoffman

Sams **Teach Yourself**

Mac OS® X Lion™ App Development

in **24** **Hours**

SAMS   800 East 96th Street, Indianapolis, Indiana, 46240 USA

Sams Teach Yourself Mac OS® X Lion™ App Development in 24 Hours

ISBN-13: 978-0-672-33581-5
ISBN-10: 0-672-33581-6

The Library of Congress Cataloging-in-Publication data is on file.

Printed in the United States of America

First Printing March 2012

Trademarks

All terms mentioned in this book that are known to be trademarks or service marks have been appropriately capitalized. Sams Publishing cannot attest to the accuracy of this information. Use of a term in this book should not be regarded as affecting the validity of any trademark or service mark.

Warning and Disclaimer

Every effort has been made to make this book as complete and as accurate as possible, but no warranty or fitness is implied. The information provided is on an "as is" basis. The author and the publisher shall have neither liability nor responsibility to any person or entity with respect to any loss or damages arising from the information contained in this book.

Bulk Sales

Sams Publishing offers excellent discounts on this book when ordered in quantity for bulk purchases or special sales. For more information, please contact

U.S. Corporate and Government Sales
1-800-382-3419
corpsales@pearsontechgroup.com

For sales outside of the U.S., please contact

International Sales
international@pearson.com

Editor-in-Chief
Greg Wiegand

Executive Editor
Neil Rowe

Development Editor
Mark Renfrow

Managing Editor
Kristy Hart

Project Editor
Andy Beaster

Copy Editor
Barbara Hacha

Indexer
Larry Sweazy

Proofreader
Christal White,
Language Logistics,
LLC

Technical Editor
Mike Givens

Publishing Coordinator
Cindy Teeters

Book Designer
Gary Adair

Compositor
Nonie Ratcliff

Contents at a Glance

Table of Contents

About the Author

Kevin Hoffman has been programming since he was 10 years old, when he got his start writing BASIC programs on a Commodore VIC-20. Since then, he has been obsessed with building software and doing so with clean, elegant, simple code in as many languages as he can learn. He has presented twice at Apple's Worldwide Developer Conference, guest lectured at Columbia University on iPhone programming, and built several iOS Apps available in the App Store. He is currently Vice President, Global Information Technology for Barclays Capital, where he is involved in all aspects of the software life cycle—from testing standards to coding standards and from architecture to implementation of powerful, high-volume, low-latency systems.

Dedication

I would like to dedicate this book to Angelica and Isabella, two of the most amazing women I have ever met who put up with me as I complain that my code samples won't work and tolerate me pacing back and forth trying to figure out how to finish a chapter. Most importantly, they encourage me to follow my dreams and do the things that make me happy.

Acknowledgments

This book would never have happened were it not for the efforts of Apple Developer Evangelists like Matt Drance and Mike Jurewitz. One day in New York City, I went into the basement conference rooms of a building a prejudiced man, convinced that no development platform was better than C# and WPF. I left NYC that day enlightened, my horizons broadened and realizing that there is a beauty that lies between the shades of gray among the many development platforms and environments.

We Want to Hear from You!

As the reader of this book, *you* are our most important critic and commentator. We value your opinion and want to know what we're doing right, what we could do better, what areas you'd like to see us publish in, and any other words of wisdom you're willing to pass our way.

You can e-mail or write me directly to let me know what you did or didn't like about this book—as well as what we can do to make our books stronger.

Please note that I cannot help you with technical problems related to the topic of this book, and that due to the high volume of mail I receive, I might not be able to reply to every message.

When you write, please be sure to include this book's title and author as well as your name and phone number or e-mail address. I will carefully review your comments and share them with the author and editors who worked on the book.

E-mail: consumer@samspublishing.com

Mail: Greg Wiegand
Editor-in-Chief
Sams Publishing
800 East 96th Street
Indianapolis, IN 46240 USA

Reader Services

Visit our website and register this book at informit.com/register for convenient access to any updates, downloads, and errata that might be available for this book.

Introduction

Building applications for Mac OS X has never been easier and—more important—has never before enabled such a wide distribution audience or such potential to make money. Because of the new App Store, the time has never been better to be a Mac OS X developer.

This book was written for those with some programming background who want to get into building Mac OS X Lion applications. Each of the 24 hours in this book is designed to quickly introduce you to a new topic that builds on the information you've learned in the previous hours. By the time you finish, you should have a firm grasp on the most important topics for Mac OS X Lion application development, and you should know enough to supplement that learning with additional references, such as Apple's documentation and more in-depth books.

Using this book, you will learn the basics of building Mac OS X Lion applications. To do this, you'll need a computer that has the latest version of Mac OS X Lion installed, and you will need access to the Internet to download and install the developer tools (introduced in Hour 2, "Introduction to the Developer Tools") and access other online resources, such as code downloads and documentation.

Audience and Organization

This book is targeted at those who have some basic familiarity with programming concepts,—but you don't have to be a professional programmer nor do you have to have any prior exposure to Mac OS X or Cocoa development.

This book gradually introduces you to the Objective-C programming language and provides you with the object-oriented programming fundamentals that you will need to proceed through all 24 hours.

The following is a list of the hours in this book with a short description of each.

Part I—Mac OS X Lion Programming Basics

Part 1 of the book provides you with the core knowledge you'll need, the foundation on which all the other hours are based. In this part you'll get an introduction to Objective-C and the development tools used to build Mac OS X applications.

1. Introduction to Mac OS X Lion

This hour provides an introduction to the new features in the Mac OS X Lion operating system, many of which you will be manipulating with code throughout this book. Some are subtle UX changes that make Mac OS X Lion the best version of Mac OS X yet.

2. Introduction to the Developer Tools

This hour introduces you to Xcode, the main development tool for Mac OS X developers. This tool is not only used for writing and compiling code, but now includes the main design tool, Interface Builder, directly within the Xcode tool.

3. Introducing Objective-C

This hour provides you with a quick and easy introduction to the Objective-C programming language, its history, philosophy, and how it differs from other C-like languages. Don't let the C lineage scare you; Objective-C is a very easy language to use and learn.

4. Object-Oriented Programming with Objective-C

This hour introduces you to some basic object-oriented programming (OOP) concepts such as classes, contracts, and polymorphism and uses Objective-C code to illustrate those concepts. After you start adding OOP to Objective-C, things really start to get fun.

5. Understanding Memory Management

This hour provides you with an overview of the various memory management techniques and technologies available to Objective-C programmers, including a discussion of manual reference counting and the newer, easier way of managing memory: Automatic Reference Counting (ARC).

Part II—Cocoa Application Programming Basics

Now that you've completed 5 hours of basics and introductory material, it's time to start building actual Cocoa applications. In this part of the book, you'll learn about Cocoa and its scope and history, how to use controls and lay out your controls within windows, use data binding, display interactive collections and lists, and support new multitouch devices and gestures.

6. Introducing Cocoa

In this hour, you will learn the basics of building Cocoa applications and get an overview of exactly what Cocoa is and how to use it.

7. Using Controls and Layout with Cocoa

This hour provides an overview of the controls available to Cocoa application developers as well as the various layout mechanisms available for organizing and displaying those controls.

8. Creating Interactive Applications

This hour builds on the previous hours and adds some interactivity to your applications by showing you how to invoke code in response to user actions and how to programmatically manipulate UI elements.

9. Creating Data-Bound Interfaces

This hour shows you how to declaratively bind properties of UI elements to underlying data, enabling more powerful and robust user interfaces that require less code to create and maintain.

10. Working with Tables and Collections

In this hour, you learn how to extend your data binding knowledge to working with lists of data that appear as tables or collections.

11. Working with Multitouch and Gestures

In this hour, you learn how Mac OS X (and especially Lion) provide developers with powerful, easy-to-use mechanisms for recognizing and responding to multitouch gestures on any number of devices, including trackpads and magic mice.

Part III—Working with Data

This section of the book deals with something that virtually every application needs to have in some form: data. It covers user defaults, core data, documents, and even Apple's new ubiquitous, synchronized data storage system called iCloud.

12. Working with User Defaults

This hour shows you how (and when) you can read and write data that is stored alongside your application as user-specific application preferences.

13. Working with Core Data

This hour shows you the power of Core Data, a framework that enables your application to store, retrieve, and query relational data in XML, binary, and SQLite.

14. Working with Documents, Versions, and Autosave

This hour extends your knowledge of data binding, collections, and Core Data to show you how to build document-oriented applications and utilize some new Lion features such as versioning and autosave.

15. Working with Apple's iCloud

This hour shows you how to extend your knowledge of document-oriented applications to illustrate how your application can store, query, and maintain documents in the cloud using iCloud.

Part IV—Building Advanced Mac Applications

In this section, you start exploring some of the more advanced features of Mac OS X Lion applications as well as some user interface elements and patterns that differentiate sample applications from real-world, commercial applications.

16. Using Alert Panels and Sheets

This hour shows you how to alert your users to important information or prompt them to supply information using Alert Panels and Sheets.

17. Working with Images

The use of images can enrich virtually any application when done tastefully. This hour shows you how to read, write, display, and manipulate images within your Mac OS X Lion application. You'll be surprised at how much you can do with images in just a few lines of code!

18. Using Popovers

This hour shows you how to display secondary windows that are anchored contextually to other windows or controls. The iPad made popover windows a familiar paradigm to millions of people, and now you can use popovers in your Mac OS X Lion application.

19. Building Animated User Interfaces

This hour shows you how to create and use animation sequences to give your applications the additional life, energy, and reactivity that people have come to expect from Mac OS X and iOS applications over the years.

20. Consuming Web Services

The Internet provides a wealth of data and functionality to enhance or support your application. This hour shows you how to take advantage of web services and how your Mac OS X application can connect to them to send and receive data.

21. Building Full-Screen Applications

This hour shows you how to take advantage of the new full-screen functionality available to all Mac OS X Lion applications.

22. Supporting Drag-and-Drop Behavior

This hour shows you how to add drag-and-drop support to your application, which can dramatically increase user satisfaction and overall user experience.

23. Building Apps for the Mac App Store

This hour introduces you to the new Mac App Store, how to create a developer account, and the process through which you can submit your application to the App Store.

24. Supporting In-App Purchases

Building on the information contained in the previous hour, this hour shows you how you can give your users the ability to buy extended functionality and features directly within your application using the StoreKit framework.

Conventions Used in This Book

The following styles are found throughout the book to help the reader with important points of interest.

This is the "Watch Out" style. These boxes present important information about the subject that the reader may find helpful to avoid potential problems.

This is the "Did You Know" style. These boxes provide additional information about a subject that may be of interest to the reader.

This is a "By The Way" style. These boxes usually refer the reader to an off-topic subject of interest.

Resource Files

All the code used in this book is available for download online. In addition to being easier than attaching a CD-ROM to the book, this gives us the ability to update the code samples as necessary.

You can download the code samples for this book from the SAMS/Pearson website. Additional information on the code downloads for this book may be available from the author's website at http://www.kotancode.com.

Keep an eye on informit.com/title/9780672335815 for updates regarding this book.

HOUR 1

Introduction to Mac OS X Lion

What you'll learn in this hour:

▶ Overview of Lion's New Features

▶ Multitouch Gestures

▶ Full-Screen Applications

▶ Mission Control

▶ The Mac App Store

▶ Launchpad

▶ Autosaving, Versions, and Resume

▶ AirDrop and Screen Sharing Enhancements

Apple refers to Mac OS X as "the world's most advanced desktop operating system" and Mac OS X Lion is the newest version of this operating system. Throughout this book you will learn how to write code that harnesses the features of this OS both old and new.

Before we get into writing code that utilizes these new features, in this hour we're going to take a tour of these features. After you know more about these features, you'll find it's easier to learn how to write code for them.

Introducing Mac OS X Lion

In this section we're going to take a tour of some of the new features of Mac OS X Lion. With this release of Mac OS X, Apple has incorporated some of the most compelling features of its mobile operating system, iOS, and the newest advancements in user interaction and technology.

Multitouch Gestures

As the popularity of devices such as the iPhone, iPod Touch, and the iPad grows, so too does the popularity of multitouch gestures. Most users of mobile devices today are already familiar with touch screens. In fact, users are so familiar with controlling applications with multitouch gestures that they have come to expect this capability.

Apple has had some support for multitouch gestures in its trackpads since Mac OS X Leopard, but Lion has greatly enhanced support for many new gesture types.

Launching Mission Control

Mission Control is a feature new to Mac OS X Lion that combines the best intentions of Spaces (providing virtual desktops) and Expose (displaying all open windows at a glance) from previous versions of Mac OS X to give you a quick look at everything running on your computer. A three-finger swipe upward activates Mission Control. Mission Control can be activated in a number of other ways, including a "hot corner," a keyboard shortcut, a mouse button, clicking the Mission Control icon in your Dock or using the Expose key (F3).

Switching Between Open Applications and Desktops

As users' lives become progressively more intertwined with the Internet and dependent on their computers, they invariably end up with more open applications and are in need of more virtual real estate on their computers.

With a three-finger swipe to the right or to the left, you can now slide the current application or desktop out of the way to make way for the adjacent application. This comes in very handy when you are running multiple full-screen applications and have multiple desktops.

Two-Finger Scrolling

Two-finger scrolling has been around since before Mac OS X Lion; however, there are a few subtle changes to scrolling with this version. The first change is that the scrollbars aren't visible unless you're actually scrolling. This experience mimics that of iOS devices. Additionally, the direction of your two-finger swipe defaults to mimic the direction you want to move the content. This new direction is called *natural* and mimics the scrolling direction and behavior of iOS. Those users used to mousewheel-style scrolling may notice that this is the *opposite* direction of the mousewheel scroll.

Double-Tap for Autozoom

In applications where zooming is applicable for the content being displayed, many now support a new double-tap gesture. Double-tapping with two fingers will perform an autozoom, which will toggle the content between a preset zoom factor and the original zoom factor.

This comes in very handy when you are browsing through photo galleries or other thumbnails and you don't feel like manually resizing the content. Simply double-tap the trackpad with the mouse cursor over the content you want to zoom, and it will automatically zoom to a preset size (determined by the application developer).

Pinch Zoom

Pinching was also available on trackpads before Mac OS X Lion, but the support for pinch zooming is now ubiquitous and available throughout the OS. Simply start touching the trackpad with two fingers touching each other, and move them apart to *zoom in*. Reverse the gesture to *zoom out*.

Navigation by Swiping

Safari on Mac OS X Lion now supports the capability to navigate forward and backward using touch gestures. With two fingers, swipe either left or right, and Safari advances forward or backward in its navigation history. As you'll see later in this book, programming support for this and other common gestures is very easy.

Working with Full-Screen Applications

As mentioned earlier, today's computer users often run many applications at once, and their desktops and screens tend to get cluttered. One solution is Mission Control, which gives users the ability to see everything at a glance.

The other solution is to allow users to focus exclusively on the one application they're working with at the time. Full-screen applications provide an immersive experience that frees users from the distraction of nearby windows, icons, and other content.

Out of the box, all the major applications in Mac OS X Lion support the capability to run in full-screen mode. Safari in full-screen mode presents the user with nothing but the web content; full-screen mail immerses the user in a completely mail-centered screen, and so on. Pages, Photo Booth, and many other applications can be run in full-screen mode.

When an application is running in full-screen mode, the user can navigate to or away from it with the three-finger application switch gesture. You'll see later in this book how to create an application that supports being run in full-screen mode.

Mission Control

Mission Control combines full-screen apps, Dashboard, Expose, and Spaces and merges them all into a single, easy-to-use feature. Think of the giant monitors in the front of the mission control room at NASA, and you get the inspiration for this feature—the capability to see everything important that's going on with your computer at a single glance.

Figure 1.1 shows a sample of what Mission Control looks like on my computer, showing multiple desktops, an application in full-screen mode, and the dashboard.

FIGURE 1.1
Mission Control.

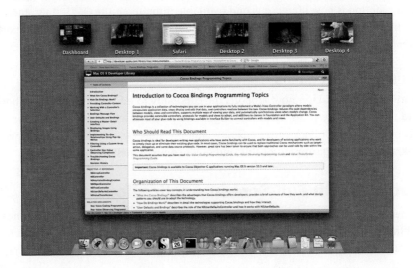

The Mac App Store

While available to Macs running Snow Leopard, the Mac App Store comes built in with Mac OS X Lion. From a developer standpoint, this is probably the most important advancement in Mac application development since the first version of Mac OS X.

As you'll learn later in the book, the Mac App store provides an application publication and distribution channel that can potentially reach every single Mac owner on the planet, all without any initial investment on your part other than the price of the annual Mac OS X Developer membership ($99/year).

> We discuss signing up for Mac OS X Developer membership later in the book.

By the Way

The only other application distribution channel with such a low barrier to entry is the iOS App Store. If you think about everything involved in trying to get your application published, noticed by users, available for download, *and* handling the credit card purchase of your application, Apple's taking 30% of each product purchase seems like a bargain considering how much traditional distribution channels can cost to get shrink-wrapped boxes into traditional brick-and-mortar stores.

Launchpad

Anyone with an iPad, iPhone, or iPod Touch is intimately familiar with the *springboard*, the main interface used for locating and launching applications on the device. All your applications are laid out in a multipage grid, and you have the option of grouping them into arbitrary groups.

Mac OS X Lion incorporates this user experience in the form of *Launchpad*. When you activate Launchpad, it will bring up a multipage grid of all the applications installed on your device. You can group applications and choose on which page and in which order they appear.

With Launchpad running, just click (or tap) and hold one of the application icons and they start wiggling, just like they do on iOS. You can drag one application over top of another application to create a new group containing those applications. A simple two-finger swipe will let you swipe between multiple Launchpad pages.

Figure 1.2 shows an example of what Launchpad looks like on my machine.

Resume, Autosave, and Versions

With Mac OS X Lion, applications will, by default, open back up in the same state they were in when you shut them down. This includes everything from the currently open file to window position and everything in between. When software updates require your computer to reboot, you no longer have to worry about saving everything, rebooting, and then trying to remember how you had everything laid out before. All your apps will start back up again in their original state after the reboot.

FIGURE 1.2
Launchpad.

By default, all Mac OS X Lion document-based applications autosave their documents. You never again have to worry about whether you remembered to save a document before you closed an application or about losing work because you forgot to press Command-S.

To complement the new autosave feature is the Versions feature. Those familiar with Time Machine will recognize some of the inspiration for this feature. The Versions feature keeps track of the autosaved snapshots of your application's documents over time and allows you to *visually* compare them side-by-side with the current version of your document. This gives users incredible flexibility but, more importantly, gives them incredible confidence to use your application to work on crucial documents without fear of accidental erasure or being unable to fix a mistake.

Figure 1.3 shows a sample application's document window being compared against previous versions. As you'll see later in this book, allowing your application to support Versions, Resume, and autosave is trivial (and in some cases requires no work at all).

AirDrop

AirDrop is a great new feature that allows for quick, encrypted file sharing among nearby computers, and it doesn't even require access to a Wi-Fi access point. Depending on the user's hardware, this icon may not show up, but for those machines supported by AirDrop, click the AirDrop icon in the Finder sidebar to start securely sharing files with other users nearby who are running Mac OS X Lion (and also looking at the AirDrop screen).

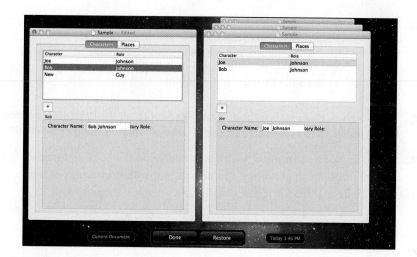

FIGURE 1.3
Comparing a document against previous versions.

Screen Sharing

Screen Sharing has been around since Mac OS X 10.5 Leopard, but it received some upgrades in Mac OS X Lion. With Lion, Screen Sharing supports full-screen mode, logging into remote screens with a different account, and several other enhancements.

Summary

This hour was an introduction to whet your appetite about the new features supported by Mac OS X Lion. These new features combine to create a powerful, appealing, incredible new operating system. As a Mac developer, you can create amazing applications for users of this operating system that will feel like native Mac applications, support the new Mac OS X Lion features, and, hopefully, even make you some money in the process.

Q&A

Q. *What new features in Lion improve the document editing experience?*

A. Autosaving, Versions, and Resume alleviate a lot of the stress usually associated with editing documents and worrying about ruining, losing, or forgetting your files.

Q. *What new feature available in recent versions of Mac OS X gives developers access to virtually every Mac user?*

A. The Mac App Store gives developers a means to market, distribute, and sell their applications with virtually no initial investment.

Q. *What feature gives you quick and easy access to all your installed applications similar to the way you can see your apps on an iPhone or an iPad?*

A. The Launchpad application, which is available on the dock and through convenient multi-touch gestures if you have a Mac with a trackpad such as a fairly modern Macbook Pro or you are using Apple's Magic Mouse.

HOUR 2

Introduction to the Developer Tools

What you'll learn in this hour:

▶ The Mac Developer Center
▶ Creating an Apple Developer Account
▶ Becoming a Paid Member of the Mac Developer Program
▶ Downloading Xcode and Other Developer Tools
▶ A Tour of Xcode

Before you can start writing applications for Mac OS X Lion, you're going to need the developer tools. In addition, you will need to know how to use the Mac Developer Center, browse the online documentation, and locate online resources.

In this hour, you learn about the Mac Developer Center, including how to become a registered Mac developer and how to use the documentation and other resources available in the Mac Developer Center.

After showing you how to establish yourself as a Mac developer, the rest of this hour focuses on acquiring, installing, and using the development tools that you will need for each of the hours remaining in the book.

Introducing the Mac Developer Center

The Mac Developer Center (Mac Dev Center) is where many Mac developers go in search of information and downloads. Think of the Mac Dev Center as a portal through which developers can access virtually everything they need for Mac development, including documentation, sample code, additional technical resources such as downloads, and a link to the areas for submitting an application to the App Store (which you'll see later in this book during Hours 23 and 24).

To reach the Mac Dev Center, open your browser to http://developer.apple.com/mac. When you first arrive at this page as a guest, you will see content that resembles that of Figure 2.1.

FIGURE 2.1
The Mac Dev Center landing page.

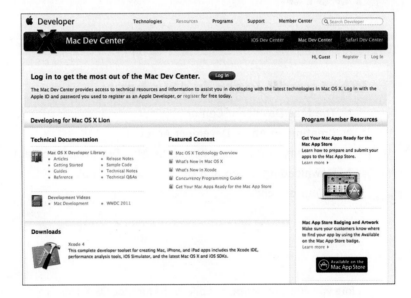

Without creating an account, guests have access to quite a bit of information on this site. Unregistered users can access virtually all documentation and sample code for non beta products like iOS and Mac OS X.

By the Way

Technically, you do not need a developer account to obtain the development tools and use them. However, it is free to register and as you'll see later in this hour, you need a registered developer account to pay for the Mac Developer Program, the program that allows you to submit apps to the App Store.

You should know that there are three different levels of access to the Mac Dev Center, all of which you will learn about in this hour:

▶ **Guest**—Anonymous users can browse documentation, view and download code samples, and download any free and publicly available tools (like Xcode).

▶ **Registered**—A registered Apple Developer has more access to technical resources and downloads. When you register as an Apple Developer, you become eligible to become part of the Mac Developer Program and the iOS Developer Program.

▶ **Mac Developer**—As someone who has a registered Apple Developer account and who has subscribed to the Mac Developer Program, you have access to pre-release versions of Mac OS X, documentation on beta and developer pre-view products. More important is that paying members of the Mac Developer Program are allowed to submit apps to the Mac App Store.

Creating an Apple Developer Account

Registering as an Apple Developer is straightforward (and more importantly, *free*). To get started, just click the Register link at the top of the landing page. (You can see this link in Figure 2.1.)

Figure 2.2 shows a sample of what you might see after clicking the Register link.

FIGURE 2.2
Registering as an Apple Developer.

Although the screenshot indicates that you get access to Xcode 3, your Apple Developer Account will have access to Xcode 4 before this book is printed.

Developer Accounts had access to Xcode 4 at the time of this book's writing; Apple just hadn't changed the content of the new developer registration page to reflect that.

Click the Get Started button to bring up the first of several screens that will ask you for your personal and professional information, as shown in Figure 2.3.

FIGURE 2.3
Registering as an Apple Developer on the Apple ID screen.

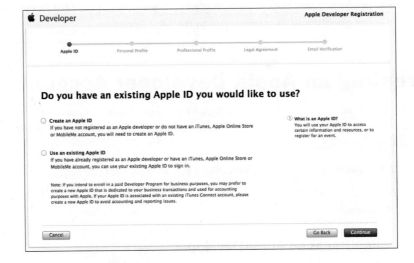

As shown in Figure 2.3, the first thing you need to do is create a new Apple ID or sign in using an existing one.

If you have an existing Apple ID that you obtained by purchasing applications from the iOS App Store or from buying music from iTunes, you can use that Apple ID, and that ID will then be configured as an Apple Developer.

Like an Xbox Live ID, a Windows Live ID, or a Google ID, the Apple ID is a catch-all identity that Apple uses for all your Apple-related activity, including buying music, applications, renting movies, and accessing developer resources.

If you want to create a new Apple ID, you can do so even if you already have an existing ID that you use for iOS apps or iTunes. After you have established the Apple ID you want to use as your Apple Developer ID, you can continue through this wizard and fill out your personal and professional information. Be *very* careful when entering this information because some information, such as your business address, is remarkably difficult to change in the future.

Many Apple Developers choose to create a new Apple ID to use exclusively for development. This way, their iTunes purchases, App Purchases, and development activity isn't all associated with the same account. Ultimately the choice is yours.

After you have created (or mapped) your Apple ID and have finished filling out all the necessary forms, you will be flagged as an Apple Developer. You will receive an email asking you to confirm your identity. You can perform this confirmation either by clicking the link sent to you in the email or by pasting the confirmation code into the designated website. Registered Apple Developers have access to more documentation and prerelease technical resources than unregistered guest users do.

Throughout the rest of this book, you may find that you need to access resources available only to registered Apple Developers. I highly recommend that before you continue with the rest of this hour, you take this opportunity to become a registered Apple Developer. The last two hours of this book will be physically impossible for you to complete without being both a registered developer and a part of the Mac Developer Program.

Becoming a Member of the Mac Developer Program

Now that you are a registered Apple Developer, you should give some very serious consideration to becoming a member of the Mac Developer Program. In addition to the obvious benefits of being able to download prerelease versions of Mac OS X and access additional technical resources, the biggest benefit of becoming a member of this program is the ability to submit applications to the App Store.

As you will see in Hour 23, "Submitting to the Mac App Store," the App Store provides Mac developers with unprecedented distribution, reach, and marketing for their applications with no up-front cost other than the annual subscription fee. Compared to traditional distribution channels and taking your chances with flaky, often-down file distribution sites or hosting your own download and update server, the benefits of being a Mac Developer are enormous.

To become a member of the Mac Developer program, you just need to sign up for it. First, make sure you're logged in to the Mac Dev Center with your Apple Developer ID.

Scroll down to the bottom of virtually any Mac Dev Center web page and you'll see some gray links, one of which is labeled Mac Developer Program. When you click this link, you'll see some content that looks similar to that of Figure 2.4.

FIGURE 2.4
The Mac
Developer
Program landing
page.

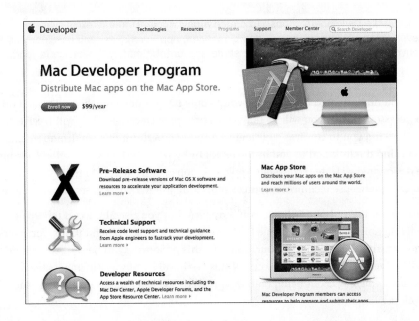

FIGURE 2.4
The Mac
Developer
Program landing
page.

Apple likes to change the look and feel of the various Developer Center websites every so often. As such, the instructions in this book may not be exactly accurate. However, Apple also makes it extremely easy to find links to things, especially links to enroll in developer programs, so even if the buttons are labeled differently or are in different places, you should have very little trouble navigating your way to signing up for the Mac Developer Program.

Click the Enroll Now link and follow the instructions. At the time this book was written, this link was a customized front-end that eventually led you to the Apple Store, where a 1-year subscription to the Mac Developer Program would be added to your cart.

You can also pay another $99/year for an iOS Developer Program subscription. Subscriptions to the Safari Developer Program are free.

Upon checkout, you will get a receipt for the payment. Within a day or so, your Mac Developer Program membership will be active; you will be able to access all the pre-release material you like and get to areas where you prep applications for submission to the App Store.

Although technically you do not have to obtain a Mac Developer Program membership to write the code for the upcoming hours in this book, I highly recommend that you start your membership now. By the time you get to Hour 23, your membership will be active, and you will be able to follow along. Hopefully, after you have completed all 24 hours in this book, you will have a great idea for an app you want to write and submit to the App Store, and your Mac Developer Program membership will facilitate that.

Downloading Xcode and Other Developer Tools

With your Apple Developer ID ready to go and as a registered member of the Mac Developer Program, you are ready to start coding. The next thing you need to do is download the Apple development tools.

With previous versions of Mac OS X, this was often a confusing and difficult process. Developers were often forced to choose among multiple prerelease versions of Xcode to download. In addition, Apple's development tools came on the second disk of the installation media for the version of Mac OS X that came with the computer, further muddying the waters with what developers should install.

All this is now straightforward and doesn't require any CDs, DVDs, or even logging in to the Mac Dev Center. To get the newest *public* release of Xcode (the one I recommend you use for the remainder of the book), all you need to do is download it from the App Store.

That's right, Xcode is now an app available through the App Store. To see this, launch the App Store from your tray and search the available apps for the word *Xcode*. Assuming everything went well, you should see a screen that looks similar to the one shown in Figure 2.5.

The version of Xcode shown in Figure 2.5 is 4.1. By the time this book is published, Xcode 4.2 (or later) should be available. Certain aspects of development on Mac OS X Lion (such as Automatic Reference Counting, which we see in Hour 5, "Managing Memory") are not available in Xcode 4.1 and are available only in Xcode 4.2 or later.

This shouldn't concern you because the version of Xcode you download will automatically be the newest. If you already have a version of Xcode that you installed for Mac OS X Lion via the App Store, make sure you check for updates and make sure that your version of Xcode is the newest possible.

FIGURE 2.5
Finding Xcode in
the Mac App
Store.

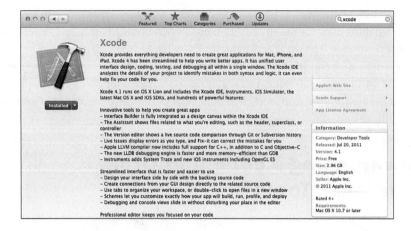

After you choose to install this application (it's a free purchase), it will download automatically. This is a very long (roughly 3GB) download, so you might want to go do something fun or read ahead in this book as Xcode downloads.

After the download is complete, you will find a new application in Launchpad called something like Install Xcode. If this application doesn't start automatically, click the application to launch the Xcode installer. This starts the Xcode installer, which will take several more minutes.

By the Way

> Not only is Xcode a 3GB download, but it expands to consume nearly 4GB of disk space. This means that if you don't have at least 7GB of hard-drive space when you attempt to download and install Xcode, you could run into trouble at the start—or even halfway through the process. Make sure you have plenty of drive space before you download Xcode from the App Store.

Now you're ready to use Xcode!

▼ **Try It Yourself**

Taking a Tour of Xcode

In the next hour, you're going to start learning how to write code in Objective-C. This section focuses on giving you a preview tour of the main development tool for Mac OS X Lion development: Xcode.

If you downloaded and installed Xcode using the Mac App Store, you should be able
▼ to find the Xcode icon by starting Launchpad.

Follow these steps to take a tour of Xcode:

1. Locate the Xcode application icon in Launchpad. If you click the Developer group, you should see the four main development tools: Instruments, Dashcode, Quartz Composer, and Xcode.

2. Click the Xcode icon to launch the application. On a typical Mac, it can take a few seconds before Xcode loads. Figure 2.6 shows the screen that appears the first time you launch Xcode. Note that in this screenshot, Xcode has remembered the list of my most recent projects.

FIGURE 2.6
Xcode's Welcome screen.

3. Make sure you spot the version (and build) number of Xcode in Figure 2.6. In the figure, it shows v4.1 build 4B110, whereas your version will more than likely be version 4.2 or later. If you are a paid member of the Mac Developer Program, you may occasionally find yourself downloading prerelease versions of Xcode. Keeping track of which version you're running is very important.

4. Click the Open Other button in the bottom-left corner of this screen.

5. Browse to the following folder, relative to the root of your hard drive (make sure you don't look for it in your personal folders): `/Developer/Examples/TextEdit` and open the `TextEdit.xcodeproj` file.

6. Click the Product menu item from the Xcode menu bar.

7. Click Run.

▼

8. The Text Edit application should now be running. You can quit this application when you're done trying out its features.

9. Click the TextEdit top-level node in the project navigator.

10. Make sure the TextEdit target is selected under the Targets node.

11. Make a note of the kind of information on this screen, as shown in Figure 2.7.

FIGURE 2.7
The Xcode
Target
Properties
screen.

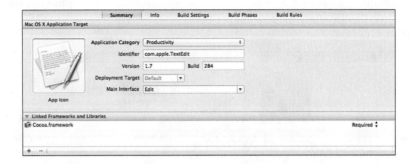

▲   Congratulations, you have just used Xcode to build and run your first project!

Summary

In this hour, you learned how to create an Apple Developer identity and how to upgrade that identity to include the Mac Developer Program, which entitles you to access prerelease software and submit applications to the Mac App Store.

Next, you learned how to download, install, and test Xcode, Apple's Integrated Development Environment (IDE). This tool will be used throughout the rest of the book to build and run all the applications and sample code you'll be writing.

Q&A

Q. *What website serves as a one-stop shop for registration, profile settings, downloads, and documentation for OS X Lion developers?*

A. The Mac Developer Center.

Q. *Does it cost money to become a Mac OS X Lion developer?*

A. You can write applications for free, but if you want to be able to sell your application in the Mac App Store, then you will need to pay the annual $99 fee. This fee is separate from the fee iOS developers have to pay annually.

HOUR 3

Introducing Objective-C

What you'll learn in this hour:

- ► History of Objective-C
- ► Doing Some Basic Math
- ► Using Strings
- ► Understanding Pointers and Equality
- ► Passing Messages
- ► Controlling Program Flow with Loops and Conditionals

It used to be that developers who wrote code in Objective-C were a small, elite group. These programmers wrote code for the Mac, building applications for a desktop OS that had very small market share and even smaller profit potential.

Today, thanks to the increasing popularity of the iPhone, iPod Touch, and the iPad, Objective-C's popularity is on the rise. Everyone from hobbyists to scientists to commercial developers and consultants are building applications for iOS using Objective-C.

During this hour you will be introduced to the Objective-C programming language, learn the basics of using variables, doing arithmetic, and building algorithms with larger blocks of code involving conditionals, looping, and the use of objects such as strings.

Overview and History of Objective-C

At its core, Objective-C is an ANSI standard version of the C programming language. Wrapped around this ANSI C core is a Smalltalk-inspired set of extensions that give the language its object-oriented capabilities, as well as several other enhancements that you don't get from the regular version of C.

Brad Cox and Tom Love created the Objective-C programming language in the early 1980s in an effort to get people to write cleaner, more modular, and clearly separated code. Contrary to popular belief, Objective-C wasn't invented by, nor is it exclusively owned by, Apple. It's actually an open standard; in the past, implementations of the Objective-C compiler existed that even ran on Windows.

If you have had any experience with C, learning Objective-C should be a breeze. Most developers find that learning the Objective-C syntax takes very little time at all, and the rest of the learning curve is devoted to learning about all the tools and controls available in Cocoa for Mac OS X.

Objective-C isn't just like C, it *is* C. If you have had any experience with C, C#, or Java, much of Objective-C's syntax should be easy to pick up. Don't let this discourage you if you are new to C-inspired languages, because Objective-C is easy to pick up for new and veteran developers alike.

Creating a New Cocoa Application

The first few steps of this section should seem familiar to you because in the previous hour we did some exercises to become familiar with the Xcode IDE and the various functions it performs. Throughout this section we'll be writing some code, predicting the output, and running the code to verify the results.

To get started with a new Cocoa application, follow these steps:

1. First, open up Xcode and when prompted create a new project. You should see a screen similar to the one shown in Figure 3.1.

2. Choose Cocoa Application as the template for the project and click Next. On the next screen (shown in Figure 3.2) you need to supply some information for your product. Use the information in Table 3.1 to fill out this form. Leave all the other values as defaults.

TABLE 3.1   Form Values to Create a New Cocoa Application

Form Field	Value
Product Name	Hour3
Company Identifier	com.sams.stylion
App Store Category	None

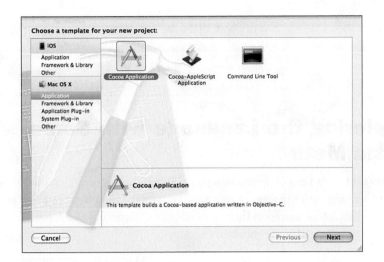

FIGURE 3.1
Creating a new Cocoa Application.

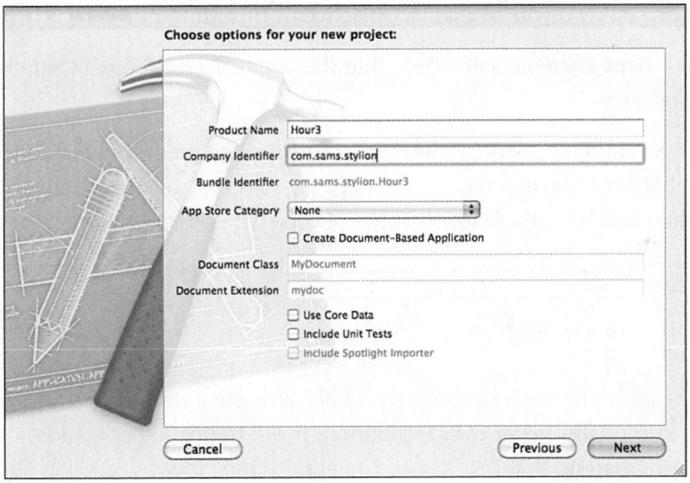

FIGURE 3.2
Providing product information for a new Cocoa Application.

3. When Xcode finishes building your new Cocoa Application, run it to make sure that you see a standard, empty window.

This is where the review starts, and we move on to covering new material and writing some actual code. If you don't feel comfortable using Xcode to create new applications, you might want to go back to review the work we did in Hour 2, "Introduction to the Developer Tools," before continuing on.

If you're curious, take a look at some of the files created automatically for you in the starter project. See what happens when you click to select each of the different files in the project navigator on the left.

Exploring the Language with Some Basic Math

Regardless of what kind of application you plan to build, you will invariably find yourself working with numbers or strings (text). Whether you want to allow your users to create a budget, report their high score in a game, or see the average of their test scores, you'll need to use numbers for that.

You have probably performed some basic math using some programming language in the past and, as mentioned earlier, because Objective-C is a superset of C, anything you can do in C you can do in Objective-C, including math.

Follow these steps to create some code that illustrates the basic use of numbers and math in Objective-C:

1. With Xcode open to the project you created in the preceding task, click the Hour3AppDelegate.m file. Locate the applicationDidFinishLaunching: method and add the following lines of code between the two curly braces:

   ```
   int a=5;
   int b=10;
   int c = a*b;
   NSLog(@"a*b = %d", c);
   ```

2. In the top-right corner of the Xcode IDE, click the button that shows a bottom tray icon. If you hover over this button, it will indicate that it hides or displays the debug area.

3. With the debug area now visible, run your application. In the debug area, below the information about the version of the debugger being used, you should see some text that looks like this:

   ```
   2011-05-29 12:16:44.916 Hour3[640:903] a*b = 50
   ```

NSLog is a function that you can call that will log text to a standard output device—in our case, the debug area of the application.

You may have noticed the little yellow triangles that appeared in the margin to the left of your code as you typed. Even before you build and run your application, as you type, the compiler is checking your code for errors or possible problems (warnings). The first warning you saw was the compiler informing you that you had declared the variable a but hadn't yet used it. As soon as you used it, that warning disappeared. This kind of instant, interactive feedback from Xcode can come in extremely handy and save you a lot of troubleshooting time in the future.

You may have noticed that there are a couple of panels you can open in the editor. Click the icon for the third (utilities) panel. You'll see a panel with a file inspector and Quick Help. Keep Quick Help open as you enter code throughout the rest of this hour and watch how it automatically figures out what information to display based on what you're typing.

By the Way

---

4. Now add the following lines of code where you left off:

```
double d = 123.00;
double e = 235.00;
double f = d * e;
NSLog(@"d*e = %f", f);
NSLog(@"d/e = %f", d / e);
NSLog(@"d/0 = %f", d / 0);
```

Note that as you type the last line of code, Xcode instantly throws a yellow caution triangle into the left margin. If you click that triangle, you'll see that the warning message says that division by zero is undefined.

By the Way

---

5. Now try to run the application, even with that warning still in place. Your output in the debug area should look like this:

```
2011-05-29 12:29:31.407 Hour3[745:903] a*b = 50
2011-05-29 12:29:31.410 Hour3[745:903] d*e = 28905.000000
2011-05-29 12:29:31.411 Hour3[745:903] d/e = 0.523404
2011-05-29 12:29:31.412 Hour3[745:903] d/0 = inf
```

Notice here that dividing by zero didn't crash our application. In many programming languages, including modern, managed runtime environments such as Java and C#, any attempt to divide by zero will crash the running application. Here, Objective-C kept on going and even managed to give the mathematically correct answer here of *infinity* rather than a crash.

When you are done with this hour, feel free to go back to this code and play around with more basic math. Remember that the data types we've used thus far are basic C types. As Cocoa programmers using Objective-C, you have the primitive numeric data types shown in Table 3.2 (as well as several others) available to you.

TABLE 3.2   Some Basic Objective-C Numeric Data Types

Type	Size	Description
int	32 or 64 bits	Basic integer. The size varies whether you're building a 32 or 64-bit application.
float	32 bits	A data type used for storing floating-point values.
double	64 bits	A data type used for storing large floating-point values.
long	64 bits	A data type used for storing large integers.
uint	2x(int)	A data type used for storing integers without a sign bit, allowing for the storage of numbers twice as big as in integer.

More numeric data types are available, but these are the ones that get used most often.

6. Add the following lines of code to the sample you've been working with:

```
float floaty = d*e;

NSLog(@"size of float: %lu", sizeof(floaty));
NSLog(@"size of double: %lu", sizeof(f));
NSLog(@"size of int: %lu", sizeof(a));
NSLog(@"size of long: %lu", sizeof(long));
NSLog(@"size of uint: %lu", sizeof(uint));
```

7. Now run the application to see the various sizes of the data types. Note that the sizeof function will work on a variable (such as floaty or f) or a data type (such as long or int).

One possible problem that you may already be thinking about is that different users have different computers, and as such, an int on the developer's computer might not always be the same as an int on the end-user's computer. There is a way to deal with these issues (and many more not-so-obvious problems with numbers and math), and you'll see one solution later in this hour when we get to a discussion of pointers.

Using Strings

Next to numbers, the other type of data that you will spend a large amount of time with is *strings*. Strings may just be pieces of text, but they are used extensively throughout every kind of application. Knowing how to use them efficiently and properly is essential to developing applications for the Mac or any other platform.

In the preceding section, you were actually using strings. Every time you wrote code that used the NSLog function, you were using strings. The @ operator in Objective-C is a convenient shortcut for the creation of a string. In addition to being a convenient shortcut, it also provides a way of distinguishing between a classic C-style string and a true Objective-C string object. Strings in Objective-C are objects, not simple values. The difference between the two will become clear in the next section on pointers and equality.

There are two different kinds of strings in Objective-C: NSString and NSMutableString. As their names imply, the former represents an instance of an immutable string, whereas the latter represents an in-memory string that can be manipulated. Many languages, including C# and Java, enforce that all strings are immutable and that anytime you "modify" a string, you are actually creating a new copy containing the modification.

> The concept of immutability is a tough one to grasp. For many languages, immutable strings are better for performance and even prevent catastrophic failures. If you can avoid using mutable strings in Objective-C, you should. Typically, you use NSMutableString when you need a single pointer to a string that will change frequently throughout your application's lifetime, and you don't want to create new strings each time it changes.

By the Way

Creating and Manipulating Strings

Now that you've had a brief introduction to strings, let's write some code to experiment with them. Follow these steps to create the sample code:

1. Add the following lines of code to the sample you've been working on:

```
NSString *favoriteColor = @"green";
NSLog(@"%@", favoriteColor);

NSString *friendlyOutput =
  [NSString stringWithFormat:
    @"Kevin loves the color %@", favoriteColor];
NSLog(@"%@", friendlyOutput);

NSString *subString = [friendlyOutput
  substringWithRange:NSMakeRange(6, 15)];
NSLog(@"substring: %@", subString);
```

There's a lot going on here that you may not be familiar with, so let's walk through it line by line.

The first line creates a new variable called `favoriteColor`, which is a *pointer* to an object of type `NSString` (again, don't worry about pointers just yet, we're building up to them slowly but surely).

The second line uses the `%@` string format character to log the string object. Just like standard C format specifiers such as `%d` and `%f` are used to represent numbers, the `%@` format string in Objective-C is used to represent an *object*. All objects in Objective-C know how to describe themselves, and whenever an object is used as a parameter to the `%@` format specifier, that object is asked to describe itself. Conveniently, the way a string describes itself is by returning its contents.

The third line creates a new string using a format string. Don't worry if the square bracket syntax looks odd; we'll get to an explanation of those in the section on message passing. Until then, try to mentally replace the square brackets with the idea that a message is being sent to an object.

Next we create a new string by extracting a substring using a range of indices. In the preceding code, we're extracting by starting at string index 6 (strings are indexed starting at 0, just like C arrays) and pulling the following 15 characters.

2. Run the sample to see what kind of output you get. It should now look something like this:

```
2011-05-29 13:10:03.351 Hour3[1076:903] a*b = 50
2011-05-29 13:10:03.354 Hour3[1076:903] d*e = 28905.000000
2011-05-29 13:10:03.356 Hour3[1076:903] d/e = 0.523404
2011-05-29 13:10:03.358 Hour3[1076:903] d/0 = inf
2011-05-29 13:10:03.359 Hour3[1076:903] size of float: 4
2011-05-29 13:10:03.360 Hour3[1076:903] size of double: 8
2011-05-29 13:10:03.360 Hour3[1076:903] size of int: 4
2011-05-29 13:10:03.361 Hour3[1076:903] size of long: 8
2011-05-29 13:10:03.363 Hour3[1076:903] size of uint: 4
2011-05-29 13:10:03.366 Hour3[1076:903] green
2011-05-29 13:10:03.367 Hour3[1076:903] Kevin loves the color green
2011-05-29 13:10:03.367 Hour3[1076:903] substring: loves the color
```

All applications use strings. They need them to display information to users and to gather information from users. As a Mac developer, you will find that you spend a great deal of time creating, manipulating, and comparing strings.

This leads to the next section on pointers and equality, which is *very* important to understand, especially when comparing things like strings.

Understanding Pointers and Equality

When most people think of a *pointer*, they think of an arrow, a sign, or even a human finger pointing in a certain direction. This is exactly what a pointer is in C or Objective-C: an indicator pointing at another location.

When your code executes, that code resides in memory. Available to your code are two types of memory: the *stack* and the *heap*. The stack, as its name implies, is a contiguous block of memory. Values can be *pushed* into the stack and they can be *popped* off of the stack. This mechanism is how functions are called: The parameters to a function are pushed onto the stack and then execution resumes within the function where the parameters are popped off the stack to make them available to the code within the function.

This works great when function parameters are small pieces of datalike integers or floats or even smaller values. What if you have a very large object (we'll cover creating classes and instantiating them in the next hour) that takes up hundreds—or even thousands—of bytes? Now the mere presence of this object on the stack is creating a headache for whatever runtime is executing your code. If you had to shovel things from one bucket to another bucket before you could do your work, would you rather shovel small fish tank pebbles or enormous boulders?

Enter pointers. Rather than placing all of the data belonging to the large object (the boulder) on the stack, we can instead write down the location of the boulder onto a small pebble and place that small pebble on the stack instead. This way, we can now quickly and easily pass all of our parameters to a function using the stack. When the function needs to access the large object/boulder, it can read the location from the pebble we put on the stack and go get the object on its own.

Obviously the Objective-C runtime doesn't write down locations on pebbles. It does, however, store memory addresses in integers and place *those* on the stack.

Far more so than in other languages like C# or Java, you will be dealing with pointers on a daily basis in Objective-C. Just remembering that pointers are merely numbers on the stack that point to a different location on the heap will serve you well as you go through the rest of this book.

To see an example of pointers in action, follow these steps:

1. Type the following code in after the last line of code you wrote for the previous section:

```
int targetNum = 42;
int bigTargetNum = 75;
int *targetNum_ptr = &targetNum;
int *targetNum_ptr2 = &targetNum;
NSLog(@"targetNum = %d, ptr points to = %d", targetNum,
```

```
*targetNum_ptr);
    NSLog(@"are two pointers equal? %d", (targetNum_ptr ==
targetNum_ptr2));
    targetNum_ptr2 = &bigTargetNum;
    NSLog(@"are two pointers equal 2nd time? %d", (targetNum_ptr ==
targetNum_ptr2));
    *targetNum_ptr2 = 42; // what did this really do?
    NSLog(@"are two pointers equal 3rd time? %d", (targetNum_ptr ==
targetNum_ptr2));

    NSString *stringA = @"Hello World";
    NSString *stringB = [NSString stringWithFormat:@"%@ %@", @"Hello",
@"World"];
    NSLog(@"Is %@ == %@ : %d", stringA, stringB, (stringA == stringB));
    NSLog(@"What about with isEqualToString? %d",

    [stringA isEqualToString:stringB]);
```

2. Before running the application, try to predict what the output might be. On the first two lines, we create two standard integers. These are standard integers and we are storing their actual values.

On the next two lines we create two pointers. First, take note of the * operator. In this case, we are not multiplying. The presence of an asterisk before a variable name in a declaration statement indicates that we are declaring a *pointer*. This informs Objective-C that the data being stored in this variable is a *memory location* (pointer to real data), and *not the actual data.*

On these same lines of code, we use the *address-of* operator (&) to obtain the memory address of the number stored in the location called targetNum. At this point, both targetNum_ptr and targetNum_ptr2 *point to the address of* targetNum.

On the next line, we use the asterisk again, but this time as a *dereferencing operator.* This means that when Objective-C expects a value and you give it a pointer variable preceded by an asterisk, Objective-C will go fetch the *value* from the memory location currently stored within that pointer.

The next set of statements attempts to get a definitive answer to the question: *Are two pointers equal if they both point to the same memory location?* Running the application shows you that this is indeed true. For example, suppose the memory address holding the value for targetNum was 100080. If we set targetNum_ptr and targetNum_ptr2 to &targetNum, we set *both* of those variables to 100080, which makes them equivalent.

The next question is a little more tricky: *If two pointers point to two different locations, but each location contains the same value, are those pointers equal?*

This is the key to understanding pointers and equality. When you compare pointers, you are essentially asking if the address of the underlying data is the same. If you want to compare whether the data itself is the same, you need to either dereference the pointers and compare the underlying data or, better yet, use classes that know how to compare themselves.

This leads us to the NSString class. The first variable, stringA, is assigned to a string literal "Hello World". Remember that the @ operator is actually a shortcut for creating an instance of an immutable string. If I had assigned stringB to @"Hello World", both stringA and stringB would be considered equivalent via the == operator because both would point to the single memory location on the heap where the immutable string "Hello World" resides.

Because we used two different methods to create "Hello World", one constant and one via concatenation, neither stringA nor stringB points to the same memory location. However, because NSString knows how to do string comparison via the isEqualToString method (there is an abundance of other related string-comparison tools for more involved scenarios), you can compare the two strings and verify that the *content* is equivalent, even though both copies of "Hello World" are sitting in two difference places on the heap.

3. When you run the application you've been working on this hour, the output related to pointers and string comparison should look like the following:

```
2011-05-29 13:31:04.788 Hour3[1325:903] targetNum = 42, ptr points to = 42
2011-05-29 13:31:04.789 Hour3[1325:903] are two pointers equal? 1
2011-05-29 13:31:04.790 Hour3[1325:903] are two pointers equal 2nd time? 0
2011-05-29 13:31:04.792 Hour3[1325:903] are two pointers equal 3rd time? 0
2011-05-29 13:31:04.793 Hour3[1325:903] Is Hello World == Hello World : 0
2011-05-29 13:31:04.794 Hour3[1325:903] What about with isEqualToString? 1
```

Finally, before moving on to the next section, it is worth noting that Objective-C strings are in fact Unicode strings. This means that these strings are not limited to storing text in English or similar 7- and 8-bit languages. Unicode strings can be used to store text in Chinese, Japanese, Hindi, Arabic, and any other language that uses text characters whose ordinal value has a value higher than 255 (often referred to as long characters or multibyte characters).

Not only do non-US versions of Mac OS X allow people to type Unicode characters directly with special keyboards, but there are also phonetic Input Method Editors (IMEs) that allow people to type phonetically and autoconvert text into Unicode. For example, someone might type 'ohayou gozaimasu' into an IME and get the Japanese Unicode: おはひょうございます. Knowing that Objective-C strings are Unicode strings can come in handy in the future, especially for languages that will support multiple cultures.

By the Way

Passing Messages

If you've never seen Objective-C before, the square brackets ([and]) might seem a little unusual. This is what is known as *message passing syntax*. Within the two square brackets are the *target* of a message and the *parameters* of that message.

The capability to send messages to objects is what lifts Objective-C above its roots in ANSI C and provides the robust, object-oriented functionality that Mac and iOS developers love today.

Let's take an example from some code that we've already written:

```
NSString *stringB = [NSString stringWithFormat:@"%@ %@", @"Hello", @"World"];
```

> If you've had Quick Help active throughout the hour, notice what happens when you click the first letter of the method name; documentation for that method appears instantly. Now see what happens when you hit the escape key with the cursor still in that same spot—a list of all the possible messages that can be sent to an object or class! This list isn't always as well-informed as the developer, so take its contents with a grain of salt.

In this line of code we are sending the NSString class the stringWithFormat: message. Note that the colon is considered part of the message name. In fact, all subsequent parameters are considered part of the name of the method being called. For example, if I had an ice cream object and I wanted to top it using a specific method, it might look something like this:

```
[iceCream topWithSauce:SauceHotFudge withCherry:YES withWhippedCream:NO];
```

In this line of code, what's the name of the method we are invoking? It isn't just topWithSauce: because that doesn't convey what we're actually doing. The method name is actually called topWithSauce:withCherry:withWhippedCream:

It might take some getting used to for programmers used to calling methods with a comma-delimited list of arguments as shown in the following line of C# code:

```
iceCream.Top(Toppings.HotFudge, true, false);
```

However, this syntax makes for highly readable, self-documenting code, and in many cases it removes all ambiguity about the name and purpose of a method's parameters without needing to consult an external document.

As an exercise, go back through the code you've written so far this hour and for every use of square brackets, determine the target being sent the message and the name of the method being called.

When you say the names of Objective-C methods out loud, you don't pronounce the colons. Instead, insert a little pause between the parameter names as you read aloud.

Controlling Program Flow

So far everything you've written has been linear. Each line of code you wrote executed immediately after the preceding line and it executed only once. What if you want to execute the same block of code 50 times? What if you want to execute a block of code over and over until you reach the end of an input file? What if you want to decide whether to execute a block of code based on some condition?

For these and many more scenarios, you have to turn to some Objective-C keywords that control your program's execution flow. In short, you will need to use looping or logic keywords.

The most common way to control program flow is through conditional branching. This can be done with the `if` statement and the `else` statement or the highly favored `switch` statement.

An `if` statement works by evaluating some Boolean expression (an expression that yields true or false or, in C terms, either zero or nonzero for false and true, respectively). If the Boolean expression evaluates to true, the body of the `if` statement is executed. If the expression evaluates to false, the body of the `if` statement is *not* executed and, optionally, an `if else` or `else` block is executed.

Follow these steps to experiment with branching and looping:

1. Enter the following code on a blank line below the code you've been writing so far:

    ```
    if ([favoriteColor isEqualToString:@"blue"])
    {
        NSLog(@"Your favorite color is BLUE!");
    }
    else if ([favoriteColor isEqualToString:@"purple"])
    {
        NSLog(@"You're into purple.");
    }
    ```

```
else
{
    NSLog(@"You don't like blue or purple!");
}
```

Remembering back to earlier in the hour, we set the value of `favoriteColor`
to "green". This means that when you execute this code, it will not execute the
body of the `if` statement or the body of the `else if` statement. It will execute
the body of the `else` statement. Play around with the value of `favoriteColor`
to get the different statements to execute. Note that every single Boolean
expression evaluated by an `if` or `else if` statement *must* be wrapped in
parentheses.

Next, let's see what a simple `for` loop looks like. As you may have guessed, an
Objective-C `for` loop works the same as it does in ANSI C.

**By the
Way**

> Later in the book you'll see a special type of `for` loop called a *fast iterator*. This is
> an elegant, clean syntax that lets you iterate through the items in a collection with
> extremely good performance.

2. Enter the following code where you left off:

```
for (int x=0; x<10; x++)
{
    switch (x) {
        case 0:
            NSLog(@"First time through!");
            break;
        case 1:
        case 2:
        case 3:
        case 4:
            NSLog(@"Not halfway there yet...");
            break;
        default:
            NSLog(@"Working on the %dth iteration.", x);
            break;
    }
}
```

When executed, this produces output similar to the following:

```
2011-05-29 17:14:07.857 Hour3[1594:903] First time through!
2011-05-29 17:14:07.858 Hour3[1594:903] Not halfway there yet...
2011-05-29 17:14:07.859 Hour3[1594:903] Not halfway there yet...
2011-05-29 17:14:07.860 Hour3[1594:903] Not halfway there yet...
2011-05-29 17:14:07.861 Hour3[1594:903] Not halfway there yet...
2011-05-29 17:14:07.861 Hour3[1594:903] Working on the 5th iteration.
```

```
2011-05-29 17:14:07.862 Hour3[1594:903] Working on the 6th iteration.
2011-05-29 17:14:07.863 Hour3[1594:903] Working on the 7th iteration.
2011-05-29 17:14:07.864 Hour3[1594:903] Working on the 8th iteration.
2011-05-29 17:14:07.865 Hour3[1594:903] Working on the 9th iteration.
```

You can see that the for loop we just executed gave us 10 iterations, with indices ranging from 0 to 9. Other kinds of loops are available to us as well, including the do loop and the while loop. These loops both execute their bodies until the associated Boolean expression evaluates to false. The only difference is that a do loop will *always* execute at least once because it evaluates the Boolean condition *after* the body executes. A while loop evaluates the Boolean condition *before* the body executes, and if the expression evaluates to false, the body will never execute. Which loop you choose is entirely up to you and should be based on how readable you want the code to be and, of course, personal preference.

Summary

In this hour, you got your feet wet with Objective-C. You experimented a little with basic mathematics and string manipulation—the building blocks of any application. You took a look at pointers, how they work, and how they affect things like equality and comparisons. You took a look at message-passing syntax and finally spent a little time creating loops and using branching and conditional logic.

Hopefully, at this point, you are excited about Objective-C and what you might be able to do with it in the next hour, where we talk about object-oriented programming and creating and consuming your own classes.

Q&A

Q. *How is Objective-C related to the ANSI C programming language?*

A. Objective-C isn't just similar to C; it is a superset of the C language. This means that any standard ANSI C code is compatible with an Objective-C application.

Q. *What function do you call to write messages to the system log and console output?*

A. NSLog(). This function will become very familiar to you as you write more and more code.

Q. *How does Objective-C message passing differ from calling methods in other programming languages?*

A. In Objective-C, the method parameters are actually part of the message name. In addition, message passing in Objective-C is dynamic, meaning you can compile code that sends messages to objects that may or may not respond to those messages at runtime.

HOUR 4

Object-Oriented Programming with Objective-C

What you'll learn in this hour:

- ▶ Creating Classes
- ▶ Adding Attributes to Classes
- ▶ Adding Behavior to Classes
- ▶ Using Objects and Classes
- ▶ Extending Classes Through Inheritance
- ▶ Using Polymorphism with Inheritance and Protocols

Some developers find it hard to believe that object-oriented programming has been around since the 1960s. In fact, some younger developers find it hard to believe that any kind of programming has been around that long.

Even back in the '60s, the complexity and size of computer programs was growing rapidly and becoming unmanageable. A solution to that program was to allow developers to create smaller, more reusable (and manageable) collections of data and functionality called *classes*.

Classes are, in general, self-sufficient modules of code that contain everything they need in terms of data and functionality to perform the task for which they were written. As a result, computer programs written this way became collections of objects that can receive messages, process messages to perform their designated task, and send messages.

Debates about the best ways to design classes and class hierarchies are numerous and span volumes of books and hundreds of websites on the Internet. In this hour, you'll learn how to create classes and allow them to do work by outfitting them with attributes and behavior. In addition, you'll learn how to extend them with inheritance and protocols.

> The first object-oriented programming language, FORTRAN (http://en.wikipedia.org/wiki/Fortran), appeared in 1957 and was followed one year later by LISP. LISP (which stands for LISt Processing) pioneered many of the object-oriented concepts that are staples for modern-day developers. LISP can even treat LISP source code as data, creating amazing potential and power for such a terse, concise language. Clojure (http://clojure.org), a popular modern programming language that runs on the Java Virtual Machine, is actually a dialect of LISP.

Creating Classes

As mentioned at the beginning of this hour, classes are reusable modules of attributes and behavior that typically work toward some fairly small, fine-grained task or that model some concept.

Before you create a class, it is generally a good idea to decide on what concept or functionality you are modeling. For the next few sections, we're going to be creating a class that models the concept of a monster, perhaps one that might belong in a video game.

To create a new `Monster` class, perform the following steps:

1. Open Xcode and create a new Cocoa application called Hour4.

2. Select the `Hour4` folder in the project navigation tree on the left side.

3. Right (or Control)-Click that folder and select New and then File.

4. Choose Objective-C Class from the template selector, as shown in Figure 4.1. Make sure that you're not accidentally selecting types from the iOS group.

5. Click Next and you should see a screen similar to the one shown in Figure 4.2. All classes in Objective-C ultimately inherit from `NSObject`, but, as we'll see later in this hour, they can inherit from other classes as well.

6. Click Next to move to the next screen, shown in Figure 4.3.

7. In the Save As field, enter **Monster** and click Save. This will create a new class called `Monster`. Your project should now have two new files in it: `Monster.m` and `Monster.h`.

Left-click each of these new files in the project navigator and take a look at the code that was created in the new, empty class.

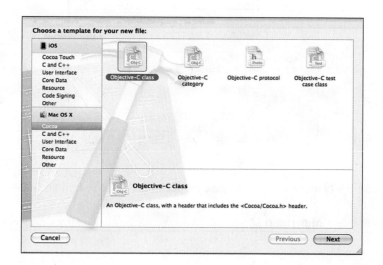

FIGURE 4.1
New Class
Wizard—step 1.

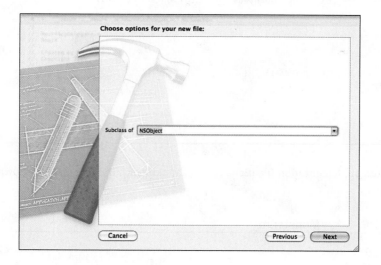

FIGURE 4.2
New Class
Wizard—step 2.

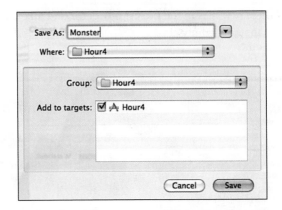

The header file (Monster.h) should look similar to the file shown in Listing 4.1.

LISTING 4.1   Monster.h

```
//
//  Monster.h
//  Hour4
//
//  Created by Kevin Hoffman on 6/2/11.
//  Copyright 2011 __MyCompanyName__. All rights reserved.
//

#import <Foundation/Foundation.h>


@interface Monster : NSObject {
@private

}

@end
```

The class implementation file (Monster.m) should look similar to the file shown in Listing 4.2

LISTING 4.2   Monster.m

```
//
//  Monster.m
//  Hour4
//
//  Created by Kevin Hoffman on 6/2/11.
//  Copyright 2011 __MyCompanyName__. All rights reserved.
//

#import "Monster.h"
```

```
@implementation Monster

- (id)init
{
    self = [super init];
    if (self) {
        // Initialization code here.
    }

    return self;
}

- (void)dealloc
{
    [super dealloc];
}

@end
```

You may have noticed that the comments header at the top of your new file contains your name and organization. If you have never set your organization name, it will appear as __MyCompanyName__.

If you want to change the company name from __MyCompanyName__ to something more meaningful, there are two easy options.

▶ Open your Address Book and set the Company name to something meaningful on your contact card.

▶ Set it on the project in Xcode. Highlight the project in the left navigation bar and then open the Utilities panel (using the panel buttons on the top right). Inside the Project Document group, change the Organization field to whatever you like. Setting the organization on a per-project basis comes in handy if you are a consultant producing code for multiple organizations.

The `Monster.h` file contains the class declaration. This file defines the attributes and behaviors that are available to other classes that will consume this class. The `Monster.m` file contains the implementation—the real code—that provides the actual functionality of the class. This combination of header file and implementation file should be familiar to developers with C or C++ backgrounds.

Languages such as Java and C# do not separate form and function in different files. The class implementation is mingled in directly with the class definition. Debates continue as to whether this is better or worse than the C/C++ way of doing things.

The `init` and `dealloc` methods that come with newly created classes are there to provide placeholders for code to be executed when a class is instantiated and when it is disposed of, respectively. In Hour 5, where we cover memory management, you will see more of these methods and how important they are. At least for this hour, however, it is safe to ignore these methods.

Build and run your application (using the Product, Run menu or the hotkey Command-R) just to make sure that the new `Monster` class hasn't done anything to break the application.

In the next few sections you will see how to add real power to classes with attributes and behavior.

Adding Attributes to Classes

When you are modeling classes, one of the first things you want to think about is the class structure—that is, the *data* that the class contains. This includes more than just defining what the data looks like but also access rules around what code can read and write that data and *how* that data is accessed.

What kind of attributes do you think we might want to give to a class called `Monster`? A few that come to mind are some simple ones like height and weight. Depending on the type of application we're planning on building, we might also want to keep track of the monster's maximum land speed and its name.

Adding Attributes with ivars

Let's get started and add some of these attributes to our monster class. To do that, we're going to create things commonly referred to as *ivars*. The word *ivar* is a shortening of two other words: *instance variable*. An instance variable is aptly named in that it is a variable that is scoped to a specific instance of a class.

For example, if we were to create four instances of the `Monster` class and send them into battle against four instances of the `Hero` class, we can expect that some of these objects are going to take some damage or perhaps die. The current condition of each instance of the `Monster` or `Hero` class would be stored in instance variables that we might call `health` or `isDead`, and the like.

Modify the `Monster.h` file so it looks like Listing 4.3 to contain some new attributes as ivars.

LISTING 4.3   Adding Attributes to the Monster Class

```
#import <Foundation/Foundation.h>


@interface Monster : NSObject {
    // Monster attributes
    int _height;
    int _weight;
    NSString *_name;
    int _maxSpeedMph;

@private

}

@end
```

The underscore preceding the name of each attribute is a convention that makes it easy to spot ivars and differentiate them from properties (we'll get to properties shortly).

With these instance variables declared as part of the Monster class, any method on this class has access to that data. For instance, we could write code in a method that looks like this:

```
_name = @"Bob";
_height = 6 * 12; // 6 feet, in inches
_weight = 225;
_maxSpeedMph = 20; // bob's a fast one.
```

The problem with these instance variables is that they are available only to code written within the Monster.m file; the class implementation. What if a Hero class needs to check the height of a monster in order to make a decision about which weapon to use? With only ivars defining the attributes of the class, you can't write code like this:

```
if (targetMonster._height > 60) { // use a bigger stick... }
```

This code won't compile because the _height variable isn't visible to any code *outside* the Monster class. To expose attributes to code other than the class itself, we need to use Objective-C *properties*.

Exposing Attributes with Properties

Properties allow you to wrap instance variables (ivars) in accessor methods that expose that data to code outside your own class. In old versions of Objective-C, before the existence of properties as first-class Objective-C citizens, exposition of an ivar involved the manual creation of methods that conformed to a specific naming convention.

For example, to expose a property called `maxSpeedMph` to consuming code, you would create a method called `maxSpeedMph` that returns an integer value and a method called `setMaxSpeedMph` that takes an integer input parameter.

Thankfully with the current version of Objective-C, the creation of these properties is easy, and Xcode can generate different types of accessors automatically for us.

To create some properties that will expose our ivars to other classes, modify the code in Listing 4.3 so that it now looks like the code in Listing 4.4.

LISTING 4.4   Monster.h with Properties

```
#import <Foundation/Foundation.h>


@interface Monster : NSObject {
    // Monster attributes
    int _height;
    int _weight;
    NSString *_name;
    int _maxSpeedMph;

@private

}

@property(nonatomic, assign) int height;
@property(nonatomic, assign) int weight;
@property(nonatomic, retain) NSString *name;
@property(nonatomic, assign) int maxSpeedMph;
@end
```

As you type the property declarations with the `@property` syntax, take a look at the little yellow triangles that appear in the left margin. As you type each property declaration, you get warnings that the corresponding read/write methods have not been set or that you haven't used the `@dynamic` or `@synthesize` keywords. This is a clue that your implementation of properties isn't yet complete.

All the `@property` keyword does is *declare* a property. This allows Xcode to know which properties your class is exposing and how it is exposing them, but it doesn't take care of the implementation of the read and write methods for accessing the underlying ivars.

Notice the two parameters to the `@property` statement. In the case of simple integers, we've used `nonatomic` and `assign` as parameters, but for the `NSString` property, we've used `nonatomic` and `retain`. Some of this won't make much sense to you until the next hour when we talk about memory management. The nonatomic parameter means that the boilerplate "set" code for the property won't bother with writing code that allows multiple threads to write to the property at the same time. The assign and retain parameters dictate the way the generated "set" accessor will manage memory.

To finish the implementation of these properties, switch over to the Monster.m file and add the following @synthesize statements after the @implementation statement:

```
@synthesize height=_height;
@synthesize maxSpeedMph=_maxSpeedMph;
@synthesize name=_name;
@synthesize weight=_weight;
```

The @synthesize statement tells Xcode to generate boilerplate "get" and "set" methods and, since we are naming ivars after the name of the property, the boilerplate code will wrap around those instance variables.

You should now be able to build your application, although it doesn't do anything particularly interesting. In this section, you actually put those properties to use.

Using Dot Notation Versus Message Passing

You can access the properties as declared in your Monster.h file in two ways. The first way is to pass messages to the class that invoke the boilerplate methods created by the @synthesize statement. The second way is to use a newer feature of Objective-C called *dot notation*.

First, let's look at how you might set and read the values of a particular instance of Monster using message passing syntax (don't worry about typing this code in now; this is just a sample):

```
Monster *m = [[Monster alloc] init];
[m setName:@"Bob"];
[m setWeight:225];
[m setHeight:72];
[m setMaxSpeedMph:25];
NSLog(@"Created a monster named %@, it weighs %d lbs and can run %dmph.",
    [m name],
    [m weight],
    [m maxSpeedMph]);
```

The first line of code creates an instance of the Monster class. The relationship between a class and instances of it is like the relationship between a cookie cutter and the cookies it presses out. We're taking the cookie cutter (the Monster class) and we're stamping (allocating memory) out a cookie in the shape of Monster. After we've stamped out that cookie, we can manipulate it however we like, including setting properties and, as you'll see shortly, invoking behaviors.

```
2011-06-02 19:57:36.875 Hour4[25471:903] Created a monster named Bob,
it weighs 225 lbs and can run 25mph.
```

Objective-C now gives us the capability to access properties in a way that looks more like the way other languages such as C# handle properties—with "dot notation." We could rewrite the preceding code to look like this:

```
Monster *m2 = [[Monster alloc] init];
m2.name = @"John";
m2.weight = 225;
m2.height = 72;
m2.maxSpeedMph = 25;
NSLog(@"Created a monster named %@, it weighs %d lbs and can run %dmph.",
      m2.name,
      m2.weight,
      m2.maxSpeedMph);
```

The end result is the same, but the code for reading and writing those properties uses fewer characters and is arguably easier to read than classic message passing notation.

> Do not forget that dot-notation syntax is merely shorthand for actual message passing. The property declarations in the class header are used to provide Xcode with enough information to allow you to use these shortcuts. The debate continues (and will continue for some time) as to whether dot notation is actually a good thing. Some claim it is confusing and misleading, and others claim it is a handy shortcut. Feel free to use it for the simplest of property read-and-write operations, but stay away from using it in other scenarios where you are truly passing messages rather than just reading and writing properties.

Adding Behavior to Classes

Now that you've had a chance to add some data to a class in the form of properties and instance variables, let's add some behavior in the form of methods.

As with deciding on the attributes that belong to a class, you should design out what behavior you would like your class to support before you actually start writing the code. This will help organize your thoughts and should lead toward a cleaner set of behaviors.

Many developers will take issue with my suggestion to design before coding, especially those who do a lot of test-driven development (TDD). Everyone works differently, and some developers need their fingers to be clicking keys in order to think
clearly. Do what suits you best, but remember that the old adage "measure twice,
cut once" also applies to good object-oriented design.

What kind of behavior might we want our Monster class to have? Like any good
monster, it should be able to move around, attack, and maybe growl. As with properties, we need to declare the methods that belong to a class in its header file.

As such, modify Monster.h so that it looks like the code in Listing 4.5

LISTING 4.5   Monster.h with Methods

```
#import <Foundation/Foundation.h>


@interface Monster : NSObject {
    // Monster attributes
    int _height;
    int _weight;
    NSString *_name;
    int _maxSpeedMph;

@private

}

@property(nonatomic, assign) int height;
@property(nonatomic, assign) int weight;
@property(nonatomic, retain) NSString *name;
@property(nonatomic, assign) int maxSpeedMph;

-(void)growl;
-(void)attack:(Monster *)target;
-(void)moveToX:(int)x Y:(int)y;

@end
```

Remember that the header file is the interface to the class—it defines the attributes
and the behaviors that are visible to code outside the class. To create the actual
implementation of these methods, we need to add them to the Monster.m file as
shown in Listing 4.6

LISTING 4.6   Monster.m with Methods

```
#import "Monster.h"


@implementation Monster
```

```objc
@synthesize height=_height;
@synthesize maxSpeedMph=_maxSpeedMph;
@synthesize name=_name;
@synthesize weight=_weight;

- (id)init
{
    self = [super init];
    if (self) {
        // Initialization code here.
    }

    return self;
}

- (void)dealloc
{
    [super dealloc];
}

- (void)growl
{
    NSLog(@"Grrr...");
}

- (void)attack:(Monster *)target
{
    NSLog(@"I, %@ the terrible, am attacking %@!!",
        _name,
        target.name);
}

- (void)moveToX:(int)x Y:(int)y
{
    NSLog(@"Look out, anybody at (%d,%d), I'm on my way!",
        x, y);
}

@end
```

These method implementations are only placeholders to illustrate how you can add behavior to the classes. As we progress throughout the book, you will learn all sorts of techniques for filling in method implementations with actual code.

Pay attention to the import "Monster.h" statement at the top of Listing 4.6. For your code to know how to use a class, it must know about that class definition. To know the class definition, it needs to import the header file. There are other ways to get around this, but for now just remember that if the compiler is complaining about unrecognized selectors or unknown classes, you might be missing a header file import.

Now that we've managed to build a simple class, in the next section we'll take a look at creating instances of objects and how we can use them.

Using Objects and Classes

As you saw earlier, to create an instance of an object you use code that looks like this:

```
Monster *m = [[Monster alloc] init];
```

The alloc and init methods will be explained in more detail in the next hour when we talk about memory management. You've already seen how to set and read properties from an Objective-C object. Type the code in Listing 4.7 into the applicationDidFinishLaunching method of the Hour4AppDelegate.m class implementation file.

LISTING 4.7   Hour4AppDelegate.m

```
#import "Hour4AppDelegate.h"
#import "Monster.h"

@implementation Hour4AppDelegate

@synthesize window;

- (void)applicationDidFinishLaunching:(NSNotification *)aNotification
{
    // Insert code here to initialize your application

    Monster *bob = [[Monster alloc] init];
    bob.name = @"Bob";
    bob.weight = 300;
    bob.height = 72;
    bob.maxSpeedMph = 10;

    Monster *joe = [[Monster alloc] init];
    joe.name = @"Joe";
    joe.weight = 225;
    joe.height = 70;
    joe.maxSpeedMph = 30;

    [bob growl];
    [bob moveToX:10 Y:8];
    [bob attack:joe];
    [joe growl];
    [joe moveToX:10 Y:8];
    [joe attack:bob];
}

@end
```

When you run your application, your debug log should contain text that looks like the following:

```
2011-06-03 11:03:02.129 Hour4[26110:903] Grrr...
2011-06-03 11:03:02.133 Hour4[26110:903] Look out, anybody at (10,8),
I'm on my way!
2011-06-03 11:03:02.135 Hour4[26110:903] I, Bob the terrible, am attacking Joe!!
2011-06-03 11:03:02.136 Hour4[26110:903] Grrr...
2011-06-03 11:03:02.137 Hour4[26110:903] Look out, anybody at (10,8),
I'm on my way!
2011-06-03 11:03:02.139 Hour4[26110:903] I, Joe the terrible,
am attacking Bob!!
```

Extending Objects Through Inheritance

So far we've only been working with a single class, `Monster`. What if we want to have different kinds of monsters and we want them to behave differently, but we also want them to inherit common functionality?

In other words, suppose we have a werewolf who does everything that a monster does, except that when the `growl` method gets called on a werewolf, he *howls*. Additionally, suppose we have a serpent and when the `growl` method gets called, he *hisses*. Other than having their own custom growls, both serpents and werewolves should behave just like other monsters.

Perform the following steps so that we can experiment with inheritance:

1. Follow the steps in the New File wizard like you did to create `Monster`, but create a new empty class called **Werewolf**. When prompted for what class this one inherits from, enter **Monster**, as shown in Figure 4.4.

FIGURE 4.4
Choosing a parent class for a new class.

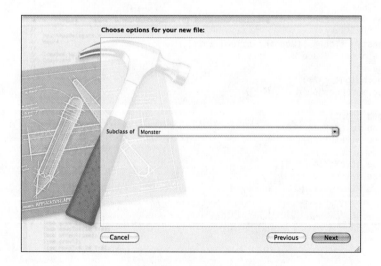

2. At the top of the Werewolf.h file add an **import "Monster.h"** statement. There should be enough examples in the code already built for this hour to give you an idea of where this statement goes. Werewolf can't inherit from Monster unless it knows about the class interface of Monster, which is in the Monster.h file.

3. Follow the steps in the New File wizard to create a new empty class called **Serpent**. Make sure it inherits from Monster, as shown in Figure 4.4.

4. Add an **import "Monster.h"** statement to the top of Serpent.h, like you did in step 2.

5. Add the following growl method to the bottom of Werewolf.m:

```
- (void)growl
{
    NSLog(@"Howl! Howl!");
}
```

6. Add the following growl method to the bottom of Serpent.m:

```
- (void)growl
{
    NSLog(@"Hisss!! Hissss!!");
}
```

7. Now go back into your Hour4AppDelegate.m file so we can see what it looks like when serpents and werewolves growl. Add the following lines of code to the bottom of the applicationDidFinishLaunching: method:

```
Werewolf *steve = [[Werewolf alloc] init];
steve.name = @"Steve"; // inherited from Monster!
[steve growl];

Serpent *wallace = [[Serpent alloc] init];
wallace.name = @"Wallace";
[wallace growl];
```

Now when you run the application, you see that you can create instances of the Monster class, which have the default growling capabilities. In addition, you can create instances of Serpent or Werewolf, each of which have its own custom growling behavior.

When you move forward to create your own applications, you probably will not be creating monsters or custom growling behavior. However, showing how child classes can override the behavior of their parents illustrates a powerful and valuable skill in application development.

Using Polymorphism

Polymorphism is one of those concepts that regularly shows up on developer interviews and sounds more complicated and intimidating than it really is. All polymorphism really refers to is the ability for code to treat different objects as if they were the same parent type (or conform to the same protocol, which we'll see shortly).

For example, you might have a method that takes as input instances of the Cat class. Other developers who invoke that method may send you instances of Cat, or they might even send you instances of Jaguar, Panther, Puma, or FatHouseCat. Polymorphism is what allows this kind of code to work. Because all those child classes inherit from Cat, they are all valid arguments when passed to methods that expect instances of the Cat class.

If this is true, we should be able to pass instances of Werewolf and Serpent to the attack: method on Monster, which expects to see instances of the Monster class.

Let's try that out and see if it works "out of the box." Add the following lines of code below your instances of Steve and Wallace, the werewolf and the serpent:

```
// Can steve attack wallace?
[steve attack:wallace];
// Can bob (a monster) attack steve (a werewolf) ?
[bob attack:steve];
// Can steve attack bob?
[steve attack:bob];
```

When you build and run this application, it should produce output similar to the following:

```
2011-06-03 11:53:27.121 Hour4[26515:903] I, Steve the terrible,
am attacking Wallace!!
2011-06-03 11:53:27.121 Hour4[26515:903] I, Bob the terrible,
am attacking Steve!!
2011-06-03 11:53:27.122 Hour4[26515:903] I, Steve the terrible,
am attacking Bob!!
```

It works! There is plenty more fun to be had with polymorphism, however.

Polymorphism by Contract

Being able to pass around instances that belong to a whole family of objects comes in *very* handy. You will see this kind of inheritance in action when we get to building user interfaces and you see how various views inherit functionality from parent views.

There is another way we can support polymorphism, and that's by contract. What if we want to be able to support some functionality that may or may not belong to different monsters?

Suppose that some of the creatures we're modeling can expose their weaknesses to their attackers. Certainly not a very bright move, but it helps illustrate the point that some classes might be able to expose weakness and some may not, and those classes don't need to inherit from a parent class that exposes weaknesses.

To see this in action let's create a *protocol*. A protocol is a contract. It doesn't contain any executable code; it only defines the attributes and behaviors that an implementing class needs to implement.

> Protocols can also contain optional properties and methods, providing for a lot of flexibility. When creating your own protocols, be careful what you mark optional and what you mark required. Many common runtime problems stem from your code assuming that an optional piece of a protocol exists on an object.

Did You Know?

To create the protocol that requires an implementing class to expose its weakness, follow the steps from the New File Wizard, but this time choose Objective-C Protocol as the type of file you're creating, as shown in Figure 4.5. Name the protocol **DiscoverableWeaknessProtocol**.

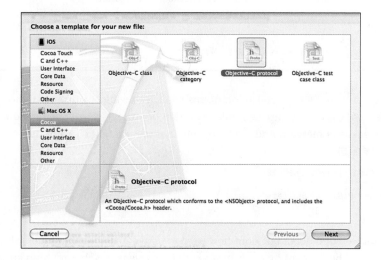

FIGURE 4.5
Creating a protocol.

Modify the code of the protocol file (protocols are usually just header files because, by definition, they only define interface, not implementation) so that it looks like the code in Listing 4.8.

LISTING 4.8   DiscoverableWeaknessProtocol.h

```
#import <Foundation/Foundation.h>

@protocol DiscoverableWeaknessProtocol <NSObject>

- (NSString *)exposeWeakness;

@end
```

Now we know that any object implementing this protocol must have the exposeWeakness method on it. Let's make sure that our Werewolf class properly exposes its weakness.

To do this, we first need to modify the Werewolf.h file so that it declares the fact that it implements the DiscoverableWeaknessProtocol, as shown in Listing 4.9.

LISTING 4.9   Updated Werewolf.h

```
#import <Foundation/Foundation.h>
#import "Monster.h"
#import "DiscoverableWeaknessProtocol.h"

@interface Werewolf : Monster <DiscoverableWeaknessProtocol>{
@private

}

@end
```

If you try to compile the application at this point, you will get warnings indicating that Werewolf is an incomplete implementation because it has not defined an exposeWeakness method. Add the following lines of code to the end of the Werewolf.m file:

```
- (NSString *)exposeWeakness
{
    return @"Silver Bullets";
}
```

This is all well and good, but right now we don't have any code that takes advantage of this. The Werewolf class is now exposing its weakness, but nothing knows how to take advantage of it.

To show the real power of protocols, let's teach the `Monster` class how to discover the weakness of other monsters. To do this, modify the `attack:` method in the `Monster.m` file to look like the following:

```
- (void)attack:(Monster *)target
{
    NSLog(@"I, %@ the terrible, am attacking %@!!",
        _name,
        target.name);
    if ([target conformsToProtocol:@protocol(DiscoverableWeaknessProtocol)])
    {
        Monster<DiscoverableWeaknessProtocol> *weakMonster =
        (Monster<DiscoverableWeaknessProtocol> *)target;
        NSLog(@"A-Ha! I've discovered %@'s weakness! It is %@",
            weakMonster.name,
            [weakMonster exposeWeakness]);

    }
}
```

By the Way

You will have to add an import for the `DiscoverableWeaknessProtocol.h` file into any class file that makes use of this protocol!

The first part of the method is identical to the previous version. Next, we check to see if the monster being attacked *conforms to* a given protocol. This means that regardless of its underlying type (`Monster`, `Cat`, `Politician`, and so on), this method will return true if the class (or any of its parent or ancestor classes) conforms to that protocol.

Next, we create a variable that is of a type that we can read as "a Monster that conforms to the DiscoverableWeaknessProtocol" (the angled brackets in Objective-C can be read aloud as "conforms to"). This lets Xcode know exactly to which messages that object will respond. In our case, it can respond to both the name method (property accessor) inherited from the `Monster` class *and* the exposeWeakness method required by the discoverable weakness protocol.

Protocols might look a little awkward to you now, but by the time we get through some basic user interface with Cocoa, they will become second nature.

When you run the application again, you'll notice that when Steve (a werewolf) gets attacked, the attacker inherits the capability to detect Steve's weakness, and the debug log gets an entry that looks like this:

```
2011-06-03 12:17:08.586 Hour4[26690:903] A-Ha! I've discovered Steve's weakness!
It is Silver Bullets
```

Summary

This hour was packed full of object-oriented programming concepts. We looked at classes, objects, attributes, behaviors, polymorphism, contracts, inheritance, and how to combine and utilize all those things in ways that make for powerful classes and class hierarchies.

Q&A

Q. *When I run my applications like the hour says, I can't find the debug log you're talking about. Where is it?*

A. The debug log shows up when you click the Hide or Show the Debug Area button in the top right of the Xcode IDE. When the debug area is visible, you can control what pieces of that area are shown with more panel visibility buttons.

Q. *When I try to compile, I get "semantic issue" errors like "Cannot find interface declaration." What causes this?*

A. This is a pretty common error that results from not importing the header file for a class that is referenced in the complaining file. Check to see if you've imported `Monster.h` from `Werewolf.h` or `Serpent.h`. You will get similar errors if you attempt to use a protocol and haven't imported the protocol's header file.

HOUR 5

Understanding Memory Management

What you'll learn in this hour:

▶ Introduction to Memory Management
▶ Creating and Fixing Memory Leaks
▶ Using Automatic Reference Counting

In this day and age of desktop and laptop computers with massive amounts of memory, tons of cores, and huge hard drives, it can be very easy for users and developers alike to take this capacity for granted.

Managing memory has always been a sticky point with developers. Whether we were manually locking every single byte of device memory on RAM-less device operating systems like PalmOS, or whether we're using modern garbage collectors like those that can be found in Objective-C, C#, and Java—developers should always have a keen awareness of how memory is being managed as they write their code.

In this hour, you'll see some of the common ways in which memory is managed in a typical Objective-C application. In classic schoolhouse style, I will walk you through doing things the hard way first and then show you the easy way afterward. As is often the case, seeing the "easy way" won't make much sense until you know how the hard way works and which problems the easy way is eliminating.

Introduction to Memory Management

In the sample code that you've been writing so far, you have been interacting with OS X Lion's memory management facilities whether you knew it or not. In this part of the hour, we'll go into more detail on memory management and show you what's going on behind the scenes.

Follow these steps to start exploring the inner workings of Objective-C's memory management:

1. Open Xcode, create a new Cocoa application, and fill in the new project form as shown in Figure 5.1

FIGURE 5.1
Creating a
new Cocoa
application.

2. By default, the version of Xcode that comes with OS X Lion turns on Automatic Reference Counting (discussed later in this hour). We are going to turn that off so that we can explore the underlying memory management system. To turn it off, click the project name in the navigation tree on the left, make sure the project is highlighted in the middle, and then type **ARC** into the search box, as shown in Figure 5.2

3. Change the Yes next to Automatic Reference Counting to No.

FIGURE 5.2
Disabling
Automatic
Reference
Counting in
Xcode.

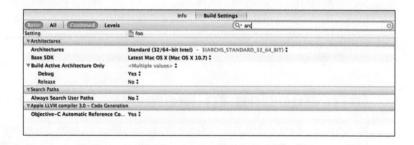

At this point, you have a Cocoa application that is managing memory the way it has been managed since Objective-C's early days, and this how we will get acquainted with memory management.

Introduction to Reference Counting

When developers started writing programs that were far less complex than the ones we write today, we had very tight control over the memory. We would explicitly call functions like `malloc` to allocate memory of a certain size, and then we would call `dalloc` (or `free`) to dispose of allocated memory.

This model worked quite well in the procedural world and in simple programs, but difficulty arose when we got into the realm of object-oriented programming, and it pretty much stemmed from one all-important question:

When is it safe to de-allocate memory?

In a modular application that could be made up of hundreds of classes that are all sending messages to each other and passing pointers to other objects around like hot potatoes, individual methods have no way of knowing whether another method somewhere else has a reference to a particular object. As a result, these methods couldn't reliably decide whether it was safe to dispose of an object.

Take the following code snippet, for example:

```
- (void)launchRocketAt:(BigTarget *)target
{
    [target takeDamage:5000];
    if ([target isDead])
        // is it safe to get rid of the target object's memory here??
}
```

In this sample, we've got an object called `target`. If this target is destroyed by the blast we launch at it, we might think it's safe to go ahead and release the memory for that object. But, what if there's a `GameBoard` object somewhere that is maintaining a list of game objects, one of which is a pointer to the same location as our target object?

If we dispose of the memory associated with the `target` object, the next time the code that runs through the list of pieces on the gameboard tries to follow that pointer to some meaningful data, it will crash.

On the other hand, we can't take the opposite approach and be afraid of deallocating memory for any object because then our programs would become so bloated they couldn't function.

The solution to this problem is *reference counting*.

Introduction to Reference Counting

Reference counting is one of many ways of solving the problem of managing, allocating, and cleaning up memory used by code in modular and object-oriented applications.

As each piece of code is given access to an object, that code gets to decide whether it needs to hang onto that object for a while. Think of an object as a pincushion that floats through the myriad execution paths of an application. Every time the pincushion floats into a new block of code, that block of code can stick a pin in the cushion. When it's done with the object, rather than destroying the pincushion directly (and possibly ruining someone else's code!), the code block politely removes a pin from the cushion. The runtime that manages Objective-C objects notices when an empty pincushion is floating around and disposes of the memory that pincushion is consuming.

As mentioned, the pincushion is an instance of an Objective-C class and the pins are *reference counts*.

From a programming point of view, a block of code declares its intent to hold onto an object by sending it the *retain* message. When the code block is done with the object, declaring that as far as it's concerned, it's ok to destroy, it sends the object the *release* message.

When an object's *retain count* reaches zero (there are no more pins in the cushion), the Objective-C runtime feels free to dispose of the memory allocated for that object.

By the Way

> You may also have heard of *root counting*. Root counting is different from reference counting. Where reference counting requires developers to explicitly declare their intent with regard to the retention of an object, root counting works by analyzing instantiation and reference paths to discover orphaned objects and is often used in garbage collection systems (discussed later this hour).

The hard part, of course, is deciding when to retain and release object references. You might wonder whether adding an object to a mutable array will add a retain/reference count to it. You might wonder what happens if you release an already released object.

The best way to satisfy curiosity is to write some code, because no amount of documentation can serve as a substitute for good, old-fashioned tinkering.

> Tinkering is more important than you might think. The more you play with a shiny new toy, the more likely you are to break it. For developers, learning what they did to break the toy and how they can fix it is an essential skill, reducing the fear of the unknown and making the developer more comfortable in the new environment. So, tinker away!

Did You Know?

To start experimenting with reference counting, open up the Xcode project you created earlier and proceed with the following steps:

1. Adapting the procedures from previous hours, add a new class to the project called **SampleClass**.

2. Open up the Hour_5AppDelegate.m implementation file by left-clicking it in the left navigation pane.

3. Modify the file so that it looks like the code in Listing 5.1.

LISTING 5.1   Hour_5AppDelegate.m

```
#import "Hour_5AppDelegate.h"
#import "SampleClass.h"

@implementation Hour_5AppDelegate

@synthesize window = _window;

- (void)applicationDidFinishLaunching:(NSNotification *)aNotification
{
    // Insert code here to initialize your application

    SampleClass *sample = [[SampleClass alloc] init];

    NSLog(@"retain count of sample: %lu", [sample retainCount]);

    NSMutableArray *array = [[NSMutableArray alloc] init];
    NSLog(@"retain count of array: %lu", [array retainCount]);

    [array addObject:sample];
    NSLog(@"retain count of sample after adding to array: %lu",
[sample retainCount]);

    // safe to release sample!
    [sample release];
}
@end
```

When you run this application, the debug log will contain entries that look similar to these:

```
2011-06-13 22:35:40.920 Hour 5[4111:507] retain count of sample: 1
2011-06-13 22:35:40.934 Hour 5[4111:507] retain count of array: 1
2011-06-13 22:35:40.936 Hour 5[4111:507] retain count of sample
after adding to array: 2
```

Let's take a closer look at what's going on here. Immediately after allocating memory for the SampleClass object, its retain count becomes 1. This means that by sending alloc and then init to an object, we're automatically declaring our intent to hang onto the object, and so we'll need to make sure we release it when we're done.

Next, we create an instance of a mutable array (whose retain count is 1 for the same reason as that of SampleClass). After adding the instance of SampleClass to the array, its retain count becomes 2. From this, we can infer that the array is declaring its intent to hang onto the object as well.

This makes perfect sense. If we add an object to an array, the array needs to be able to count on the fact that the object will remain accessible as long as the object is in the array. If the object can be disposed of without ever being removed from the array, it can easily cause the array code to crash.

A general rule is that you should never release an object that you didn't instantiate yourself using an alloc, new, or copy method. Although exceptions exist to every rule (such as specific APIs where you know that you need to release something you didn't allocate), this is a good guideline to follow and comes directly from Apple's memory management guide.

Detecting and Fixing Memory Leaks

In an effort to keep each of these hours as close to an hour of your time as possible, we're not going to be able to explore the depths of memory leak creation, detection, debugging, and repair. Rather, we'll take a look at some very quick and easy samples of what memory leaks are, what some look like, and how we fix them. After you finish this book, if you are still eager to find out more information on memory management and memory leaks, a multitude of online and printed references can help.

If you do want extra details on memory management in Cocoa applications, check out the following URL: http://developer.apple.com/library/mac/#documentation/Cocoa/Conceptual/MemoryMgmt/Articles/MemoryMgmt.html

What Is a Memory Leak?

A memory leak is a piece of allocated memory to which nothing refers. To bring back the beleaguered pincushion analogy, think of a memory leak as a pincushion with no pins that is hiding so well that it can't be destroyed. Eventually, if your application leaks enough memory, it will run out of free memory and crash.

Thankfully, modern applications like those built for Mac OS X Lion won't bring down the entire operating system if they are leaking memory, but it can slow the computer down and will certainly create a terrible experience for your application's users.

Detecting Memory Leaks

There's actually a little bit of a memory leak in the previous code sample. In fact, it's such an easy to spot memory leak that Xcode's Analyze feature will be able to spot the offending code very quickly.

To see this in action, switch over to Xcode, go to Product and select Analyze. If you're looking at the `Hour_5AppDelegate.m` file, you'll immediately see a blue line appear.

There is an error message displayed on the offending line of code. If you click the little blue button next to the error message, something truly amazing happens. Xcode draws arrows showing you the code path that creates an object leak, as shown in Figure 5.3

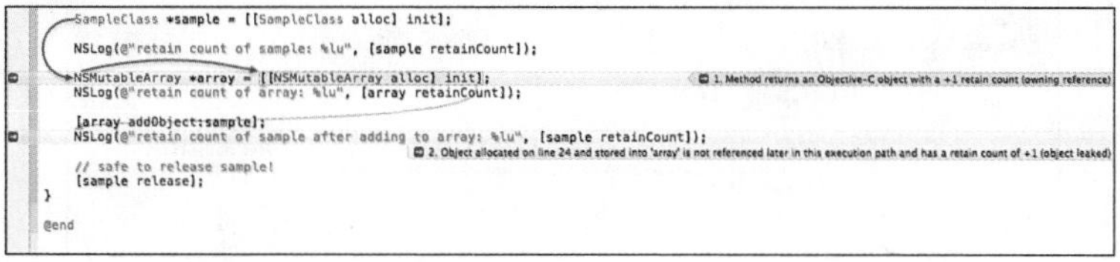

FIGURE 5.3
Xcode's Analyze feature illustrating an object leak.

This figure shows us that the instance of `SampleClass` is created with a reference count of one, which means that we've created an *owning reference* to this variable called `sample`.

We then add that object to an array, increasing its reference count to 2, as we've already seen. What this bit of code analysis then tells us is that the reference count never drops to 0, so the object is being leaked.

This is a classic example of an object having too many references; as such, it is never de-allocated. Another type of memory leak is when an object is set to `nil` before its reference count hits zero, creating a piece of allocated memory to which nothing refers (the hiding pincushion).

Here's a classic loop that will leak a whole bunch of objects:

```
// Loop to leak a pile of objects
for (int x=0; x<20; x++)
{
    SampleClass *theSample = [[SampleClass alloc] init];
    // pretend to do something useful here...
    NSLog(@"sample: %@", theSample);
    // we're done so set the object to nil, right? :)
    theSample = nil;
}
```

Now when we run Product, Analyze we don't get any errors. To detect this kind of memory leak, we're going to have to run the application and use a different kind of instrument, the Leaks profiler.

In Xcode, click the Product menu and then Profile. When prompted, choose the Leaks instrument, as shown in Figure 5.4.

FIGURE 5.4
Choosing the Leaks instrument.

After the application runs for a while, you can click the Stop button. Expand the Leaks portion of the tree view, and you'll see that it has detected that `SampleClass` has been leaked 19 times, as shown in Figure 5.5. Coincidentally enough, that is exactly the number of iterations in the `for` loop from the preceding sample.

Entire hours, or even books, could be written about the proper use of the various instruments available when profiling Xcode applications. For now, we're going to have to keep moving so we can take a look at a few ways to fix the memory leaks we've seen so far.

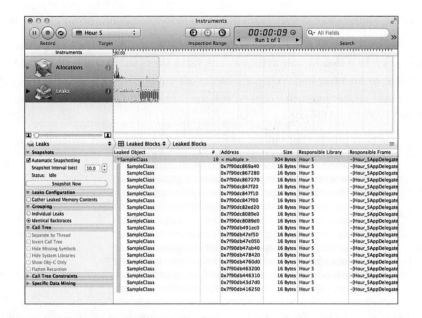

FIGURE 5.5
Results of running the Leaks instrument.

For more detail, see the "Debugging and Analyzing Your Code" section of the Xcode user guide here: http://developer.apple.com/library/ios/#documentation/ToolsLanguages/Conceptual/Xcode4UserGuide/Debugging/Debugging.html#//apple_ref/doc/uid/TP40010215-CH3-SW1

Did You Know?

Fixing Memory Leaks

As you saw in the previous section, one of the ways you can find memory leaks is through the use of the Analyze tool. This tool performs static analysis on your code and finds common problems without you even needing to run your application.

The first leak we found, the one indicating that we never got rid of all the references to the SampleClass instance, is fairly easy to fix. The problem stems from the fact that our code has an *owning reference* to the object, and when we added it to an array, the array also had a reference to it. If you look back at the code, you'll notice that we never released the array or removed the item from it to drop its reference count.

To fix this leak, add the following line of code right after the line where we release sample:

```
[array release];
```

Rerun the Analyze tool to make sure that it no longer complains about leaking the `sample` object.

Next, let's take a look at how to fix memory leaks where we've accidentally lost track of objects. In the preceding (extremely contrived) sample, we foolishly set our objects to nil before reclaiming their memory, and the Leaks instrument told us that we leaked the object 19 times.

We can go back into the code and make sure we release the object inside the loop before we set it to nil:

```
// Loop to leak a pile of objects
for (int x=0; x<20; x++)
{
    SampleClass *theSample = [[SampleClass alloc] init];
    // pretend to do something useful here...
    NSLog(@"sample: %@", theSample);
    // we're done so set the object to nil, right? :)
    [theSample release];
    theSample = nil;
}
```

Rerunning the profiler with the Leaks instrument now shows that we're not leaking any memory. Again, this is a cursory coverage of memory leak debugging; hopefully, after you see what's in the next section, you won't have to worry too much about it.

> There is a facility called an autorelease pool that allows us to gather up logically related objects, and we can send the `release` message to the *pool* rather than individual objects. When the pool is released, all the objects in the pool are released. There is a little overhead penalty for using pools, but they can vastly simplify the task of managing memory and reducing leaks when used appropriately.

Using Automatic Reference Counting

I'm sure most of us remember being in school when the teacher showed us the tedious, painful, hard way to do something. Then, after we'd struggled through doing things the hard way, the teacher showed us the easy way. This is when we vowed revenge.

As hard as it may be for us to admit, the teachers were right. If I simply showed you the easy way (Automatic Reference Counting) without explaining regular reference counting or memory leaks, you wouldn't have any way of knowing how much good stuff is being done on your behalf and, more importantly, you wouldn't know *why*.

Doing things the manual (I try to avoid calling "difficult") way involves paying very close attention to which objects our code owns, which objects we sort of need to keep track of, and which objects we don't particularly care about at all. Even with all of that tracking being done in our heads, we still need to make sure that we call `release` at the right time.

A brand new feature available in Mac OS X Lion (as well as iOS 5.0, much to the enjoyment of iPhone and iPad developers) is Automatic Reference Counting (ARC). It does just what you think it might do given its name: it takes care of retaining and releasing references for us. Make no mistake, reference counting is still being done under the hood—we are just being insulated from it as developers.

By the Way

> Automatic Reference Counting is not the same as Garbage Collection, a feature
> that has been available since the release of Objective-C 2.0. Garbage Collection is
> a dominant feature of languages like C# and Java and works by having a back-
> ground process periodically traverse graphs of managed objects and clean up the
> orphans. ARC requires a little more forethought on the developer's part but should,
> in general, be faster than Garbage Collection.

Developers still need to declare how they want to hold onto the objects, but the plumbing of retaining and releasing is hidden from us.

Follow these instructions to experiment with Automatic Reference Counting:

1. Highlight the project (Hour 5) in the folder view of the project browser.

2. Find the Automatic Reference Counting setting we disabled at the beginning of the hour and set it to Yes.

3. Rebuild the application.

4. Note all of the errors that show up. Xcode complains every time you use the `retainCount` message or the `retain` or the `release` message.

5. Let's clean up the code so that we remove all references to `retain`, `release`, and `retainCount`, as shown in Listing 5.2

LISTING 5.2   Removing Reference Counting from Hour_5AppDelegate.m

```
#import "Hour_5AppDelegate.h"
#import "SampleClass.h"

@implementation Hour_5AppDelegate

@synthesize window = _window;
```

```
- (void)applicationDidFinishLaunching:(NSNotification *)aNotification
{
    // Insert code here to initialize your application

    SampleClass *sample = [SampleClass new];

    NSMutableArray *array = [NSMutableArray new];

    [array addObject:sample];

    // Loop to leak a pile of objects
    for (int x=0; x<20; x++)
    {
        SampleClass *theSample = [[SampleClass alloc] init];
        // pretend to do something useful here...
        NSLog(@"sample: %@", theSample);
        // we're done so set the object to nil, right? :)
        theSample = nil;
    }
}
@end
```

Did You Know?

> We don't actually have to send the class the `alloc` message and then send the instance the `init` message. We can send the class the `new` message as a shortcut—for example, `[SampleClass new]`.

6. Now let's add some properties to the `SampleClass` class. Listing 5.3 shows the modified `SampleClass.h` file. Note the options when we declare the properties now.

LISTING 5.3   SampleClass.h

```
#import <Foundation/Foundation.h>

@interface SampleClass : NSObject

@property(nonatomic, strong) NSString *firstName;
@property(nonatomic, strong) NSString *lastName;

@property(nonatomic, weak) SampleClass *parent;

@end
```

7. The `strong` keyword indicates that when the property is set, the object will retain it (add 1 to its reference count). Note that we don't have to do the reference count manipulation ourselves. The `weak` keyword will allow the assignment to take place without increasing reference count. If the object is deallocated, the property will be automatically set to nil, which is really

helpful. Finish out this class by adding the `synthesize` statement to the implementation file:

```
@synthesize firstName, lastName, parent;
```

We aren't limited to declaring our object lifetime intentions to properties. You can prefix variable declarations with lifetime hints like __strong, __weak, __unsafe_ unretained, and __autoreleasing. By default, variables are declared with the __strong lifetime hint.

> Automatic Reference Counting will be used by default in every sample throughout the remainder of the book. This should not only make the samples easier to read and experiment with, but should get you used to Apple's new recommendation for development on OS X Lion.

Strong Versus Weak References

As you saw in the preceding code, we can choose to declare objects with strong references or weak references. A strong reference is a retained reference. When this variable or property is set, the value to which it is assigned will be sent the `retain` message automatically. By declaring a variable as a strong reference, we are indicating that we intend to own that object after it has been assigned.

A weak reference is one that is not retained when the variable or property is set. In this case we're just hanging onto the reference, but we don't plan on using it for very long, or we know that we aren't the owner of the object so we don't need to waste resources by messing with that object's retain count.

A *zeroing* weak reference is a weak reference that, when deallocated, will set the object to *nil*. This means that if we have a weak reference to the parent object, as with the code in Listing 5.3, and the parent object is released by some other code, the `parent` property will automatically be set to nil. This is a tremendously helpful feature that will save developers a lot of time spent debugging errors they get when attempting to access previously released objects (also called *zombies*).

Summary

This was a very dense hour, and we tried to pack an awful lot of information about memory management into it. We started with an overview of how Objective-C handles reference counting and how reference counting mistakes can lead to memory leaks. Finally, we wrapped up the hour with a discussion of Automatic Reference

Counting, Apple's preferred memory management scheme for new applications developed for Mac OS X Lion and iOS5 and beyond.

This hour finishes up the foundational section of the book. In the next hour, we'll move on to create some actual user interface, and we can stop using the NSLog function to keep tabs on what we're doing.

Q&A

Q. *Information online suggests that we should be using Garbage Collection and doesn't mention ARC. Which one should I use and when?*

A. If you are building a brand new application targeting Mac OS X Lion, Apple recommends that you use Automatic Reference Counting. If you are building on a previous version of Mac OS X, ARC is not available, and you'll probably want to use Garbage Collection. If you are writing for iOS 4 and earlier, neither ARC nor Garbage Collection is available as an option, and you have to manage memory the "old-fashioned" way.

Q. *Does the Leaks instrument still work with an ARC application?*

A. Yes. Although it should be substantially harder to do so, it is still possible to create memory leaks with ARC enabled. Remember that ARC is just doing the reference counting for you, it isn't replacing reference counting with another mechanism like Garbage Collection does. All of the profiling and analysis tools should work just fine with ARC, GC, and traditional memory management applications.

HOUR 6

Introducing Cocoa

What you'll learn in this hour:

▶ What Cocoa Is and Where It Came From

▶ The Basics of Using Interface Builder

▶ How to Use Interface Builder's Inspectors

▶ How to Add and Configure Controls in a Window

Now that you have a solid foundation, built by the previous hours, of the tools and the Objective-C programming language, in this hour you'll start building your first graphical user interface (GUI) with Cocoa.

In this hour, you learn what Cocoa is, where it came from, and what it includes. You'll see the various inspectors and tools used in creating user interfaces for Mac OS X Lion. Then, to wrap things up and solidify all this information, you'll build and manipulate your own UI using the design tool.

A Brief Overview of Cocoa

In the late 1980s and 1990s a company called NeXT was working on a revolutionary new operating system called NeXTSTEP and application development frameworks for that operating system, called Application Kit and Foundation Kit (among other frameworks, also commonly labeled as "kits"). In 1996 Apple acquired NeXT and all of its intellectual property.

Apple's new operating system (to be called Rhapsody) was to have a Mac emulation layer called Blue Box, and the application frameworks and base libraries for development were called Yellow Box.

The Blue Box eventually became the first release of Mac OS X, and the Yellow Box set of libraries and frameworks became Cocoa.

By the Way

> If you've been wondering why so many of the basic classes, such as NSString, start with the two-letter prefix NS, it should no longer be a mystery. Most of the classes in Cocoa use this prefix, which stands for the origins of the API, NeXTSTEP.

Cocoa is made up of multiple frameworks, but two frameworks make up the majority of what you're going to use in this book:

▶ **Foundation Kit**—Foundation Kit is based on Core Foundation. Many of the classes at this low level are prefixed with CF, for Core Foundation. Much of the user interface that makes Cocoa applications possible relies on low-level facilities provided in the Foundation Kit.

▶ **Application Kit (often simply called AppKit)**—This framework is a direct descendent of the original UI framework developed for NeXTSTEP. AppKit is built on top of the foundation libraries, and its classes all use the same NS prefix.

By the Way

> Although this book focuses exclusively on Cocoa development using Objective-C, it is possible to write Cocoa applications in several other languages, including Ruby, Python, and even C#. Documentation on Ruby and Python for Cocoa is sketchy, and Apple no longer distributes project templates for those languages. For information on writing Cocoa applications in C#, check out the Mono Project's CocoaSharp tool at http://www.mono-project.com/CocoaSharp.

Understanding the Model-View-Controller Pattern

One of the many defining characteristics of the Cocoa API is the use of the Model-View-Controller (MVC) pattern. This pattern is a way of separating the various components of an interactive application to make them easier to build, maintain, debug, and enhance. The MVC pattern has been around since the days of the Smalltalk language and divides application code into the following three roles:

▶ **Model**—The model is, as you may have guessed, where the data resides. For example, an address book application might have a model that contains a list of contacts, or a stock trading application's model might contain the most recent buy and sell quotes for a list of stock symbols.

▶ **View**—The view is the user interface. This is what the users see and what they interact with using the mouse, trackpad, or touch device like an iPhone or iPad. Views in their purest form should have very little embedded logic and should know very little about anything other than the UI.

▶ **Controller**—As its name implies, the controller is responsible for orchestrating the user interface as a whole. It responds to user input when the view forwards that information to the controller, and it can manipulate the view in response to changes in the model.

You will see a lot more of the MVC pattern as you progress through this book. Controllers are pervasive throughout Cocoa, and in many cases developers often find it difficult to *not* adopt the MVC pattern. Don't worry if it doesn't quite make sense yet—in the next few hours, we'll create several models, views, and controllers, and it will all become much clearer.

Understanding the Cocoa Views System

The first and most important thing to know about the Cocoa view system is that *everything is a view*. A view is a rectangular region of the screen that is either in a window or contained within another view. All views are ultimately derived from the NSView class.

Unlike many other UI frameworks where interactive controls inherit from disparate inheritance hierarchies, all controls, knobs, widgets, images, and everything in between is a view. This consistency makes learning the basics of Cocoa very easy.

Did You Know?

The Cocoa View system is both rich and deep. There's a lot of information to grasp, and there just isn't enough time in this hour to cram it all in. If you want the full story on Cocoa Views, check out Apple's *View Programming Guide for Cocoa*, which you can find on its Mac developer site or at this shortcut URL: http://tinyurl.com/cocoaviews.

Views can also contain other views. Sometimes this is to provide simple nesting; at other times, the parent view enforces some kind of layout or special behavior on its subviews. In these cases, the parent view is called a *container view*. Container views can do things like allow subview content to be scrollable, separate multiple views as tabs in a tab control, or enable subtle functionality like wrapping subviews in a box to logically separate them from the container view's peers.

Understanding View Coordinates and Hierarchies

Each view in Cocoa has its own private coordinate system. Any subviews that are positioned within it or any custom drawing that takes place in that view takes place in the view's local coordinates.

The coordinate system is a standard Cartesian plane, but unlike the ones many of us remember from high school math class, the origin is *not* in the center. Center-based origins make for really difficult drawing because you have to deal with negative numbers.

To make drawing and positioning as easy as possible, each view's *origin* is in the bottom-left corner of the view. The X axis extends horizontally to the right of the origin, and the Y axis extends vertically above the origin, as shown in Figure 6.1

FIGURE 6.1
Cocoa view
coordinates.

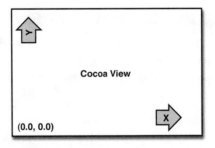

When you place a subview within a parent view, its position is given relative to the parent or container's origin. However, if that subview also has its own subviews, those views are positioned relative to that view's origin.

What that really means is that every view is responsible for the views underneath it and isn't responsible for the view in which it resides, called the *superview*.

By the Way

> There are several fairly easy ways that you can convert coordinates local to one view to coordinates relative to the superview's origin and back again. These helper functions get used frequently when reacting to touches, clicks, and mouse movement.

When views render, they render from the *bottom up*. This means that the topmost view in the hierarchy will appear on the bottom of the user interface. Its subviews are rendered *on top* of the superview, and those subviews are rendered atop their subviews, and so on.

Figure 6.2 shows a mock-up of a view hierarchy.

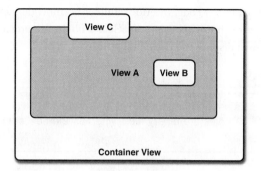

FIGURE 6.2
Sample view
hierarchy.

From this picture, we can gather that the container view is the topmost view in the hierarchy and is probably the sole subview (or *content view*) of the window.

The container view has two subviews, *View A* and *View C*. The order in which you add a subview to the parent view determines whether it will render above or below its peer views. The last view added as a subview will be the one that renders topmost in the UI. *View B* is a subview of *View A*. Each of these views has its own local coordinate systems, but coordinates within each of those views can be translated into the coordinate system of any of the superviews.

The hierarchy rendering might seem confusing at first, so this mnemonic may help keep things straight: Think of the programmer adding views to the hierarchy as though you're putting cards down on a table. If you put a queen down *after* you put a jack down, and you've put them both in the same place, the only card you can see is the queen, even though both cards are on the table. Cocoa's rendering system is like an observer looking straight down at your card table.

Did You Know?

Taking a Tour of Interface Builder

Before we can start putting controls in our user interface, we should probably get familiar with the tool that allows us to do just that. Interface Builder is the tool that allows us to visually design our user interfaces.

Versions of Xcode older than 4.x did not include Interface Builder as part of the Integrated Development Environment (IDE). Interface Builder used to be a separate tool that had its own windows, its own interface, and often caused confusion or lost time when developers got their interfaces out of sync with their code. Keeping track of the code and interface also became a chore for developers with small monitors or laptops because of the sheer number of windows, trays, inspectors, and panels that could be open at any given time.

With the current version of Xcode, Interface Builder is embedded directly into the Xcode tool. This means that whenever you select a file in the project files list with the .xib extension, it will display Interface Builder rather than the code editing view on the right.

> Interface Builder files used to be stored only as .nib files, which stands for NeXT Interface Builder. .nib files are binary files, whereas the new standard, .xib, is an XML file.

Follow these steps to create a new project and see what Interface Builder looks like:

1. Open Xcode and create a new Cocoa application project called **Hour6**.

2. In the project navigator on the left, select the MainMenu.xib file.

3. On the right, you should see an Interface Builder screen that looks similar to the one in Figure 6.3.

FIGURE 6.3
Interface
Builder.

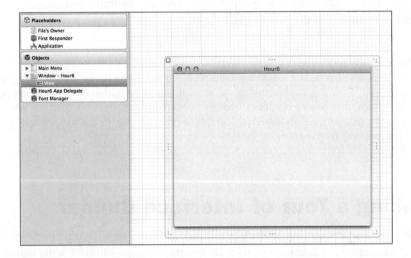

On the left side of the Interface Builder screen is a tray containing placeholders and objects. The three placeholders you will see in every xib file are the File's Owner, First Responder, and Application. We won't spend too much time on these now, but they will become increasingly important in later hours.

Below the placeholders is a list of objects contained within the file. In the default file we have a main menu, a window titled Hour 6, an object representing the Hour6 App Delegate, and an object representing the Font Manager.

In the next section, we take a closer look at some of the ways you can inspect and manipulate user interface objects within Interface Builder.

Using the Utilities Panels and Inspectors

Interface Builder is an extremely powerful tool, and even the most user-friendly of tools can take some getting used to before you feel comfortable with it. The goal of this next section is to give you a tour of the various panels and inspectors that you will use daily as a Mac OS X Lion developer so that you will feel comfortable maneuvering through the many layers of Interface Builder.

To get started, click the Hide or Show Utilities icon in the top right of your Xcode window (the one that shows a panel docked to the right side of a window). This will cause the utilities panel to appear.

The file inspector is the first tab in this panel and shows properties and information about the file you're editing. We won't spend much time on this inspector. The next inspector tab is the quick help inspector. We saw this in previous hours, and you can leave this inspector open while coding to get live, auto-adjusting help as it relates to the classes you're using. There is also a view effects inspector that we won't be covering in this hour because Hour 19, "Building Animated User Interfaces," is devoted to animation and effects.

The Identity Inspector

The identity inspector allows you to view and manipulate various aspects of the *identity* of the object currently selected. The object could be anything from a window to a control to a placeholder to one of the "blue cube" objects representing object instances that have no user interface.

Figure 6.4 shows the identity inspector with the main window selected. Before continuing, select all the different objects on the left in the placeholders and objects panel to see how it affects the contents of the identity inspector.

One of the features you will use most on this tab is to choose a custom class from which the object derives.

Never underestimate the power of inline documentation available directly in the IDE. Make use of the Notes field and provide Xcode-specific labels for your views and controls. When working in Interface Builder, document your work as if you intended it to be viewed by a developer who had never looked at your project before. This way, when you come back to your code after a long vacation or a trip to the bar, you will still be able to discern what's happening and why.

FIGURE 6.4
The identity
inspector.

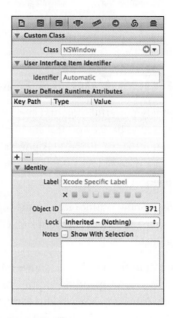

The Attributes Inspector

The attributes inspector allows you, as the name implies, to view the attributes of a selected object. If you are familiar with other development IDEs, you might think of this tab as a "property grid" or a property editor.

The list of attributes available for viewing and editing is entirely dependent on the type of object you have selected. For a window, you can change the title, the autosave name (we'll get to autosave in a few hours), and which controls appear on the window frame (minimize, close, and resize). In addition, you can change the window's behavior and appearance in many ways.

In short, if you ever find yourself looking for a way to "set up" or configure a particular view or control, make the attributes inspector the first place you go.

Figure 6.5 shows the attributes inspector with the main window selected.

As you did with the identity inspector, select of the different objects and placeholders and take note of the various attributes that you can edit for each.

Did You Know?

Whenever you're looking at an inspector in Xcode, especially on a small monitor, make sure you give the trackpad or mouse a quick flip to cause it to scroll. Often, additional properties and groups are hidden by other panels, and you can't see them until you scroll.

FIGURE 6.5
The attributes
inspector.

The Size Inspector

The size inspector allows you to view and control the size and layout characteristics of a control, including a window. When you select a view, the size inspector provides you with knobs and input fields that control everything from the control's starting size to how it should stretch in relation to nearby views to how it should lay itself out within the parent container. You can even change its origin (although I don't recommend doing this unless you absolutely have to).

Figure 6.6 shows the size inspector in action.

The Connections Inspector

The connections inspector is another area within Interface Builder where you will probably spend a great deal of time. You will see a lot more about connections in Hour 8, "Creating Interactive Applications." For now, think of connections as a way of linking aspects of a view's behavior to code.

In other IDEs you might double-click a button that then pulls up a blank piece of boilerplate code, allowing you to start coding. Cocoa applications take a slightly different approach in that you need to *connect* a UI behavior with an *action* in code. Likewise, if you want to connect data rather than behavior, you need to plug a UI connection into an *outlet* in an underlying Objective-C class.

FIGURE 6.6
The size
inspector.

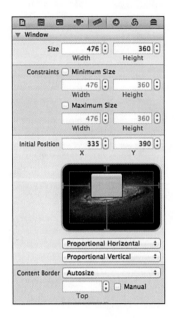

You will get plenty of hands-on experience with connections, outlets, and actions in Hour 8.

Figure 6.7 shows the connections inspector for an NSButton class that has been selected. Note the empty (hollow circle) connection point for handling the button's performClick: action. If we had code plugged into that action, the circle would appear solid.

The Bindings Inspector

The bindings inspector allows you to bind all sorts of attributes of a particular object to values stored in code properties. Bindings are different from connections, and you'll see that difference more clearly as you go through both Hour 8 and Hour 9.

For example, you might want to bind the text of a button to the value of a string property stored in an instance of an object. In another instance, you might want to bind the contents of a table control to an array of customers, and so on.

Figure 6.8 shows the binding inspector for a selected button with the Title property expanded to give you a taste of some of the power available in the bindings system.

FIGURE 6.7
The connections inspector.

FIGURE 6.8
The bindings inspector.

The Object Library

As you have been clicking around through the various inspectors, you may have noticed that some of the content below these inspectors has stayed the same throughout this hour. When you have the utilities panel open, the top portion (it is resizable if you need to make room) contains the inspectors and the bottom portion contains the libraries.

The File Template Library contains all the templates available for adding new files of a certain type to a project. The Code Snippet Library contains a wealth of useful snippets for facilitating the creation of code that performs very common tasks, such as creating classes, performing background tasks, and even fetching data from local databases.

The Object Library (represented by the cube icon) is where you'll find all of the visual elements that can be added to an interface. Everything from buttons to images to progress bars and placeholders for custom views is found inside the Object Library. This area of Interface Builder is used constantly during the creation of Cocoa applications.

> The first thing many developers do when setting up Xcode is switch the Object Library view from a detailed list to an icon view. If you have plenty of real estate (such as a 27" monitor or multiple monitors) this may not be an issue, but if space is a concern, the icon view gives you quicker access to the controls with less scrolling. It's easy enough to switch back to list view when you need details.

Figure 6.9 shows the Object Library after having been toggled to the icon view.

FIGURE 6.9
The Object Library.

The Media Library

The media library contains a unified view of the media (images, videos, audio files, and so on) you have added to your application, as well as the stock media that comes with Xcode.

Apple is very big on consistency; as you'll see when we get to the last two hours of the book on the Mac App Store, straying from Apple's consistent guidelines when it comes to user interaction can sometimes be grounds for rejection from the App Store.

By the Way

> Required reading for any Mac developer includes Apple's *Human Interface Guidelines*. This document gives you extremely detailed instructions on how to build an application that feels "at home" on the Mac. You can find these guidelines at this URL: `http://tinyurl.com/apple-hi-guide`.

Using the stock icons, images, and other media from the media library automatically gives your application consistency and makes it gel with other applications that perform similar functionality. For example, if your application makes use of Bluetooth, you should use the stock Bluetooth icon available in the system Media Library, as shown in Figure 6.10.

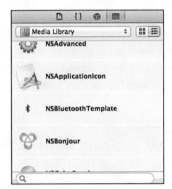

FIGURE 6.10
The Media Library.

Try It Yourself

Adding and Configuring Controls

Now that you've seen Interface Builder and have had some exposure to the inspectors and libraries that developers most often use, it's time to put that into practice and create your very first user interface.

Follow these steps to experiment with adding and configuring controls:

1. Make sure Xcode is open to the Hour6 project that we created earlier.

2. Select the MainMenu.xib file in the project navigator. This should bring up Interface Builder in the right-side editor.

▼

3. Select the Hour 6 window in the objects and placeholders tray.

4. Using the Object Library, drag a box onto the Hour 6 window.

5. Using the Object Library, drag two buttons and a label into the box you created in step 4.

6. Change the Xcode-specific identity of the box to **Main Box**.

Did You
Know?

> Remember that you'll need to select the control you want to modify, and then choose the appropriate inspector before you can change aspects of an object.

7. Change the ToolTip of the first and second buttons to **First Button** and **Second Button**, respectively.

8. Change the Xcode-specific identity label of the buttons from step 7 to **First Button** and **Second Button**, respectively.

9. Change the title of the NSLabel control to **This is a label**.

10. You should see that the label is too small to print all of its text. Change the size of the control *from inside an inspector* (you can also change it by getting the sizing grip as you hover over the edge of a view) so that there is enough room to display the entire title.

Did You
Know?

> If you set the label's width to something more than 90, there should be enough room.

11. Click the button to expand the objects and placeholders tray (it is a right-facing disclosure indicator button at the bottom of the tray). When it expands, you should see the entire hierarchy of views, which looks like the one shown in Figure 6.11.

12. If you've been following along and have done all the steps properly, you should be able to run your application (the Play button at the top left). If you hover over one of the buttons that you set as a tooltip, you should see that text show up in a little yellow box, as shown in Figure 6.12.

This is just a tiny taste of the kinds of things you can do with the stock Cocoa controls. In the next hour, we'll tour through all the standard controls to see what they look like and what they're typically used for.

▼

FIGURE 6.11
Expanded view
hierarchy in
Interface
Builder.

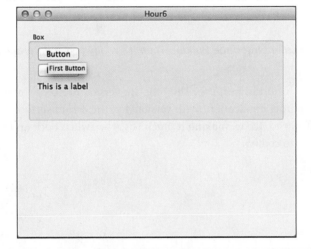

FIGURE 6.12
A running Cocoa
application.

Summary

In this hour we started with an overview and history of Cocoa, the API for building
graphical applications on Mac OS X. From there, we took a look at Interface Builder,
the tool that allows you to graphically design your user interfaces, including a tour
of the available inspectors and libraries.

At this point you should now have a solid foundation of Objective-C skills. You have
received an introduction to Cocoa and building graphical applications for the Mac,
so you should be ready (and hopefully eager!) to move on to the next hour, where
we start diving deeper into building rich user interfaces.

Q&A

Q. *Can I use Cocoa to build server applications or something other than desktop applications?*

A. Cocoa is a User Interface framework. While it contains a ton of utilities and helper classes, it is not meant to be used for anything other than desktop development.

Q. *Creating custom controls in some other desktop application frameworks can be really hard—is it that hard with Cocoa?*

A. Remember that everything visual in Cocoa derives from a view, so if you understand the view hierarchy, how views are rendered, and the basics of the NSView class, you should be able to create your own controls with little difficulty.

Q. *Why is it called Interface Builder when it's really just a different view inside Xcode?*

A. This is for historical purposes. Until the 4.x version of Xcode, Interface Builder was a separate application. With version 4.x, the design surface of IB is now integrated into Xcode, making it much easier to switch back and forth from designing to coding.

HOUR 7

Using Controls and Layout with Cocoa

What you'll learn in this hour:

▶ Laying Out Controls with Springs and Struts
▶ A Tour of the Basic Controls
▶ Laying Out Controls Using Automatic Layout

In the past hour, you were introduced to the primary design tool for building applications in Cocoa: Interface Builder. You saw all the different inspectors and libraries.

In this hour, we tour all the basic controls and the default layout system, typically referred to as "springs and struts." After the tour of basic controls, you'll see a new layout system that is available only on Mac OS X Lion: Automatic Layout.

> Some of the more advanced controls, as well as custom controls you may develop on your own, are often made up of groups of primitive controls. Rather than taking several hours talking about every possible control combination, in this hour we'll talk about the basic controls and those used as building blocks for more advanced controls.

A Tour of the Basic Cocoa Controls

The expression, "when you're a hammer everything looks like a nail," is appropriate in many scenarios when building software. If you know only one way to solve a problem, that's the only solution you'll attempt to use. Likewise, if you know about only one or two controls, those are the only ones you'll put in your applications.

In this next section, we tour the basic Cocoa controls.

> Remember that all these controls are actually subclasses of NSView. I call them controls for convenience, but you should remember that everything is a view, so if you know how to create custom views, you know how to create custom controls.

We'll see how to do all of the basics of any simple user interface: display information, prompt the user for information, and provide feedback to the user.

Displaying and Editing Text

Whether you're building a game, an application that allows you to edit documents, a financial reporting tool, or anything else, one thing you will always have to do is display text and allow your users to enter text. In this section we'll discuss some of the common controls for displaying and editing text.

Figure 7.1 shows a sample user interface composed of some of the controls we'll discuss in this section.

FIGURE 7.1
Controls for displaying and editing text.

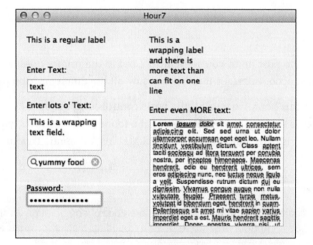

Label

The label is one of the basic building blocks of any user interface. Labels allow you to display text in very flexible ways. You can choose the alignment (centered, left, right, and so on), the foreground color, the type and shape of its border, and many other things. As you'll see in Hour 9, "Creating Data-Bound Interfaces," you can bind many of the properties of controls (such as the displayed text) to data stored in Objective-C objects.

Wrapping Label

A wrapping label is just a label with the ability to wrap text. You can control the wrapping behavior as well as the height and width of the label. These controls come in handy when you need to display some read-only text and a simple one-line label is too small to hold the information.

Text Field

The text field is the most basic facility for allowing users to enter text. It provides users with a powerful control that accepts a single line of text input. Note that the text can be Unicode input, and labels can display Unicode text as well.

By the Way

Unicode input can come from character map tools, pasted from the clipboard, typed manually on a foreign keyboard, or from a tool that translates phonetic typing styles like Pinyin for Chinese and Romaji for Japanese into Unicode that represents native-language characters. You should feel comfortable in knowing that Unicode characters are supported pretty much anywhere data can be accepted as input or displayed by a control.

Wrapping Text Field

A wrapping text field is a text field that has been preconfigured to accept and display multiple lines of text. It also properly handles when the user presses the Enter key to allow for multiline editing.

Did You Know?

The Label, Wrapping Label, Text Field, and Wrapping Text Field controls are all instances of the NSTextField class. Labels are just read-only text fields. Knowing this can come in handy when it comes to interacting with this controls from your Objective-C code.

Text View

The text view is actually a composite control. Anytime you see a text view, its contents are wrapped in a scroll view. When you're editing your window or view in Interface Builder, the first time you click this control you will notice that you've selected the embedded scroll view. If you click again, you will select the text view control itself. This pattern of repetitive single-clicks (not double-clicks!) is used throughout Interface Builder (IB) to reach nested subcontrols. When you get to Hour 10, "Working with Tables and Collections," you'll use this same pattern to edit the properties of individual cells within the outer table or outline view.

Search Field

The search field is a special type of text field that is designed specifically to facilitate searches. You can configure it to invoke search code when the user is done typing in the search field, or it can perform the search dynamically as the user types.

Token Field

The token field looks like a regular text field until the user starts typing into it. Every time the user presses Tab or Enter, it takes the string they just typed and turns it into a "token." You see this kind of behavior when editing contacts in the Address Book application.

Secure Text Field

The secure text field uses a masking character to prevent users from seeing the field's contents. These text fields are typically used to prompt users for passwords or other sensitive information that should not be displayed on the screen and should not be available to the clipboard for copying and pasting.

Number Formatted Text Field

The number formatted text field is a shortcut that will put a regular text field into a container and then associate it with a number formatter. This will ensure that anything a user types into this text field can be converted into a valid number.

By the Way

> Several other types of formatters are available, and you can even write your own. Some of the stock formatters include the date formatter, number formatter, and custom formatter that lets you control the shape and underlying data type of the information being entered by the user.

Pushing Buttons

Now that your users are capable of providing your application with input and seeing information provided by your application, they will expect to be able to *do* something with your app. For this, users generally resort to pressing buttons; fortunately, Cocoa has a wide variety of buttons available.

They all follow the same pattern of allowing a user to press a button to perform an action, but they can differ in implementation and subtleties. Figure 7.2 shows a window with several types of sample buttons on it.

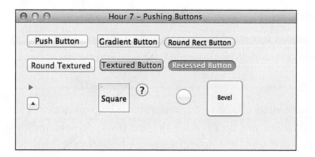

FIGURE 7.2
Button controls.

Push Button

The push button is the standard button used for soliciting action clicks from a user. This type of button has a slightly more squarish appearance in Mac OS X Lion than in previous versions of Mac OS X.

Gradient Button

The gradient button is a square-bordered button. As with all the other buttons, its border, style, coloring, and image can be configured.

Rounded Rect Button

The rounded rect button generally has a shorter appearance than the other buttons with rounded edges.

Round Textured Button

The round textured button looks a lot like the push button control and, from Figure 7.2, it might be hard to tell the difference. When you press down on the button, you'll notice that the push button displays its "down" state with a familiar blue overlay gradient.

When you press down the round textured button, a very subtle change indicates the button has been pressed. When you push the gradient button, the default behavior is to fill the button with gray. Many of the differences between these buttons are very subtle.

For more information on when it is appropriate to use each type of button, consult Apple's *Human Interface Guidelines*: http://developer.apple.com/library/mac/#documentation/UserExperience/Conceptual/AppleHIGuidelines/Intro/Intro.html

Did You Know?

Textured Button

The textured button has an older looking appearance and starts with a gray background fill that gets darker when you press the button down.

Recessed Button

The recessed button starts looking sunken into the background view. The default behavior is that when you click it once, the text becomes bold and the button no longer looks recessed until you hover the mouse back over it.

What this looks like in practice is that clicking a recessed button toggles on and off whether the button is sunken. This type of button makes a great way of providing the user with big, easy-to-hit targets for turning on and off Boolean data without using a check box.

Disclosure Triangle

The disclosure triangle starts out as a simple triangle pointing to the right. When the user clicks this triangle, it animates and points down. This allows you to expose additional user interface at the user's request. Apple's guidelines are very clear that disclosure triangles should be used only to disclose UI *below* the triangle and shouldn't be used to toggle the visibility of seemingly unrelated information elsewhere in the view.

Disclosure Button

The disclosure button has the same purpose as the disclosure triangle—to optionally hide or reveal additional UI elements. However, the disclosure button starts by pointing up and toggles to be pointing down. You often find that these buttons will *animate* or *slide* down below the UI elements they reveal, and then slide back up over them when those same UI elements are hidden again.

Round Button

The round button is, as its name implies, a circle. These types of buttons generally look better when they contain iconic images rather than text because of the shape of the button, although there are no restrictions against placing text within a round button.

Bevel Button

The bevel button is a rectangular button with slightly rounded corners that has a beveled appearance. In general, it looks to be slightly closer to the user (or "further off the page," depending on your frame of reference) than other buttons.

Did You Know?

All the buttons in this section are implementations of the NSButton class. The variations come from choosing the button's *style*, which can be any of the following: Bevel, Push, Check, Radio, Round, Square, Disclosure Triangle, Textured, Help, Gradient, Round Textured, Disclosure, Round Rect, Recessed, and Inline.

Choosing Values and Dates

Allowing the user to enter free-form, password, and lengthy text is great for many applications. However, at times users need shortcuts or specialized controls to allow them to select values of different types, such as dates, selecting yes or no, choosing from among a group of values, incrementing or decrementing values, and so on.

The controls in this section provide the user with simple, easy-to-use facilities for these kinds of input, as shown in Figure 7.3.

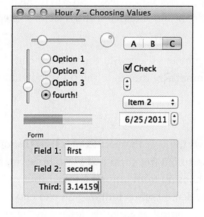

FIGURE 7.3
Controls for choosing values and dates.

Radio Button

Radio buttons exist as part of a radio group. Only one of the options in the group can be selected at any given time. You typically use this type of control when the user needs to select from among a *relatively short* list of available options. Because all the available options are displayed, this type of control shouldn't be used for picking from lengthy or indeterminate lists of options.

Check Box

The check box is a straightforward control that has been around since the dawn of graphical user interfaces. It allows the user to choose between checked (yes or true) and unchecked (no or false).

Combo Box

A combo box, as its name implies, is a combination of a drop-down list and a text field. This control allows the user to type directly into the box as well as select from among a list of available options. You can use this control to allow users to automatically add new possibilities to a list, or you can use the text field as a shortcut for helping the user find the appropriate option.

Date Picker

Date pickers allow users to select dates, and the date the user chooses is available directly from the control as an instance of the NSDate class, freeing the developer from having to manually convert from freeform text into dates.

You can choose three types of date pickers:

▶ **Textual**—A simple text field that limits users to entering only valid dates.

▶ **Textual with Stepper**—A simple text field where each component of the date can be incremented or decremented using a stepper (steppers are discussed shortly).

▶ **Graphical**—This provides users with the familiar calendar view, allowing them to scroll through month by month to select an individual date.

Pop-Up Button

The pop-up button allows the user to select from a fixed list of available options. They cannot pick items using a free-form text view; however, the list of items can scroll, so it is ideal for choosing from among a larger (but not massive!) list of options. Despite being called a pop-*up* button, you can choose whether the list of options pops up from the control or expands downward.

Segmented Control

A segmented control appears as a rectangle with multiple segments. You can use Interface Builder to create additional segments and configure their titles. Like a radio group, the segmented control presents a "one among many" option to users and can have only one segment selected at any given time.

The tab view control uses a segmented control to allow users to pick which tab is the currently selected (and visible) tab.

Stepper

The stepper control is a simple control that provides two opposite-facing arrows that allow the user to *step* a value in a particular direction. You can control the minimum and maximum value as well as how much the value is incremented or decremented every time the user clicks one of the stepping arrows. As you'll see in Hour 9 when we talk about bindings, steppers are often bound to the same numeric value as a number-formatted text field, allowing users to choose whether they enter values directly or whether they make small changes to the existing value.

Level Indicator

As its name implies, the level indicator control is designed to visually indicate a numeric value or *level*. The level indicator is an extremely flexible control and can be used to allow users to edit levels as well as give them feedback. You can choose a simple progress-bar style level or a level that changes from yellow to red depending on its current value and configurable warning and critical threshold values.

Horizontal, Vertical, and Circular Sliders

Sliders of all kinds allow users to click, hold, and then drag to manipulate some underlying numerical value. You can define how much change occurs for each segment the slider is dragged, as well as the maximum and minimum values. The circular slider, although it can be used to select from any arbitrary range, is ideal for letting users select angles because the rotating animation and control is already built in to the button.

Form

The form provides the user with a matrix of inputs. If you need to render a row-and-column style input form where you have a label and a corresponding input field in every row, this control will do the job for you. Remember to use the "repetitive, slow, single-click" technique to drive your selection from the parent control to the individual elements within the form.

Grouping Areas of the UI

When you start building more complex screens, you may find that they get cluttered as you add more and more controls to them. One way of handling that complexity and making your user interfaces easier to use at the same time is using some controls that logically split or group your user interface.

Figure 7.4 shows a very simple example of some ways to logically group UI elements by using a tab view and making use of expanding and contracting split views. Although this UI is certainly not going to win any design awards, it shows off some of the power of these container controls.

FIGURE 7.4
Controls for grouping and splitting views.

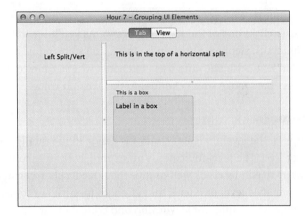

Vertical and Horizontal Split View

The vertical and horizontal split views do as their names imply—split the container in which they reside into two pieces, either vertically or horizontally. By default, the split views come with little gripping bars that allow the user to resize the split. Note that the two views remain next to each other at all times, so when you use the resize bar to expand one side of the split, the other side shrinks accordingly.

Box

The box is a very simple control, yet, when used in the right places, it can have a very powerful effect on the UI. It provides a way of encapsulating its child controls in a box with an optional text label. You see this in Figure 7.3, where the form control resides within a box, and in Figure 7.4, where the bottom half of a nested split view contains a box.

Scroll View

Scroll views are simple, yet powerful, controls. They are designed to facilitate content that is larger than the view containing it. To allow the user to see the large amount of content, scrollbars enable the user to move through the content. You can control the maximum size of the content as well as many other factors.

Scrolling behavior can be triggered automatically by users with trackpads on their laptops, external Apple mice or trackpads, or external mice with scroll wheels. On Mac OS X Lion, the default scrollbar behavior is to remain invisible until scrolling actually takes place, which is also the default behavior for the iPhone and iPad.

Tab View

The tab view allows you to provide multiple views of interface in the same window without cramming all of it onto the visible area at once. Each tab represents one smaller logical grouping of UI elements that all belong to the whole (the container in which the tab view resides). For example, you might use a tab view to provide access to multiple categories worth of information all belonging to a single person in an application.

> Even while not visible, the controls within tab views are active, and so they can change in response to activity of controls in the visible tab. For example, you can have the person's contact information tab change in response to a selection that occurs on the person's main tab.

Providing Feedback

When your application is doing something, whether it is doing it in the foreground or in the background, users typically want to know about it. You can provide the user with feedback in the form of progress indicators (spinners) and many of the various flavors of level indicators to inform the user that work is taking place.

Figure 7.5 shows a sample UI with a couple of progress indicators and level indicators used to either provide or solicit feedback from users.

> Editable level indicators are some of the most easy-to-develop controls that provide some amazingly powerful input possibilities for users. Make sure you keep them in mind as you build your applications.

Progress Indicators

You can display progress in several ways. The standard progress indicator can be displayed as a *bar* or as *spinning*. When the progress indicator is set to be *indeterminate*, it means that your application is doing something, but it doesn't know how long it is going to take. In this case, a spinning indeterminate progress indicator ticks off hashmarks in a circle indefinitely until the work is done.

A spinning *determinate* progress indicator shows the amount of progress between the minimum and maximum value as a fraction of a circle. Likewise, the bar indicator either shows the "barber shop" style rotating progress bar when it is *indeterminate,* or it shows a partially filled bar corresponding to the amount of progress that has been completed thus far.

FIGURE 7.5

Providing feed-
back with level
and progress
indicators.

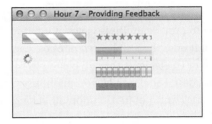

Comparing Traditional and Automatic Layouts

When we place controls on a window or in a container view, we have some options with regard to how those controls are laid out. Up until the most recent version of Mac OS X, the only layout model available to developers was the "springs and struts" model.

With the release of Mac OS X Lion, we are able to write applications that make use of automatic layout, a system that hopes to simplify the act of building user interfaces that behave and lay out intuitively. Automatic layout is available to applications that target *only* Mac OS X Lion, however, so applications targeting older versions of the operating system will still have to use the "springs and struts" layout.

Overview of "Springs and Struts" Layout

"Springs and struts" gets its name from how developers control the size and layout of individual controls. As you can see from Figure 7.6, you control how a control can expand using springs, and you control how it is attached to its parent container walls using struts.

The control of the sizing and constraint of a particular view is done from within the size inspector in Interface Builder. You can't tell from the figure, but the example window in the size inspector continually expands and contracts to show you how your view will behave within the confines of the container view.

There is definitely nothing wrong with this method of view layout, and it has worked for Apple since Cocoa's beginning. However, each control needs to be constrained individually, and developers have to write an awful lot of custom code to get controls to behave in groups, relative to other controls, or in other intuitive ways the users expect.

FIGURE 7.6
The "springs and struts" layout.

Overview of Automatic Layout

To give the developer a more natural way of expressing layout, allow Interface Builder to do more, and reduce the amount of custom layout code that developers typically need to write, Apple created the new automatic layout system for Mac OS X Lion.

Automatic layout allows developers to define where controls should be relative to each other, allows views to automatically size to contain the content within, and even allows the definition of high-level layout concepts such as indicating that a button should appear *no less than* one standard spacing unit from another button, but can expand with the UI as needed.

To enable automatic layout for a specific Interface Builder file, follow these steps:

1. Select the file (typically `MainMenu.xib` for simple Cocoa applications) in the project navigator.

2. Open the file inspector with that file still selected.

3. In the Interface Builder Document section, check the Use Autolayout option.

4. If your application is not currently set to deploy specifically to Mac OS X Lion (10.7), you will see the dialog in Figure 7.7. Click Continue and Upgrade if this dialog appears.

5. With automatic layout now active, drag a couple of buttons onto the window surface and experiment with dragging them near walls and near the other button.

6. Notice that the blue lines are first-class objects within the Interface Builder (IB) file. They are *constraints* and can be edited and manipulated after they are created. IB creates constraints automatically for you by guessing at your intention based on where you drag your controls, but you can edit and create them yourself manually.

7. Use the various inspectors you learned about in the previous hour to see all the options for configuring constraints by selecting each constraint and viewing its properties.

FIGURE 7.7
The Upgrade
Target
Deployment
dialog.

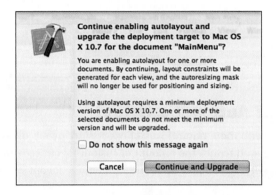

Continue enabling autolayout and
upgrade the deployment target to Mac OS
X 10.7 for the document "MainMenu"?

You are enabling autolayout for one or more
documents. By continuing, layout constraints will be
generated for each view, and the autoresizing mask
will no longer be used for positioning and sizing.

Using autolayout requires a minimum deployment
version of Mac OS X 10.7. One or more of the
selected documents do not meet the minimum
version and will be upgraded.

☐ Do not show this message again

Cancel   Continue and Upgrade

▼ **Try It Yourself**

Creating a Dynamic, Automatic Layout

In this section, we're going to create our own automatically laid out user interface. The sample application won't do anything; we're just going to lay out some controls relative to each other and to the window.

We're going to have a content area (where we can pretend we have content) at the top and then some buttons on the bottom for manipulating this content, such as an Add button, a Remove button, and a Details button.

If you have ever tried to create flexible user interfaces on other platforms that handle window resizing in a smooth, elegant way, you know that it can be pretty time consuming and very difficult to debug if the custom sizing and positioning logic is embedded in your code and not handled by the design tool.

Follow these steps to experiment with automatic layout:

1. Create new Cocoa application called **Hour7DIY** and accept all the defaults for the new application dialog.

2. Select the `MainMenu.xib` file and configure it to use automatic layout, using the steps learned in the preceding section.

3. Add a box to the window. Using the automatic guides that appear, size and position the box so that it is a standard space from the top, left, and right and has some room at the bottom (more than 50 points).

4. Run the application, paying close attention to what happens to the box when you resize the window. Make sure you try to shrink the window to a size smaller than the box, as well as expand the window bigger than the box.

▼

5. When you've seen how the application handles layout, quit and come back into Interface Builder. Add a push button to your window by dragging it to the far left, below the box. Make sure the automatic guides kick in before you let go of the button. You should see a constraint created between the button and the left window wall and the bottom of the window.

6. Change the text of the button to **Add**. Note how the size of the button automatically changed.

7. Add another button by dragging it just to the right of the Add button, making sure the automatic guides kick in to create constraints. Change the text of this button to **Remove**.

8. Add a button called **Details** to the bottom right of the window. Make sure you use the guides to put it in place, which will create the default constraints for you.

9. Now run the application and see what happens when you shrink the window. Note that it's still possible to shrink the window to hide the buttons and the box, and the buttons also overlap each other when you shrink the window to the left. When you're done, quit the application and go back into Interface Builder.

10. Click the Add button, then Shift-click the box above it. You should now see the constraints for both controls.

11. Click the Editor menu, click Add Constraint, and then choose Vertical Spacing. This will add a vertical spacing constraint between the Add button and the box. Figure 7.8 shows what IB should look like after adding this constraint.

12. Use the attributes inspector to change the constraint from Equal to Greater Than or Equal and leave the value as is.

13. Now when you run the app, you can expand the window to grow the box down and to the right, but you cannot shrink the window vertically past the box height. Also, note that the box doesn't grow, and we can still overlap buttons when we shrink the window.

14. Click the Remove button and then Shift-click the Details button.

15. Click the Editor menu, select Add Constraint, and then choose Horizontal Spacing.

16. Modify the newly created constraint to be Greater Than or Equal and then check the Standard check box. This sets the constraint to be greater than or equal to a single standard space.

FIGURE 7.8
Adding con-
straints to UI
elements.

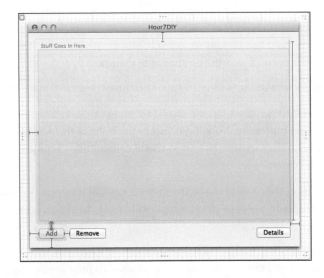

The definition of a standard space varies depending on whether you're talking about the distance between a control and a window border, two views, and so on. The best part is that the Autolayout runtime figures this out automatically for you to adhere to the *Human Interface Guidelines*.

17. Run the application and see what happens when you try to shrink the window horizontally and vertically. Quit and return to IB when you're done.

18. Modify the vertical constraint on the box to be Greater Than or Equal and leave the number the same.

19. Run the application to see if the box grows vertically when the window does the same. Before continuing to step 20, see if you can figure out why it isn't growing.

The reason it's not growing is because even though we've said that it *can* grow (a height constraint of type *greater than or equal to*), we don't have any other constraints on the box that *ask* or *force* it to grow. Step 19 adds this constraint, which makes the box grow.

20. Add a constraint to the box of type "Trailing Space to Bottom of Superview." This is just like a strut from the old system. Leave it as "Equal." This will force the box to always size itself to be 55 points (the number may be different for your application) from the bottom of the window.

21. Now run the application. Notice how you can expand to the right and to the bottom, and you can compress the window, and the buttons will slide closer to each other but never overlap. The UI is now predictable and intuitive, and you didn't have to write *any* custom code to make this possible!

There is a way to programmatically create and manipulate constraints. To keep these constraints as easy to work with in code as they are to work with in Interface Builder, Apple created a special string format for specifying constraints called the Visual Format Language (VFL). Apple has quite a bit of documentation available on VFL, so feel free to consult that whenever you feel like learning how to build code-driven layouts.

> Documentation on the VFL can be found here: http://developer.apple.com/library/mac/#documentation/UserExperience/Conceptual/AutolayoutPG/Articles/formatLanguage.html

A simple example of a VFL string might look like this:

```
|-[addButton]-[removeButton]-[detailsButton]-|
```

In this VFL string, we're saying that the Add button appears a standard length away from the "wall" (the edge of the super view or window), followed by a standard space, followed by the Remove button, followed by a standard space, followed by the Details button, which is followed by a standard distance away from the edge of the superview.

Summary

In this hour, we took a tour through the stock controls available to Cocoa developers that come with Xcode out of the box. You saw a little bit about how these controls look, where and when you might use them, and how they can help you create powerful and compelling user interfaces.

Next, you learned about the default "springs and struts" layout system available on all versions of Mac OS X, as well as the new automatic layout system that is available only on Mac OS X Lion.

Finally, you created your own dynamic layout. This layout responded automatically to the resizing of the window and positioned buttons where they should be, resized a box intuitively, and even prevented certain aspects of the UI from overlapping each other when the window shrinks. All this was possible without writing a single line of code.

In the next hour you'll put all the knowledge you've gained so far to practical use and start building user interfaces that can react to user input.

Q&A

Q. *How do I decide between using springs and struts or using the automatic layout system?*

A. If you are starting a brand new project, you should try and use automatic layout. If you have the choice, you should get in the habit of using automatic layout because the layout format language is incredibly powerful. If you are working on an existing application, you may be forced to use the traditional springs and struts layout system.

Q. *How do I know which control to use to display certain types of data or get certain types of feedback from my users?*

A. The best source of this information is the Apple Human Interface Guidelines.

HOUR 8

Creating Interactive Applications

What you'll learn in this hour:

▶ The Basics of Connections and Outlets
▶ How to React to User Input
▶ How to Manipulate Controls with Code

Even the most beautiful user interface won't do your users much good if they can't interact with it. Users need to be able to type text into forms, press buttons, drag sliders, and generally prod everything that looks like it can be manipulated with a mouse, trackpad, or touch gesture.

In this hour, you'll learn the basic building blocks that make interactive applications possible. Interaction is made possible by user actions triggering code and in turn by code manipulating the user interface. We'll go through both of those scenarios in this hour.

Introducing Connections, Outlets, and Actions

As mentioned in the introduction to this hour, the essential building blocks of creating interactive user interfaces start with the ability to trigger code from the UI and to manipulate the UI from code.

These two tasks are made possible by the fundamentals of Cocoa user interfaces: outlets and the connections made to them and actions.

Using Connections and Outlets

Electrical wall outlets are something that we are all very familiar with. You plug things into the wall that need power, and (assuming you haven't overloaded a circuit) power will flow freely to that device.

Cocoa outlets are similar to wall outlets in that they advertise to all who may be interested that *something* can be plugged into said outlet. A better analogy might be the connections on the back of an audio/video receiver. As shown in Figure 8.1, some devices are plugged into the *inputs* in the back of the receiver (Wii, Xbox, BluRay player), and the receiver is responsible for taking those inputs and sending the appropriate output to the TV, the subwoofer, speakers, and so on.

FIGURE 8.1
Inputs and outputs for a home stereo.

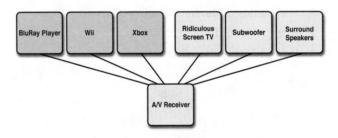

Cocoa works in a similar manner. If your code needs to access a particular UI object, an *outlet* must be created within the code. A *connection* is then made from the code outlet to the destination object. With a connected outlet, your code can access the outlet to manipulate the object to which it is connected.

You define outlets in the header files of your classes and you connect them to Interface Builder objects using Interface Builder's design surface. Let's assume that you have a text field and you need to be able to manipulate it with code. You might want to programmatically set the contents of the field or read its current value.

The first thing we would do in this situation is open up the `xib` file we're interested in, select the control to which we want to establish a connection, and then activate the assistant editor.

Did You Know?

> The icon for the assistant editor is one of my personal favorites in all of Xcode 4—it is an icon of a bow tie and suit. The assistant editor is like a little code butler, standing ready to attend to your every need!

The assistant editor will attempt to figure out which file corresponds to the `xib` file you're working with, but if it ends up on the wrong header file, you can manually choose the file with which the editor will assist. Figure 8.2 shows an Interface Builder design surface with the assistant editor window open to the right.

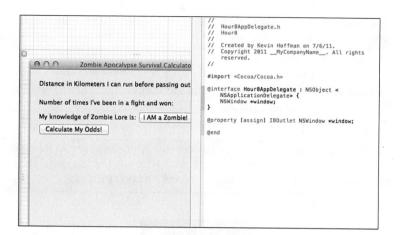

FIGURE 8.2
Opening the
assistant editor.

You may have noticed that the window property pointing to the main window has the word IBOutlet in front of it. If you guessed that the Interface Builder window is connected to the code via this outlet, you're right.

By the Way

Cocoa has a special keyword called IBOutlet that is used before class member declarations and used solely by Interface Builder (IB). A member variable decorated with this keyword will show up as a potential connection target.

Xcode 4 and the assistant editor have a convenient shortcut method that allows you to create a code outlet *and* connect it to the IB object at the same time.

To do this, Ctrl+click and hold on the IB object (like a text field, button, table, grid, and so on) and then drag the mouse into the code in the header file where you would like the outlet declared.

Figure 8.3 shows the little outlet creation dialog that pops up when you let go of the mouse after this operation.

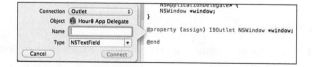

FIGURE 8.3
Creating and
connecting a
new outlet.

When you type the name of the outlet and press Enter, the outlet is created and automatically connected to the UI element that originated the drag-and-drop operation.

To see the newly created connection and all other connections (inbound and outbound) associated with a control, you can either right-click the control to bring up the Connections HUD (Heads-Up Display), or you can select the control and open the connections inspector in the utilities panel. Figure 8.4 shows an example of this connections HUD. In this figure you can see that the sample text field has been connected to a code outlet called `maxRunDistance`.

Did You Know?

Newcomers to the Mac often have trouble with the right-clicks, especially on trackpad-only devices. A simple Control-click will suffice as a right-click, and a default on most trackpads is to place two fingers on the pad and then click.

FIGURE 8.4
Displaying a control's connections.

With the outlet declared in the header file and with the connection established in Interface Builder, the code in the class implementation should be able to access and manipulate the control.

Using Actions

Now that you've seen how to connect individual UI elements to code, let's take a look at how we might trigger the execution of code as a result of a user performing an action.

You connect actions the same way you connect outlets. Select the control that performs an action (different controls perform different actions, but each one has a default action that is the easiest to connect to your code). After it is selected, perform the control-drag from the control to the header file in the assistant editor. Click the pop-up button and change its selected value from Outlet to Action (this may happen automatically depending on what type of control you selected when you started the drag).

Type in a name for the action that will eventually become the name of the method that is executed when the control's action is performed. Figure 8.5 illustrates connecting a button to a method called `calculateOdds`.

Interface Builder will automatically handle putting the colon at the end of the method name, so you don't need to enter it when creating actions this way.

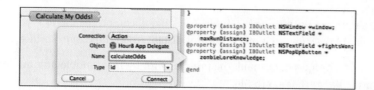

FIGURE 8.5
Connecting an Action to code.

After the action is connected, the method will be executed every time that action is performed on that control. The default action on buttons is a click.

To recap: You create outlets (indicated by the `IBOutlet` keyword) in code and connect them with Interface Builder to grant your code access to the control. You create actions (indicated by the `IBAction` keyword) in code and connect them with Interface Builder to invoke those methods when the control's action is triggered.

In the next section, you'll get to build a user interface that makes use of both outlets and actions.

Try It Yourself

Building an Interactive Interface

This section will put to use all the skills you've learned so far in this book. You will create a window-based application that gets values from text fields, uses them to perform calculations, and reports those results back to the user.

The application we're going to build is a new twist on an oft-used sample: the calculator. Rather than building a regular calculator, we will build a calculator that takes some basic information about us and computes our chances of surviving the impending zombie apocalypse. One can never be too prepared, and a tool like this may save a few lives.

▼

Our tool will ask for the following information:

▶ Distance in Kilometers that the user can run before passing out. This will be a text field with a numeric formatter preattached.

▶ Number of times the user has been in a fight and won. This will also be a text field with a numeric formatter preattached.

▶ The user's familiarity with zombie lore. This will be a pop-up button that presents a menu of three options ranging from unfamiliar to intimately familiar.

Follow these steps to create your own interactive application:

1. Create a new Cocoa application using the standard Xcode template and call it **Hour8**.

2. Open up the MainWindow.xib file. Click the x icon on the menu if you need room. Make sure the main window is displayed on the design surface.

3. Using techniques you should be familiar with by now, enable automatic layout for the MainWindow.xib file.

4. Add labels to the window for each of the three pieces of information we need to prompt for: distance in kilometers before passing out, number of fights won, and zombie lore knowledge.

5. Add a Text Field with Number Formatter control next to the first two labels you added in the previous step. Size them so that it looks like they should only hold a few digits each.

6. Add a Pop-Up Button control next to the label prompting for zombie lore knowledge. Stretch it out fairly big so it has enough room to display the larger options.

7. Edit the Pop-Up Button control so that it contains three menu options for knowledge levels reflecting little knowledge, some knowledge, and lots of knowledge, respectively. Feel free to get creative with the labels.

Figuring out how to edit the available options in a Pop-Up Button control can be difficult. Start by expanding the object hierarchy view so you can get an outline view of all the controls within MainWindow.xib. Expand the Pop-Up Button node and then expand the Pop-Up Button Cell node. You should now see a node called Menu—OtherViews. When you select this, a menu appears showing the options. You can now click each option and change its title.

▼

8. Add a button to the window that will calculate the results. Feel free to name it whatever you like—the outlets you'll be creating aren't affected by the titles or labels of controls.

9. Add a box to the window with a title of **Results**. Stretch the box so it fills the window and you see autolayout constraints created on both sides of the box. You'll know autolayout is working if you resize the window in Interface Builder and the box shrinks and grows accordingly.

> If you can't get this constraint to appear automatically, select the box, then select Editor, Add Constraint, Trailing Space to Superview. This will force the box's right edge to always be as far from the window's right edge as it was when you added the constraint.

Did You Know?

10. Add a label inside the box that contains text similar to `Your chances of surviving the apocalypse are:`

11. Add another label to the right of this one (IB should create a constraint for you between these two labels if the blue guides appear). Leave this label alone because its text will be manipulated programmatically.

12. When you run your application (without any outlets or actions yet), it should look something like the one shown in Figure 8.6. Feel free to get creative here and style the UI however you like. Now is a great time to play some more with autolayout constraints.

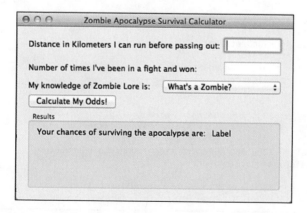

FIGURE 8.6
Preliminary Zombie Apocalypse Calculator UI.

13. Now it's time to start creating outlets. Use the control-drag technique with the assistant editor to create appropriately named outlets for the first two text fields (name suggestions: `maxRunDistance` and `fightsWon`).

▼

14. Create another outlet for the pop-up button and call it something like
zombieLoreKnowledge.

> There is a never-ending debate about whether to include type clues in the names
> of controls, outlets, and other member variables (for example, calling the outlet
> **zombieLoreKnowledgePopupButton** instead of just zombieLoreKnowledge).
> Today's IDEs provide us with all kinds of type information, and Xcode even does
> documentation lookups when we click on variables. You should make up your own
> mind, but remember that many of the reasons behind this and other "hungarian"
> style notations are no longer concerns with today's modern tools.

15. Now create an action for the Calculate Odds button; this should prompt you to
name a method rather than a member variable. Note that if you've done this
properly, you will not only see the method in your header file, but you'll also
see an empty stub implementation of that method in your implementation
(.m) file.

16. Create an outlet for the results label, calling it **resultsLabel**. Note here I
chose to use the suffix "Label" not to conform to hungarian notation but to
clarify its purpose as a read-only output of text and to distinguish it from the
box whose title is also Results. Listing 8.1 shows the header file as it should
appear after creating all of the outlets and actions.

LISTING 8.1   Hour 8 AppDelegate Header After Outlets and Connections

```
#import <Cocoa/Cocoa.h>

@interface Hour8AppDelegate : NSObject <NSApplicationDelegate> {
    NSWindow *window;
    NSTextField *maxRunDistance;
    NSTextField *fightsWon;
    NSPopUpButton *zombieLoreKnowledge;
    NSTextField *resultsLabel;
}

@property (assign) IBOutlet NSWindow *window;
@property (assign) IBOutlet NSTextField *maxRunDistance;
@property (assign) IBOutlet NSTextField *fightsWon;
@property (assign) IBOutlet NSPopUpButton *zombieLoreKnowledge;
- (IBAction)calculateOdds:(id)sender;

@property (assign) IBOutlet NSTextField *resultsLabel;
@end
```

▼

You may be wondering why the properties are marked as `assign` rather than strong. Just to keep up the variety, I chose not to use Automatic Reference Counting for this sample.

17. With all the outlets in place, write some code that pulls the integer values from the two text fields and pulls the currently selected value from the pop-up button. This algorithm should then compute a percentage and set that into the `resultsLabel` outlet's text. The algorithm and math don't matter here—feel free to make it all up. The important pieces are reading from the text fields and pop-up buttons and changing the label text.

The `integerValue` method will give you the numeric value currently stored in a text field with a number formatter. The `titleOfSelectedItem` method will, as its name implies, give you the title of a pop-up button's currently selected menu item.

Listing 8.2 shows one way to write the code to compute the odds of surviving the zombie apocalypse.

LISTING 8.2   Completed Sample Code for Calculating Survival Odds

```
- (IBAction)calculateOdds:(id)sender {
    NSLog(@"You wanted to calculate the odds.");

    NSInteger runDistance = maxRunDistance.integerValue;
    NSInteger wonFights = fightsWon.integerValue;
    NSString *loreValue = [zombieLoreKnowledge titleOfSelectedItem];

    NSLog(@"About to calculate odds with a run distance of %ld, [ccc]
win count of %ld, and a lore knowledge of %@",
          runDistance,
          wonFights,
          loreValue);

    NSInteger raw = runDistance * wonFights;
    if ([loreValue isEqualToString:@"What's a Zombie?"])
        raw -= 150;

    double ratio = raw / 880.0;
    NSInteger odds = ratio * 100;
    resultsLabel.stringValue =
        [NSString stringWithFormat:@"%d%%", odds];
    [resultsLabel setBezeled:YES];
}
```

▼

Figure 8.7 shows a sample run of the application.

FIGURE 8.7
Completed sample application.

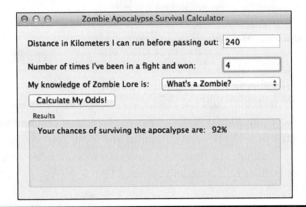

▲

This sample showed you how to create outlets, create actions, and put them all together to build your first interactive application.

Manipulating Controls at Runtime with Code

As you saw in the preceding example, the one prerequisite for manipulating a control at runtime is the need for a pointer to that control. You can either get that pointer by creating an instance of the control manually (we haven't covered this, so don't worry about that scenario) or when Cocoa creates an instance of the control for you by reading from an Interface Builder file and you have created a connection between the control and your outlet.

You've already seen how to perform simple control manipulations in the preceding sample. The following line of code, taken from the previous section, shows how to set the string value of the label (which is really an instance of NSTextField) at runtime:

```
resultsLabel.stringValue = [NSString stringWithFormat:@"%d%%", odds];
```

This is just the tip of the iceberg. Any method available on the control and any property publicly accessible on the control is at your disposal after you have created the connection to that control in Interface Builder.

I can easily invoke methods to change the appearance and behaviors of controls at runtime the way I might use Interface Builder and the Inspectors to change behavior and appearance at design time.

For example, the following line of code will change the appearance of the results label to be bezeled:

```
[resultsLabel setBezeled:YES];
```

As you progress throughout the book, you will see more and more examples of manipulating the user interface at runtime. The essential thing to remember is that you use Interface Builder to connect controls to outlets and actions, and you can then write code against those outlets that will, in turn, manipulate controls.

Summary

In this hour, you took your first steps toward building truly interactive applications. You learned about two fundamental Cocoa concepts: outlets and actions and the glue that holds those together with code, connections.

Using outlets and actions, you learned how to link member variables in classes to their corresponding visual controls, and you learned how to write code that will execute when a control's action (such as a button click) is performed.

In this hour, you used practically all the skills you've learned up to this point, and you should be ready to continue exploring Mac OS X Lion development for your next hour, when you will create data-bound applications.

Q&A

Q. *What is Interface Builder really doing when I create connections or outlets?*

A. When Cocoa loads information from an XIB file, it sifts through the connections and outlets and executes code that programmatically sets up those links at runtime. A general rule of thumb is that everything you can do in IB, you can do in code yourself (though you certainly may not want to).

HOUR 9

Creating Data-Bound Interfaces

What you'll learn in this hour:

▶ The Model-View-Controller Pattern
▶ Introduction to Cocoa Bindings
▶ Building a Data-Bound Interface
▶ How Bindings Work Under the Hood

In the previous hour you learned about outlets, actions, and connections, and the power they give us to connect our code to our user interfaces. In this hour, we're going to learn how to take that knowledge a step further and create automatic bindings between code objects and controls.

This hour covers how to bind individual properties of a control to values exposed by objects such as controllers, but before you learn how to bind to a controller, we'll explore one of the guiding principles of Cocoa's architecture: the Model-View-Controller pattern.

Introducing the Model-View-Controller Pattern

First described back in 1979 by Trygve Reenskaug, one of the people originally responsible for the SmallTalk programming language, Model-View-Controller is a principle that influences virtually all aspects of Cocoa.

> There are several flavors of Model-View-Controller and other related patterns, such as Model-View-ViewModel. If you're interested in design patterns, you should check out the "Gang of Four" book, *Design Patterns: Elements of Reusable Object-Oriented Software*. It is considered by most to be the bible of design patterns books. It is available for purchase here: http://www.amazon.com/Design-Patterns-Elements-Reusable-Object-Oriented/dp/0201633612/ref=sr_1_2?s=books&ie=UTF8&qid=1319298264&sr=1-2

Model-View-Controller (MVC hereafter for brevity) is a pattern that prescribes a way to cleanly separate the three main components of applications with user interfaces. It splits the roles and responsibilities into these three categories and, by separating your own application according to these roles, you will find that the application is easier to develop, maintain, and troubleshoot.

To understand the various roles, let's walk through a sample user interaction:

First, the user is presented with an interface. What appears on the screen and is available to the user for interaction is the sole responsibility of the View. The user then interacts with the interface by clicking a button. The Controller is notified of this button click through some means (remember Actions from the previous hour?) and can respond to this event accordingly.

If a model change is necessary as a result of this action, the controller will then manipulate the Model, which is responsible for maintaining *interface state*.

> People often confuse the model in MVC with a model as it might be retrieved or stored in a database. Although it *can* be the same model, in many cases it is not. It is easier if you think of the model in this scenario as an *object to store user interface state*.

The view then updates to reflect the new state of the model. As we saw in Hour 8, "Creating Interactive Applications," this can be done manually by directly manipulating control properties (such as a label's stringValue property), but it can also be done with bindings, as we'll see during this hour. Bindings allow the view to update automatically in response to changes in the model and can also make changes to the model in response to changes in the view.

The one direction of communication that you shouldn't see in a typical MVC application is a model that talks to the controller. This should always be top-down communication from the controller to the model, as shown in Figure 9.1. The other thing to keep in mind is that while Figure 9.1 shows two-way communication between the view and the controller, the view should only communicate with the controller to relay information about user interaction events and little else.

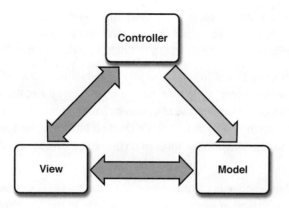

FIGURE 9.1
Model-View-
Controller com-
munication.

As we go through the information throughout the rest of this hour and build our own application that utilizes bindings, we'll point out the individual roles in the MVC architecture as we build them.

Introducing Cocoa Bindings

The simplest way to describe Cocoa bindings is that they provide a way for you to synchronize your view and your model. If you look back at Figure 9.1, you'll see that there is a two-way communication between the view and the model, and this is almost always facilitated with some sort of binding system.

By the Way

> If you've been looking up design patterns, you may have also noticed the *Observer* pattern, which is an abstract way of describing code that monitors other code and reacts to changes. In essence, this is the pattern that underlies the implementation of Cocoa bindings.

Think back to the sample Zombie Apocalypse calculator you built in the previous hour. This sample had no model—only a view and a controller. The controller (in that case, it was the Hour8AppDelegate class) responded directly to events and read values directly from the view. This is usually considered bad practice because it gives the controller too much direct knowledge of how the view works. For example, if you change how you represent a piece of data in the view, you would then have to modify all references to that data in the controller as well.

A better way would have been to create a model object. This model object could have been an instance of the ApocalypseCalculation class and could have been a property of the controller called calculationModel. When we have this type of scenario, we say that the controller *presents* the calculationModel object.

Before we get into a full sample of using bindings, there's a trick you can use that isn't really a binding but can come in handy if all you want to do is connect two controls on the same view without going through a model or controller.

For example, suppose I want to connect a label's text value to the current angle represented by a circular slider. To do that, first I would create a circular slider and set its mode to *continuous* (to make it send updates about its current value even while I'm still holding the mouse down). Then I'd create a label. Finally, I would control-drag from the circular slider to the label and choose the `takeStringValueFrom:` connection.

Figure 9.2 shows a sample of what this type of UI looks like. The slider and the label are connected to each other *without bindings* and without the intervention of a model. If this is all you need, it is generally quicker and easier than going through a model to store the current value in the slider and allow the label to bind to that.

FIGURE 9.2
Connecting two controls without bindings.

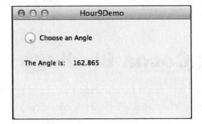

This is great, but what we're really after is the ability to connect these two controls to the *same model object*. This allows the value (the current value of the slider) to be available to the controller code as well as other controls on the view.

You don't need to worry about following along for this part; in the next section you'll see detailed steps to help you do this yourself. The first step to upgrade this project is to add a model object, which is just an Objective-C class that inherits from `NSObject`.

We'll need a property on this class called `currentAngle` of type `double`. Then we use Interface Builder to add an object instance of this type to the xib file.

Did You
Know?

To do this, scroll down in the object library until you see the blue cube for object. Drag it into the object tray and then open the identity inspector. Set the class name of this new object to the name of the code class you just created. In our case, this was a class called `SliderModel`.

After Interface Builder knows about the instance of this model object, you can start binding your controls to it. To bind the slider, select it and then open the bindings inspector. Expand the value node and choose to bind against the object we just added to Interface Builder. Under the Model Key Path label, type the name of the property to which we're binding: currentAngle.

Figure 9.3 shows the bindings inspector for the sample I created (this code is available with the rest of the code for this hour).

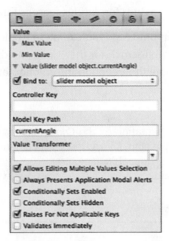

FIGURE 9.3
Bindings inspector for simple bindings example.

Next, we're going to want to bind the label to the same value. You can go through the same process to bind the label's value to the currentAngle property of the SliderModel instance. Now when we run the application it looks just like the other one and behaves the same way, but instead of linking the two values without giving us (or rather, our controller code) access to the data, now the value is being stored in code.

To prove that the value is available to the controller as well as to the view, we can create an outlet in the project's App Delegate class and connect it to the instance of the model object (this is done the same way we created and connected outlets in the previous hour). Now we can drop a button onto the view, create an action for it, and use that action to interrogate the value of the model object using code that looks like this:

```
- (IBAction)checkSliderValue:(id)sender {
    NSLog(@"current slider value: %f", sliderModel.currentAngle);
}
```

When we run the application now, we can see the value of the slider change by look-ing at the text of the label change. When we click the new button, we get output that looks like this:

```
2011-07-08 21:34:09.360 Hour9Demo[6920:707] current slider value: 123.347450
```

Cocoa bindings is an incredibly broad and deep topic and we could spend many hours exploring all of its intricacies. In order to keep things moving and give you just the highlights, we'll skip over some of the lower-level details of how bindings work and we'll also revisit bindings for various reasons later in the book.

For more information about bindings, you can go to Apple's Mac Developer Center, go to the developer library and search for the "Cocoa Bindings Programming Topics" guide. This will give you more than enough information on all of the facets of this detailed topic.

You can find Apple's documentation on the *Cocoa Bindings Programming Topics* here: http://developer.apple.com/library/mac/#documentation/Cocoa/Conceptual/CocoaBindings/CocoaBindings.html

▼ **Try It Yourself**

Backing Views with Bound Models

In the preceding section you got a brief introduction to how to synchronize models with views. In this section you're going to get a chance to build your own applica-tion that uses a model object and bindings.

The Zombie Apocalypse Calculator application is functional but hardly elegant. The controller shouldn't be reading values directly from the view objects, and it is a com-mon practice to make sure that you *avoid* giving your controllers direct references to individual controls. What we'd really like to do is upgrade this application to make use of bindings.

Use the following steps to upgrade the Zombie Apocalypse Calculator application to use bindings:

▼

1. Create a new Cocoa application with the same options we've been using up to this point and call it Hour9.

You might be tempted to copy the calculator application from Hour 8, but you would spend more time tracking down all the references to "Hour8" and renaming them than you would creating a new application from scratch.

2. Open up the `MainWindow.xib` file and add three labels for the three pieces of data we will be prompting the user for: kilometers run without passing out, number of fights won, and zombie lore knowledge.

3. Add two Text Field with Number Formatter controls next to their corresponding labels.

4. Add a pop-up button for the zombie lore knowledge and populate it with the same values that we used in the previous hour. Feel free to look back to the steps in Hour 8 if you don't remember how to set the values in a pop-up button.

5. Add a button to the window and set its text to **Calculate Odds**.

6. Add a box below the button you added in step 5.

7. Add a label to the box with the text **Your chances of surviving the apocalypse are**.

8. Add another label right next to the label from step 7 and leave its text as the default.

9. Now we're going to create a model class. From the Xcode menu select File, New, New File. When prompted, choose the Objective-C Class template and accept the default inheritance of NSObject. Name the new class **ApocalypseCalculatorModel** and make sure it generates both a header (.h) and an implementation (.m) file.

10. Add two properties of type NSInteger to the class called maxRunDistance and fightsWon. Make sure you declare the property in the header file and synthesize it in the implementation file.

11. Add another NSInteger property to the model class called **loreKnowledgeSelectedIndex**. We're going to use this number to store the selected index of the zombie lore knowledge pop-up button.

12. Add a property of type NSString * to the class called resultsText. We'll be using this to display the results of the calculation.

13. You should be able to compile and run your application now. It won't do any-thing, but at least you should be able to tell whether you've defined your model class properly. Listings 9.1 and 9.2, respectively, show what my calcula-tor model looked like when I was done (yours might differ slightly if you're using Automatic Reference Counting).

LISTING 9.1   ApocalypseCalculatorModel.h

```
#import <Foundation/Foundation.h>

@interface ApocalypseCalculatorModel : NSObject

@property(assign) NSInteger maxRunDistance;
@property(assign) NSInteger fightsWon;
@property(assign) NSInteger loreKnowledgeSelectedIndex;
@property(retain) NSString *resultsText;

@end
```

LISTING 9.2   ApocalypseCalculatorModel.m

```
#import "ApocalypseCalculatorModel.h"

@implementation ApocalypseCalculatorModel

@synthesize maxRunDistance, fightsWon,
loreKnowledgeSelectedIndex, resultsText;

- (id)init
{
    self = [super init];
    if (self) {
        // Initialization code here.
    }

    return self;
}

@end
```

14. Now that we've got a model class, we need to create an instance of that class and make it available to Interface Builder. To do that, drag an Object (the blue cube) from the object library into the object tray. Use the identity inspector to change the class of the object to `ApocalypseCalculatorModel`.

15. Select the text field for the maximum run distance and open the bindings inspector. Bind the `Value` node to the `ApocalypseCalculatorModel` object. Set the Model Key Path value to `maxRunDistance`. Figure 9.4 shows what this inspector looks like.

FIGURE 9.4
Setting the
Model Key Path
for a binding.

> If you type a character in the box for Model Key Path and then wait a second, you'll see that Xcode gives you a list of potential candidates for properties. Also keep in mind that you can nest key paths—binding to a property of an object that is the property of a parent object, and so on.

Did You Know?

16. Do the same for the `fightsWon` property of the model, binding it to the appropriate text field.

17. Bind the `Selected Index` node of the pop-up button to the `loreKnowledgeSelectedIndex` property of the model object.

18. Bind the value of the results label to the `resultsText` property of the calculator model object.

19. Use the control-drag technique with the assistant editor to create an action for the Calculate Odds button.

20. Write a method that calculates the odds using the same algorithm as the one we used in the previous hour. Listing 9.3 shows a sample method; feel free to experiment and get creative with how you compute the odds.

LISTING 9.3   Calculating the Odds of Surviving the Zombie Apocalypse

```
- (IBAction)calculateOdds:(id)sender {
    NSLog(@"max run distance: %ld", calculatorModel.maxRunDistance);
    NSLog(@"fights won: %ld", calculatorModel.fightsWon);
    NSLog(@"lore knowledge index: %ld",
calculatorModel.loreKnowledgeSelectedIndex);
```

▼

```
    NSInteger raw =
calculatorModel.maxRunDistance * calculatorModel.fightsWon;
    if (calculatorModel.loreKnowledgeSelectedIndex < 1)
        raw -= 150;

    double ratio = raw / 880.0;
    NSInteger odds = ratio * 100; // completely arbitrary calculation

    calculatorModel.resultsText =
[NSString stringWithFormat:@"%d%%", odds];
}
```

21. Notice how much more straightforward it is accessing the data. We don't have to manually interrogate the controls for their values because our model object already contains the data we need through the power of Cocoa bindings.

Now we should be ready to run our application. Note that you have to tab out of each text field for the value to be stored in the bound model object. Figure 9.5 shows a sample of the new bindings-enabled application in action.

FIGURE 9.5
Zombie
Apocalypse
Survival Odds
calculator.

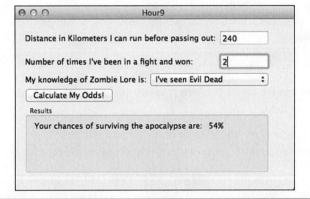

▲

Under the Hood with KVC and KVO

Now that you've seen how to create a model object and how to use Interface Builder to create a binding between the object and properties of controls, you might be wondering, how does it all work?

If you want to know all the tiny details, Apple's documentation on Cocoa bindings should be more than sufficient, so here we'll stick with a short overview.

The core of bindings is made possible by the ability for code to write values to properties and read values from properties without knowing the names of the accessor methods ahead of time.

The ability to write values to arbitrary (in our case, the model) objects is made possible with a technology called Key-Value Coding (KVC). If you recall the steps where you configured the bindings, you told the binding which property on the model object to use with a value called the Model Key Path. Key-Value Coding works by allowing code to set values for arbitrary key paths using methods such as `setValue:forKeyPath:`.

For example, if I wanted to set the `maxRunDistance` property on my model object, I could set it directly or I could use KVC:

```
[modelObject setValue:22 forKeyPath:@"maxRunDistance"];
```

Underneath the hood, as the values in your interface change, those values are stored (coded) into the model object with KVC methods like the one in the preceding example.

Likewise, we can obtain the value for a key path with a similar method:

```
[modelObject valueForKeyPath:@"maxRunDistance"];
```

This is how the other half of the data binding works when values change in the model that need to be reflected in the user interface.

Now you know how values are read and set for bindings, but there is one more key technology that makes bindings possible: Key-Value Observing (KVO). KVO allows one object to *subscribe* to the changes in another object. This allows the object to *observe* changes as they happen.

When a binding is created between a control and a model object, the control *observes* changes to the model object and the model object *observes* changes in the control. When a change is detected, KVO and KVC are used to synchronize the model and the control.

To manually observe changes in another object, we can send the object being observed the `addObserver:forKeyPath:options:context:` message.

Objects that are being observed notify their observers of changes with the `observeValue:forKeyPath:ofObject:change:context:` message. The great part about Cocoa Bindings is that if you're using properties and synthesizing them, you never have to worry about manually notifying observers of changes—that is handled for you automatically.

Summary

In this hour, you built on your Interface Builder skills and your growing Objective-C skills to create a model class, and you bound the properties of that model to your interface objects. You were able to make changes in the UI appear in your model object and likewise make changes in the model object appear in the UI. You put all this to work by rewriting the Zombie Apocalypse Calculator application from Hour 8 to use Cocoa bindings. Finally, we wrapped up the hour with a brief overview of some of the technology that makes Cocoa bindings work.

As you'll see in many of the forthcoming hours, Cocoa Bindings are an essential part of application development for the Mac, and what you've learned in this hour is just the beginning of harnessing the power of data-bound interfaces.

Q&A

Q. *Do I have to follow the Model-View-Controller pattern when building my applications?*

A. There is nothing specifically that will force you to do so, however, all of Cocoa is designed this way and you will be making your life far more difficult than it has to be by resisting MVC.

Q. *Why would I use data binding when I can just set a control's properties manually?*

A. The same reason we don't want to walk thirty miles when we can drive. Use binding everywhere and at every opportunity you can and you will find that you write less code (a good thing) and your application is easier to troubleshoot and maintain.

Q. *Do I need to use KVC and KVO?*

A. Usually you can set up your bindings in IB and not have to worry about the plumbing that makes it possible. However, knowing about observing value changes in objects can come in handy when you least expect it.

HOUR 10

Working with Tables and Collections

What you'll learn in this hour:

▶ Working with Bindings and Collections
▶ Using Table Views
▶ Using Collection Views
▶ Using the Outline View

In the previous hour you got your first real taste of building a data-bound Cocoa application for Mac OS X Lion. In this hour, we're going to build on those data-binding skills and expand your abilities to work with collections of data.

Being able to bind a single text field to a property of an object is incredibly useful, but many applications also need to be able to work with lists of objects: customers, stock quotes, onscreen monsters in games, and much more.

In this hour you'll see some of the different types of controllers designed to facilitate collection binding and some of the controls that provide a user interface around working with collections.

Working with Bindings and Collections

Before we get into the code that shows *how* we deal with collections and bindings, it's worth it to examine *why* we're going to do these things.

Take a moment and think about the tasks involved in a typical user interface that involves a bound collection. Suppose you're building an application that maintains a list of recipes. On the main window of the application you have a view of some kind that displays a list of recipes. It shows the title and calorie count of each recipe, and when you select a recipe from the list, more detailed information, such as ingredients, appears below the list. This is a fairly common user interface.

Let's break down some of the tasks that an interface like this needs to handle:

▶ **Query the list of recipes**—We will need an object to maintain the list of recipes so that our user interface can query that list for display.

▶ **Add a recipe to the list**—Most native Mac applications have a plus (+) or Add button that adds an item to a list of items.

▶ **Remove a recipe from the list**—Likewise, there is usually a [minus] (–) or Remove button that removes the currently selected item from the list.

▶ **Identify the currently selected recipe(s)**—When the user clicks an item in the list, the item should change visually to reflect this. In addition, we need to know the currently selected item so we can delete it and display its details.

▶ **Display the recipe title in a list view**—Within a list view, we need access to individual properties of the bound items so we can display values such as the recipe title or calorie count.

▶ **Display recipe details in a detail view**—Using the currently selected item, our controls need access to individual properties so they can display (and possibly edit) details on the selected item.

▶ **Optionally sort the list of recipes by calories**—When looking at a list of items, users generally like to be able to sort those lists, especially when there is a large number of items. In our sample case, we want to be able to give the user the ability to sort by calorie count.

Thankfully, we don't have to reinvent the wheel: we don't have to write all the code that makes the preceding tasks possible. In fact, Apple has encapsulated all the preceding tasks in some form within specialized controllers such as the `NSArrayController`, the `NSTreeController`, and the `NSDictionaryController`.

These controllers provider wrappers around lists of data. For example, the `NSArrayController` provides a bindings-aware wrapper around a mutable array. The `NSTreeController` provides a bindings-aware wrapper around a tree structure that can support nodes with arbitrary data.

The `NSArrayController` does more than just create an array for you, it also maintains a `selection` property as well as `selectionIndexes` for multiselect list views, and it exposes methods like `add:` and `remove:` that are already tagged as possible actions for Interface Builder so you can control-drag directly from your Add button to the array controller, as you'll see in this hour.

Using Table Views

If the data you plan to present to the user is spreadsheet-style data where you have an obvious layout of rows and columns, chances are you're going to want to use an NSTableView to present that data.

There are many variations of the table view and some very clever things you can do with single-column table views, so before you dismiss this control because your data doesn't look like traditional "row and column" data, play around with some of the options and give it a second chance. You might be surprised.

As mentioned earlier, it is technically possible to bind your table view to data without using Apple's NSArrayController. However, the scenarios where you might want to avoid the stock array controller are beyond the scope of this book, so we're going to focus on *not* reinventing the wheel and will discuss how to bind a table view to an array controller.

To use a table view, the first thing you're going to need is a model object that represents a single row of data. This model object can be a dictionary (this is actually the default), but in many cases you will be working with Objective-C objects (especially if you're using Core Data, which we discuss in Hour 13, "Working with Core Data").

Let's assume we have a KHRecipe class that contains all the details we could possibly need for a single recipe.

Apple developers, especially companies, tend to prefix their classes and libraries with two letters. This is to avoid potential naming conflicts with any Apple or third-party libraries that may share the same name as your class. In this case, the prefix of KH stands for Kevin Hoffman, a common practice for independent developers.

After we have a model object, we create an array controller in Interface Builder. To do that, we drag the array controller object from the object library (it looks like several blue cubes in a row, inside a green bubble) into the object list. Using the techniques we've learned from previous hours, you can change the Xcode label for this controller to something like **Recipe Array Controller**.

Next, we need to tell the array controller the kind of objects that will be in the array. To do this, select the array controller, go to the attributes inspector, and change the Class Name value to the name of the class that we're representing. In this sample it would be **KHRecipe**, as shown in Figure 10.1.

FIGURE 10.1
Configuring an
Array Controller.

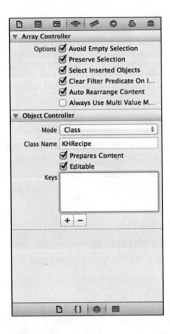

Now that we've got an array controller capable of controlling an array of recipes, we already have the ability to add new recipe objects, remove existing recipes, and even sort them and keep track of which recipe objects are currently selected.

The last step is to set up the table view. To do this, we put a table view on our window and then do the "slow sequential left clicks" trick until we've selected the first column in the view.

Did You Know?

> To add columns to the view, select the table view (this should take two slow left clicks, or just pick it from the object tree view) and in the attributes inspector set the number of columns. The view will update automatically.

With the first column selected, the attributes inspector will have a few settings available under the Table Column heading. Here you can set the title. In this sample, we might set the title to "Recipe Name." In the bindings inspector, we bind the Value node to the array controller (which could be labeled "Recipes Array Controller" or whatever you choose). The controller key is arrangedObjects and the Model Key Path is whatever we want to display in this column. For the recipes sample, we might choose a property called recipeName, as shown in Figure 10.2.

FIGURE 10.2
Configuring a
bound table
column.

Notice the little gray exclamation point in the Model Key Path field. This is a warning letting us know that Interface Builder doesn't know how to find that property, but that's okay—at runtime that property is available on the objects being managed by the array controller.

We repeat the same process until we've configured all our table columns. Last, we need to make sure that the table view's content array is properly bound (it should be if we bound the individual columns), but we also want to make sure that as the currently selected row changes in the table view, the array controller is notified. This will allow controls bound to the *selected object* within the controller to change their values immediately when the selection changes.

Take a look at Figure 10.3, which shows the bindings inspector for the table view itself. Note that the Content node is bound to the array controller's `arrangedObjects` property and the Selection Indexes node is bound to the array controller's `selectionIndexes` property. The `arrangedObjects` property is one of those fantastic pieces of code that we don't have to write ourselves—it contains the list of objects in the array controller as they would appear given the current sort options.

Where the `arrangedObjects` controller key refers to the sorted list of items, the `selection` controller key points to the single selected row and will give you back an object that is of the underlying type of the array controller.

FIGURE 10.3
Table view
bindings.

This means that you can write the following line of code to obtain a reference to the currently selected recipe in this sample:

```
KHRecipe *currentRecipe = (KHRecipe *)recipeArrayController.selection;
```

With the information in this section about array controllers and table views, you should now be ready to put some of this knowledge into practice.

▼ Try It Yourself

Creating a Data-Bound Table UI

In this section, you'll be creating an application that has a data-bound table view. This table view will display a list of contacts (to keep things simple, the contacts only have a first name and last name). There will be a plus (+) button for creating new contacts, a minus (–) button for deleting contacts, and labels that display the first and last name of the currently selected contact. Finally, to prove that everything is as it should be under the hood, we'll add a button that iterates through the contents of the array controller and displays that to the standard output via NSLog().

To create this application, follow these steps:

1. Create a new Cocoa application called **Hour10**. Make sure it is not a document-based application and doesn't use Core Data.

▼

2. Enable autolayout in the MainWindow.xib file and make sure that Automatic Reference Counting is enabled. You can verify this by noting that the IBOutlet pointer window is a strong property and not a retain property.

3. Open up the MainWindow.xib interface and add a table view to the main window. Resize the table view so that it is stuck to the top, left, and right sides of the window, but make sure you leave some room at the bottom for the details area and buttons.

4. Add a box below the table view and title it **Contact Details**.

5. Add two labels to the inside of the box, the first left-justified and the second attached via constraint to the end of the first label (this should happen automatically if you drag the second close enough to the first).

6. Add a square button below the box and change its image via the drop-down box to **NSAddTemplate**.

7. Add another square button next to the add button and set its image to **NSRemoveTemplate**.

8. Go back up to the table view and change the title of the first column to **First Name**.

9. Change the title of the second column of the table view to **Last Name**.

10. Add a regular push button to the window, titled **Check Contents**.

At this point your interface should look something like the one shown in Figure 10.4.

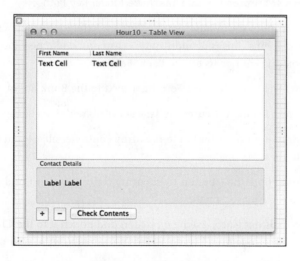

FIGURE 10.4
Sample contact application UI.

11. Create a `Customer` class. To do this, follow the steps you learned in previous hours to create a new Objective-C class.

12. Add two `strong` properties to the customer class called **firstName** and **lastName**, respectively.

13. Add an `assign` property called **bankBalance** (to make this easy, just make the value of type `NSInteger`).

14. Add an `NSArrayController` to the `MainWindow.xib` file and, using the steps you learned about earlier, set its class type to `Customer`.

15. Now go back to the table view and bind the First Name column's value to the array controller. Remember to set the Controller Key to `arrangedObjects` and the Model Key Path to `firstName`. Also remember there are a couple of ways to select the first column in the table view.

16. Select the Last Name column and bind its value to the `lastName` Model Key Path of the array controller's `arrangedObjects` key.

17. Select the table view and ensure that the content is bound to the `arrangedObjects` array (this should already be set). Now bind the Selection Indexes value to the array controller's selection indexes.

18. Select the first of the two labels in the Contact Details box. Bind its value to the array controller by choosing `selection` for the Controller Key and `firstName` for Model Key Path.

19. Select the second label in the Contact Details box. Bind its value to the array controller's `selection` key and `lastName` Model Key Path.

20. To illustrate that we can have more values underlying the table view than there are columns (this is actually quite common), add a new label to the details box and change its text to **Bank Balance**.

21. Add a Text Field with Number Formatter next to the Bank Balance label.

22. Bind this text field to the currently selected customer's `bankBalance` property.

23. Control-drag from the + button to the array controller object and create a connection to the `add:` method.

24. Control-drag from the − button to the array controller object and create a connection to the `remove:` method.

25. Using the assistant editor, create an action and attach it to the Check Contents button. Use the code from Listing 10.1 as a sample to write your own code.

LISTING 10.1   **Examining the Contents of an Array Controller**

```
- (IBAction)checkContents:(id)sender {
    for (Customer *cust in self.customersArrayController.arrangedObjects)
    {
        NSLog(@"customer %@ %@, bank balance: $%ld",
            cust.firstName, cust.lastName, cust.bankBalance);
    }
}
```

> Notice the reference to `customersArrayController` within the
> `Hour10AppDelegate` class. You'll have to create this outlet yourself before this
> code will work!

**Watch
Out!**

26. At this point you should have a completely bound table view, a functioning array controller, and two labels and a text field that are bound to properties of the currently selected item within the array controller. Build and run the application. You should be able to produce output similar to the screenshot in Figure 10.5.

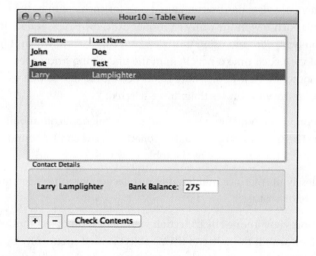

FIGURE 10.5
A running data-bound table view application.

When you run the application, you should be able to push the Check Contents button and receive output that looks similar to this:

```
2011-07-11 21:45:36.324 Hour10[13468:407] customer John Doe,
➡bank balance: $500
2011-07-11 21:45:36.330 Hour10[13468:407] customer Jane Test,
➡bank balance: $800
2011-07-11 21:45:36.333 Hour10[13468:407] customer Larry Lamplighter,
➡bank balance: $275
```

After completing this exercise, you should be feeling pretty good about your Cocoa application skills. You've been able to use Interface Builder to create interactive applications, and now you've created an application that maintains a list of contacts and their details and does it all with binding and no code (other than what we used to dump the array contents to the log).

Using Collection Views

If the kind of data you want to display to your users might be more appropriately displayed as a somewhat loose collection of items rather than in strict table-and-row form, a collection view might be just what you need.

A collection view allows you to define a grid (rows and columns), but individual items flow from top to bottom and then wrap horizontally when room runs out. You typically see this kind of behavior when you're looking at a list of thumbnails of photos in a picture folder, or you might be browsing through a list of contacts by picture and name.

Collection views bind to array controllers just like table views. The main difference is that where the table view has preconfigured cells for each column, the collection view represents each row in the array controller as its own view. It does this by maintaining a prototype view and using that view as a source from which it instantiates an individual view each time a new item in the underlying array needs rendering. You can configure the view to alternate colors between items, as well as whether clicking items in the view causes them to be selected.

To see collection views in action, we can add one to the application built in the previous section. The Content property of the collection view can be bound to the array controller in much the same way as the table view was.

If you look closely at Interface Builder after a collection view has been added, you'll see two additional objects:

▶ **Collection view item**—The collection view item is an object that represents a single item within the collection. This object is used specifically by the collection view and, as you'll see shortly, is primarily used as a bindings target.

▶ **View**—This is the prototype view from which all views in the collection view are created. Think of this as a stamper that is used to stamp out each item as it needs to be rendered.

If we open up the view, we can see that it's an empty slate. Within this view you can create anything you like: images, text, editable content, you name it. For example, if you wanted to display the first name of a contact in this view, you might add a label for that. To bind this label, you need to know about a special property of the collection view item called `representedObject`. This is the actual object that is being represented by the collection view at the time. If we were doing this for our contact example, the `representedObject` instance would be an instance of the `Customer` class. As a result, we could bind to the `firstName` or `lastName` properties. To do this, you pick the Collection View Item from the binding target drop-down and choose `representedObject.firstName` for the Model Key Path.

Figure 10.6 shows what the application built in the preceding section might look like if we also had a collection view bound to the customer contact array controller.

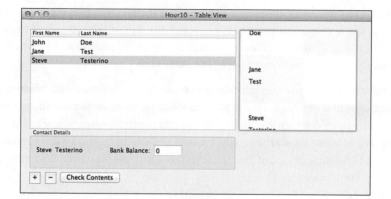

FIGURE 10.6
Collection view and table view bound to same array controller.

Using the Outline View

The table view and collection view are both great controls if you are planning to display a flat list of data or a list of data that lends itself to being displayed in rows and columns. But what if you want to display a hierarchy of data?

In this situation, you have rows that look very much like the rows that belong in a table view, except that these rows are actually *parents* to child rows. Using an outline view, a disclosure triangle appears next to every row that has child rows. When you click this disclosure triangle, child rows appear beneath the parent row.

This kind of control comes in handy in many scenarios. One of the most common is where you are displaying a tree of data that you want to allow your user to navigate, such as a file directory browser or a media catalog. Another very common use for the outline view is in the traditional "parent-child" scenario. For example, you might have an application that displays invoices and their total dollar amounts. For each of these invoices, there might be multiple line items, and you could use the outline view control to allow the user to expand and collapse invoices to see the individual line items.

Because outline views represent hierarchical data, a simple array controller isn't enough to hold the underlying data. We need something that can represent arrays as well as child arrays of individual items. This job falls to the `NSTreeController`.

Fortunately, binding columns of an outline view to a tree controller is almost as easy as binding table views to array controllers. Using the slow left click trick (or navigating the object tree), drill down to the first column in your tree controller and switch to the bindings inspector. There, you're going to use the special property `representedObject` like you did with the collection view.

To bind the outline view's column, you bind the column to the tree controller and set the Controller Key value to `arrangedObjects`. If the data you're attaching to an individual tree node for this column has a property called `nodeName`, you would set the Model Key Path to `representedObject.nodeName`.

There are many ways you can get data into a tree controller, including binding the tree controller to a database, as you'll see in Hour 13 when we work with core data. Listing 10.2 shows another way to populate a tree controller—manually using `NSTreeNode` objects and your own custom data objects. In Listing 10.2, we're using a class called `TreeNodeData`, but you could just as easily use whatever class makes sense for your application.

LISTING 10.2   Method to Fill a Tree Controller

```
- (NSArray *)generateTree
{
    NSString *rootStrings[] = {@"Cool", @"Sorta Cool", @"Not So Cool", @"Lame"};
    NSMutableArray *roots = [NSMutableArray array];
    for (int i=0; i<4; i++)
    {
        TreeNodeData *nodeData = [TreeNodeData new];
        nodeData.nodeName = rootStrings[i];
        NSTreeNode *node =
[NSTreeNode treeNodeWithRepresentedObject:nodeData];
        for (int j=0; j<10; j++)
        {
            TreeNodeData *level2Data = [TreeNodeData new];
            level2Data.nodeName =
[NSString stringWithFormat:@"node %d", j+1];
            NSTreeNode *level2Node =
             [NSTreeNode treeNodeWithRepresentedObject:level2Data];
            [[node mutableChildNodes] addObject:level2Node];
        }
        [roots addObject:node];
    }
    return roots;
}
```

The generateTree method creates a set root nodes based on some arbitrary strings and then, for each of those root nodes, adds 10 child nodes. To set the content of a tree controller, just call its setContent method, as shown next:

```
[self.sampleTreeController setContent:[self generateTree]];
```

When the application runs, the bound outline view will read the top-level nodes from the tree controller. For each of those nodes, it will decide whether that node has child nodes. This determines whether a disclosure triangle will be displayed next to the node in the outline view.

Did You Know?

> The methods to invoke on the node to determine if it has child nodes or if the node is a leaf node are configurable properties of the tree controller. This allows developers to maintain flexibility in controlling the types of objects managed by the tree controller.

Figure 10.7 shows a sample outline view bound to a tree controller that was populated by the method shown in Listing 10.2

FIGURE 10.7
An outline view bound to a tree controller.

Summary

In this hour you continued to build and extend your Cocoa application development skills by working with lists or collections of data. We took a look at some controllers designed specifically to facilitate binding controls to lists such as the `NSArrayController` and the `NSTreeController`. We took a tour of the controls designed to present lists for user interaction such as the `NSTableView`, the `NSCollectionView`, and the `NSOutlineView`.

Now that you've had experience building applications that create interactive user experiences, and you know how to bind individual controls to model objects as well as controls to lists of model objects, you are ready learn more advanced techniques.

Q&A

Q. *How do I know when to use a table view versus a collection view?*

A. Your first resource for questions like this should always be Apple's Human Interface Guidelines. After that, always try and opt for the most minimal interface that will suit your needs—it's easier to start small and expand than it is to shrink it later.

Q. *Are trees just as easy to bind as table and collection views?*

A. They are fairly easy to bind, but you need to make sure that you can represent your data as a tree, which often takes a little more work and sometimes involves a translation step between your real data source and the source you bind to your tree.

HOUR 11

Working with Multitouch and Gestures

What you'll learn in this hour:

▶ Introduction to Multitouch on Mac OS X Lion

▶ Responding to Gestures and Multitouch Events

It seems lately that the marketing material for virtually every new device claims multitouch as a primary feature. Whether you're talking about the iPhone, an iPad, trackpads for the Mac and Macbooks, or tablets and laptops of all shapes or sizes—the ability to touch and tap user interfaces is becoming as ubiquitous as the mouse.

Mac OS X Lion is not without its support for multitouch gestures. Whether you're swiping, panning, rotating, zooming, or double-tapping, your applications can take advantage of these new forms of interaction to create new, compelling interfaces.

In this hour, you will be introduced to Mac OS X Lion's support for multitouch gestures and learn how you can write code to take advantage of those gestures in your application.

Introduction to Multitouch on Mac OS X Lion

Whether you're using a Magic Mouse, a wireless trackpad, or the built-in trackpad from a Macbook Pro or Macbook Air, Mac OS X Lion has full support for multitouch built in.

To see the kind of gestures available with your particular device, open up System Preferences and then choose Trackpad. Here you will see all the different kinds of gestures available. Each of the gestures comes with a handy little video demonstrating the gesture as it appears on your device and the visual effect it might have on an application or an application's content.

Some of the gestures available are

- ▶ **Scrolling**—By dragging two fingers up or down across the surface of the trackpad, you can scroll content. A change from Mac OS X Snow Leopard to Lion is that the default scrolling direction has changed. The new direction, called "natural," allows content to move in accordance with your fingers the way scrolling works on the iPhone or iPad.

- ▶ **Zoom**—You can zoom either by spreading your thumb and another finger apart or you can use a new "smart zoom" feature by double-tapping the trackpad.

- ▶ **Navigate**—With two fingers held down on the trackpad, you can swipe to the left or right to control navigation. For example, in Safari this gesture will navigate forward or backward through your browsing history.

- ▶ **Full-Screen Applications**—With three fingers held down on the trackpad, you can swipe to the left or right to navigate between virtual desktops or, if an application is in full-screen mode, between full-screen views.

You might be wondering how any of this should impact your application. Just because the operating system supports several multitouch gestures doesn't necessarily mean that your application should.

However, consider that users are creatures of habit, and their expectations are raised or lowered by the operating system and applications they use. If, as they are navigating around Lion, they get used to being able to do three-finger swipes, double-tap zooms, and two-finger rotates, they will try these gestures on your application. If there's a spot in your user interface where the user thinks one of these gestures might be appropriate and your application doesn't support it, the user will remember that lack of functionality more than any other amazing features you might provide.

When you are designing your application and its main screens, take a moment to consider where gesture support might provide the user with a better, more satisfying experience than standard point-and-click mouse interaction. As you'll see in the rest of this hour, adding support for the basic gestures is straightforward; considering the kind of enhanced experience gestures provide for your users, adding support where appropriate is well worth the effort.

Responding to Gestures and Multitouch Events

In this section of the hour you'll learn about the tools you'll need and code you need to write to make a gesture-aware application. In addition, you'll learn about the most commonly used types of gestures and how easy they are to support in your application.

To understand how gestures work, you first need to understand how multitouch events are handled and interpreted by Mac OS X Lion. Gestures are just logic applied on top of a series of touches and movements on a trackpad.

A touch sequence typically starts when a user presses a finger down on the touch-pad. From there, the finger can move in arbitrary directions, it can lift up off the trackpad, or it can stay still. Additional fingers can be added anytime during the touch sequence.

We now take many of these gestures for granted because of technological advance-ments like the iPhone, the iPad, touch-aware computer monitors, tablet devices, and trackpads on modern laptops.

Think about a gesture many of us use regularly: the *pinch*. To do a pinch we need to put two (and usually *only* two) fingers down on a trackpad. Then, we move the fin-gers inward toward each other. This pinch gesture is usually interpreted as *zoom in*. The inverse of this gesture, where two fingers start together and spread apart, is usu-ally interpreted as *zoom out*.

While this might seem like a simple gesture, think about the fact that you need to keep track of the number of fingers (*touches*) on the trackpad and the relative dis-tance between the touches. While this is going on, you need to make sure that the number of touches neither increases nor decreases to make sure you've detected the right gesture. To complicate things, you need to be vigilant in detecting other ges-tures that might seem similar to the one you're looking for.

Things get even more complicated when you think about gestures like *rotate*. In this gesture, you need to track two points and make sure that they are maintaining velocities in (somewhat) opposite directions—the two fingers rotate along the bounds of an invisible circle. We can't expect users to have perfect dexterity, so we need to know that if those two fingers start drifting toward each other *while rotating*, we can tell the difference between a rotate and an accidental zoom.

Creating a Custom View

Touches, and the gestures they combine to create, are conveyed to a view in the form of methods that belong to the NSResponder object. These methods are invoked when significant events occur in the lifetime of a touch. Fortunately, methods exist that allow us to respond to high-level gestures without doing all the complicated math and state management involved in detecting the gestures manually.

The view object contains the code that responds to touches and gestures. Therefore, for us to write gesture-reactive code, we need to put it in the view.

> This is a simplification. Technically, we can designate a delegate other than the view to handle the events destined for this view, but that gets complicated and usually results in code that is difficult to troubleshoot and maintain.

Creating a custom view might seem like a daunting task if you've ever done this on another platform or with other languages, but it's fairly straightforward to create a custom Cocoa view.

To create a new custom Cocoa view, add a new Objective-C class file to your project. When prompted for the class from which the new class derives, type NSView instead of NSObject.

To make the view respond to low-level touch events, make the code for the initWithFrame: method look like the code that follows:

```
- (id)initWithFrame:(NSRect)frame
{
    self = [super initWithFrame:frame];
    if (self) {
        // Initialization code here.
        [self setAcceptsTouchEvents:YES];
    }

    return self;
}
```

> Note that you have to do this only if you want to receive the individual, low-level touch events such as the start, movement, and completion of touches. Gestures such as magnify, rotate, and swipe will register in your view even if you don't call setAcceptsTouchEvents:.

To use the view, you need to drag the "custom view" object from the object library onto your design surface. Using the identity inspector for that view, you set the view's class to the `NSView` subclass you just created.

Typically, developers create custom views when they need to control the rendering behavior of the view, when they need to perform custom drawing, or when they need custom event-handling for that view.

Responding to Multitouch Trackpad Events

To respond to individual touch events, you will need to enable touch responses in your view. In the preceding code block, you saw the use of the method `setAcceptsTouchEvents:`. After your view is able to accept touch events, you can write code to respond to the various touch events, as shown in the following code:

```
- (void)touchesCancelledWithEvent:(NSEvent *)event
{
    // NSLog(@"Touches canceled!");
}
- (void)touchesBeganWithEvent:(NSEvent *)event
{
    //    NSLog(@"Touches began!");
}

- (void)touchesMovedWithEvent:(NSEvent *)event {
    // NSLog(@"touches moved!");
}

- (void)touchesEndedWithEvent:(NSEvent *)event  {
    //  NSLog(@"Touches ended!");
}
```

After you have the touch event, you're going to need to extract the list of touches from the event.

Keep in mind that every touch event could involve multiple touches. As such, you will always be operating on an `NSSet` of touches that you can pull from the single touch event.

To extract those touches, you can use the `touchesMatchingPhase:inView:` method, as shown next:

```
- (void)touchesBeganWithEvent:(NSEvent *)event
{
    NSLog(@"Touches began!");
    NSSet *touches = [event touchesMatchingPhase:NSTouchPhaseBegan inView:self];
    for (NSTouch *touch in touches)
```

```
    {
        NSPoint normalizedPosition = touch.normalizedPosition;

        NSLog(@"[Touch %@]: Got a Touch at (%g, %g)", touch.identity,
            normalizedPosition.x, normalizedPosition.y);
    }
}
```

First, we use `touchesMatchingPhase:inView:` to extract an `NSSet` of `NSTouch` object instances. For each of those, we can access the `normalizedPosition` property, which gives you a decimal value indicating the *fraction* of the maximum distance along that axis the user's finger is pressing.

For example, if you touch directly in the middle of your trackpad, the `normalizedPosition` property should report a coordinate position of (0.5, 0.5) with the origin of the graph at the bottom left of the trackpad.

Many gesture types, such as when you use a two-finger swipe to advance or go back pages in Safari, speed up or slow down the corresponding UI animations based on your finger velocity. The `normalizedPosition` is essential in determining this. Trackpads and touchable surfaces come in many shapes and sizes, and if you had to manually account for these variances every time you started detecting gestures, life would be miserable and you would spend more time coding gesture recognition than you did building your application's functionality.

Fortunately, as you'll see in the next few sections, Apple has already taken care of the majority of the legwork for detecting three of the most common gesture types: magnify/zoom, swipe, and rotate.

Using the Magnify Gesture

There are several gestures that contribute to allowing users to zoom:

▶ **Pinch to zoom out**—By dragging fingers closer together, users indicate they want to shrink whatever was underneath the mouse cursor at the time of the gesture.

▶ **Unpinch to zoom in**—By pulling fingers apart, users indicate they want to zoom in on or expand whatever was underneath the mouse cursor at the time of the gesture.

▶ **Double-tap to quick zoom**—Two quick two-finger taps on the trackpad counts as a *zoom reset*. Applications often choose to handle this gesture by toggling between two preset zoom levels (e.g. normal and large).

To make your view respond to a magnify gesture, you need to supply an implementation for the `magnifyWithEvent:` method:

```
-(void)magnifyWithEvent:(NSEvent *)event {
    CGFloat magFactor = event.magnification;
    NSLog(@"Magnify gesture detected, zoom factor: %f", magFactor);
}
```

> Remember that the magnification factor here counts as an adjustment value, not as an absolute value. Therefore, you should *adjust* your current scale factor by the value received in the event, not just set the scale factor to the magnify factor outright.

When the user double-taps to do a quick zoom, the magnification factor will be 0. It is then up to you to decide how you want to handle that value.

Using the Swipe Gesture

A swipe gesture from an application standpoint is a multifinger swipe. It involves a multifinger starting touch event, followed by those same fingers moving in a single direction. We don't have to track the individual touches, and we can respond to a swipe as shown in this code:

```
- (void)swipeWithEvent:(NSEvent *)event {
    NSLog(@"swipe detected");
    CGFloat dX = event.deltaX;
    CGFloat dY = event.deltaY;

    if (dX > 0) {
        // swiped left
    }
    else if (dX < 0) {
        // swiped right
    }
    else if (dY > 0) {
        // swiped up
    }
    else {
        // swiped down
    }
}
```

The `deltaX` and `deltaY` properties of the `NSEvent` object indicate the *change* in X (horizontal) and Y (vertical) position that occurred during the swipe. As you can see from the preceding code, all you have to do is check these two values to detect the overall direction of the swipe.

Using the Rotate Gesture

Rotation is a fairly complicated gesture to detect if all you have to work with are the low-level touch events. Fortunately, we don't have to use those events and can skip right to the corresponding rotation event:

```
- (void)rotateWithEvent:(NSEvent *)event {
    CGFloat newRotation = [event rotation];
    NSLog(@"requesting rotate to %f", newRotation);
}
```

This couldn't be much easier: the event comes with a value called `rotation` that indicates the angle of rotation desired by the gesture. When the gesture first starts, the angle is pretty low, but the more you turn, the more the gesture recognizes the difference between where your fingers started rotating and where they stopped—giving us the desired rotation angle.

Every view comes with a property called `frameCenterRotation`. To make a view rotate according to a rotate gesture, you add the gesture's rotation to the view's current rotation and set the view's rotation to that value:

```
[targetView setFrameCenterRotation:currentRotation + newRotation];
```

You will use this technique in the next section, where you build an application that responds to magnifications, swipes, and rotations.

▼ **Try It Yourself**

Creating a Gesture-Aware Application

Now that you know the mechanics behind multitouch gestures, responding to touch events, and responding to gesture events, it's time to put that to work. Use the following steps to build a gesture-aware application, referring to earlier pages for reference:

1. Create a new Cocoa application called **Hour11** using the same defaults that you've been using throughout the book.

> Do *not* enable Automatic Layout for the `MainWindow.xib` file. Doing so will interfere with some of the code you're going to be writing.

2. Add a new Objective-C class to the project called **GestureView**, making sure that it inherits from `NSView`.

3. Open up the `MainWindow.xib` file and make sure that the window object is selected.

▼

4. Drag a custom view object from the object library onto the window and resize it to fill most of the window (the blue guides should tell you when to stop expanding the view).

5. Using the identity inspector, set the class of the custom view to `GestureView`.

6. Add an image well to the custom view by dragging it from the object library and centering it within the view.

7. Now we need to add an `IBOutlet` for the image so that the `GestureView` class can refer to it. Add an `IBOutlet` declaration for the property in `GestureView.h` and make sure you synthesize the property in `GestureView.m`. Because the code that comes with the book uses the Mac OS X Lion logo as an image, I called the outlet **lionView**.

8. Connect the outlet you just created by opening the connections inspector of the custom view and dragging from the connection point to the image view.

9. Now we need to pick an image for the image view. You can use the image that came with the code samples for the book, or you can pick your own. To add an image to the project, right-click the project and choose Add Files to Hour11.

10. Configure the image view to display the image you just added to the project. In the attributes inspector, the image is the first configurable property for an image well. Set the image to the one you added, and while you're there, set the border value to None.

11. At this point you should have an application that displays a custom view that contains an image. Now we can write some code to manipulate this image with gestures. Add the following code to the `GestureView.m` file to manipulate the image with a rotate gesture (remember to change the name of the view if you didn't call yours `lionView`):

```
- (void)rotateWithEvent:(NSEvent *)event {
    CGFloat currentRotation = [lionView frameCenterRotation];
    CGFloat newRotation = [event rotation];
    NSLog(@"requesting rotate to %f", newRotation);
    [lionView setFrameCenterRotation:currentRotation + newRotation];
}
```

12. Run the application. Notice that as you rotate your fingers on the trackpad, the image rotates along with it!

13. Now let's add support for the pinch gesture. Add the following code to the `GestureView.m` file:

```
-(void)magnifyWithEvent:(NSEvent *)event {
    CGFloat magFactor = event.magnification;
    NSLog(@"Magnify gesture detected, zoom factor: %f", magFactor);

    NSSize newSize = lionView.frame.size;
    newSize.height = newSize.height * (magFactor + 1.0);
    newSize.width = newSize.width * (magFactor + 1.0);
    [lionView setFrameSize:newSize];
}
```

14. Now run the application again. You should be able to both rotate *and* zoom the image. The two gestures are detected at the same time so, if you are dexterous enough, you should be able to expand and contract the zoom while rotating the image.

15. As an optional exercise, add in some logic that detects the zoom double-tap (remember this occurs when `event.magnification` is 0). When the user double-tap zooms, toggle between the image's current size and a quick zoom size (either its original size or a 2× scale size).

16. Next, add code that will handle a swipe gesture to the `GestureView.m` class. For each possible direction, move the `lionView` as far as it can go in that direction. For example, on a swipe left, set its X coordinate to 0 but leave the Y the same. You can do this by setting the view's `frame` property to the results of an `NSMakeRect()` function call:

```
- (void)swipeWithEvent:(NSEvent *)event {
    NSLog(@"swipe detected");
    CGFloat dX = event.deltaX;
    CGFloat dY = event.deltaY;

    if (dX > 0) {
        // swiped left
        lionView.frame = NSMakeRect(0.0, lionView.frame.origin.y,
                                    lionView.frame.size.width,
                                    lionView.frame.size.height);
    }
    else if (dX < 0) {
        // swiped right
    }
    else if (dY > 0) {
        // swiped up
    }
    else {
        // swiped down
    }
}
```

17. Run the application again. You should now be able to rotate, zoom, and swipe, and the image should respond accordingly.

▼

> The swipe gesture is a bit tricky. Mac OS X Lion itself responds to quite a few swipe gestures, and those are evaluated *before* your application sees them. If you have trouble recognizing swipes, turn off the system swipe gestures, and your app should then recognize swipe gestures.

By the Way

You now have a fully interactive application that responds to multiple gestures and illustrates the power of multitouch and the ease with which you can add multitouch support to your applications.

▲

Summary

In this hour you learned that Mac OS X has had multitouch support built in for some time now and learned how Mac OS X Lion improves on that support with new gestures.

You learned about creating custom views so that you can write code that responds to multitouch events and high-level gestures like the zoom, rotate, and swipe. You went through the exercise of building your own highly reactive, gesture-aware application.

Multitouch and gesture-based UIs are gaining popularity and momentum. Today, users are surrounded by touchable devices like iPhones, iPads, tablets, trackpads, and touch-screen monitors. Taking the relatively small amount of time to add gesture recognition to your application could set it apart from its competitors and give the user that rich, satisfying experience they crave from all Mac apps.

Q&A

Q. *What are the most common types of gestures that are easily recognized by writing code in a Mac OS X Lion application?*

A. Pinching to zoom, swiping to indicate direction or navigation, multi-finger vertical gestures for scrolling, and two-finger rotation to indicate rotation angles.

Q. *How many potential Mac users actually have access to a multi-touch device?*

A. Anyone who has purchased a Macbook Pro or a Macbook Air in the last few years will have gesture recognition, as well as those iMac and Mac Pro users who have purchased an Apple Magic Mouse peripheral. In short, you should expect the vast majority of your potential users to have some form of touch gesture recognition.

HOUR 12

Working with User Defaults

What you'll learn in this hour:

▶ Introduction to User Defaults and Preference Panes

▶ Reading and Writing User Defaults

▶ Binding to the User Defaults Controller

▶ Building a User Preferences Window

This section of the book deals with the storage and retrieval of data in Mac OS X Lion applications. Your application can interact with data in many ways, and in this hour, we're going to focus on giving your users the ability to set application preferences.

In this hour we'll discuss user preferences and how users typically expect to interact with them in Mac OS X applications. From there, we'll move on to a discussion of how to read and write preferences programmatically, and finally, we'll build an application preferences window to put all that information together in a real-world example.

Introduction to User Defaults and Preferences Panes

If you've been using Mac OS X for a while, you are familiar with the Preferences menu option. In most applications with a native Mac look and feel, the application's menu typically has an option called Preferences. Clicking this menu option opens a preferences window that allows users to configure application-specific options.

For example, a preferences window for a Twitter application might prompt users for their Twitter account password and other options for displaying feeds, network activity, and so on.

The preferences window for Pages, Apple's word processor, allows the user to configure text editing defaults, page layout, autocorrection, change tracking information, and more.

You may want to use user defaults to remember which record the user was last editing or the position of the window at the time the application closed, as well as other more obvious settings like credentials and network and connectivity options.

User Defaults Versus System Preference Panes

Some applications integrate their settings with the System Preferences window, an OS-level window that controls OS settings from user accounts to security to Wi-Fi, trackpads, and everything in between.

For example, if you use the application Growl to provide a nice pop-up notification system to let applications alert you when important events occur, you will see a Growl icon at the bottom of your System Preferences window.

Applications that add panels to the system preferences area of the OS are making changes to system-level files and executing some code that is beyond the scope of this book. In addition, the App Store submission rules at the time this book was written prohibit you from selling an application through the App Store that makes such system-level modifications.

Reading and Writing User Defaults

They are called user defaults in the API because they are most often used to control the default state or behavior of an application when that application first starts up. Users can later customize those defaults, but their purpose as initial start-up values is clear.

To access these values, we use the NSUserDefaults class. This class provides us with the ability to *register* defaults (provide initial values for the application's first launch), *read* defaults, and *write* defaults.

Suppose that our application has the following two user defaults:

► **Favorite Number**—Allows users to indicate their favorite number. At application startup, this value should default to "42" and remain 42 until the user specifies otherwise.

► **Coin Preference**—Allows users to indicate the type of coins they would like to use in the application. At application startup, this value should default to "gold" and should remain that way until the user changes it.

The first thing we need to do is *register* our defaults. This provides default values for each of our application's default settings. This registration will allow us to access these values safely, even if the user has never opened the application's preferences window.

The following code registers these two defaults:

```
[[NSUserDefaults standardUserDefaults] registerDefaults:
    [NSDictionary dictionaryWithObjectsAndKeys:
        [NSNumber numberWithInt:42], @"favoriteNumber",
        @"gold", @"coinPreference",
    nil]];
```

The `standardUserDefaults` class method of the `NSUserDefaults` class is a *singleton*, meaning that there is never more than one instance of the singleton object. Although you can create your own custom instances of the user defaults object, using the `standardUserDefaults` object gives you the simplest access to user defaults functionality.

In this code, I'm passing in an instance of a dictionary that contains the default values we want. At this point, these settings are *not* being stored on disk anywhere, they are being used as defaults only for when the application tries to read values that have not yet been configured.

> You don't have to hand-code the defaults dictionary yourself. If you have a lot of settings and default values, you can store the dictionary as a resource and load it from your application bundle at runtime as an instance of a dictionary. If you're interested, research the `dictionaryWithContentsOfFile` method of the `NSDictionary` class to get started. The documentation for the `NSDictionary` class can be found here: http://developer.apple.com/library/mac/#documentation/Cocoa/Reference/Foundation/Classes/NSDictionary_Class/Reference/Reference.html

By the Way

With the defaults registered, we are now free to try to read values from the `NSUserDefaults` object:

```
NSInteger favNumber = [[NSUserDefaults standardUserDefaults]
                          integerForKey:@"favoriteNumber"];
NSString *coinPref = [[NSUserDefaults standardUserDefaults]
                          stringForKey:@"coinPreference"];
```

Setting these values is just as easy. In the following lines of code, we're setting defaults based on values contained in text fields in a window:

```
NSInteger newValue = favNumberTextField.intValue;
[[NSUserDefaults standardUserDefaults] setInteger:newValue
forKey:@"favoriteNumber"];
```

```
NSString *newValue = coinPrefTextField.stringValue;
[[NSUserDefaults standardUserDefaults] setObject:newValue
forKey:@"coinPreference"];
```

When your application terminates normally, the values currently in the user defaults object will be persisted to disk. The emphasis here is on *normally*. If your application crashes, or if you are in debug mode and you stop the debugger from Xcode rather than doing a normal application quit, these settings will *not* be saved to disk.

If you need to manually save the settings to disk in response to some event, you can do so by calling the synchronize method on the user defaults object. Call this only if you absolutely must because it is called periodically without your intervention.

By the Way

> When user defaults are saved to disk, they can be found in the following location: ~/Library/Preferences, in a file named the same as your application's ID (for example, this hour's would be in com.stylion.hour12) with the extension .plist, which is Apple's *property list* file format. So, a tennis game written by a company called FunCorp might store its preferences in the file ~/Library/Preferences/ com.funcorp.tennis.plist. These files are binary files and can't be viewed using a standard text editor, but you can view and edit plist files using Xcode.

Binding to the User Defaults Controller

In the previous section, you saw how you can programmatically set and query user default values to allow users to customize and configure your application.

If you want the user to be able to edit these preferences, there is an easier way of doing so other than manually copying values from text fields into the user defaults object and back again.

The NSUserDefaultsController class is a bindings-aware class that you can use to provide a binding target for UI elements so they can be bound to user preferences. Remember that bindings work for more than just simple input fields. For example, you could bind the color of a view to the user's favorite color.

To bind a value to the user defaults controller, open up the bindings inspector of whatever control you're working with. When you choose to bind, one of the options for a binding target is called Shared User Defaults Controller.

When you select this, the *controller key* becomes values and the *model key path* should be set to the name of the setting to which you want to bind. For example, to bind the value of a text field to the favoriteNumber user default, you would configure the binding as shown in Figure 12.1.

FIGURE 12.1
Binding to the
Shared User
Defaults
Controller.

The binding that you configure here will read the same values that you would be reading using the `stringForKey:` or `integerForKey:` methods on the `standardUserDefaults` object. As such, these values will be *empty* if you don't register them first using the `registerDefaults:` method.

To recap, your application should register the default values for user defaults *every time the application launches*. When users change values, they can do so either using values directly bound to the shared user defaults controller or programmatically with methods on an instance of the `NSUserDefaults` class.

The values the user chooses (either through bindings or indirectly via code) will be stored on disk when the user defaults object synchronizes automatically, or on demand when you call the `synchronize:` method.

Try It Yourself

Building a User Preferences Window

In this section we're going to build an application that allows the user to configure defaults for an application. This application will maintain two values: a favorite color and a favorite number. Instead of doing this all programmatically without any UI, we're going to build on some of our newfound Cocoa skills and create a user preferences window.

This user preferences window will look very much like the user preferences windows used by thousands of other Mac OS X applications and, as such, the users of your application will feel right at home making use of this window to change their application preferences.

▼

Follow these steps to create an application with a user preferences window:

1. Create a new Cocoa application called **Hour 12** using the standard options that you've been using for most of the book (no Core Data support, do not create a document-based application, and so on).

2. Add a new file to the project called **PreferencesWindowController** (include both the .m and .h files). Make sure this file derives from NSWindowController.

3. Add a new .xib file to the project. To do this, choose to create a new file but instead of choosing Objective-C as the template group, select User Interface on the left of the new file template dialog (as shown in Figure 12.2), and then select Window as the file type. Call this new window **Hour12PreferencesWindow.xib**.

FIGURE 12.2
Adding a new window to an Xcode project.

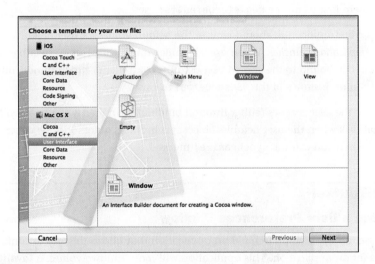

4. Open up the Hour12PreferencesWindow.xib file and, using the designer, change the identity of the File's Owner object to be PreferencesWindowController.

5. Create a connection between the window outlet of the File's Owner object to the window in the .xib file.

By the Way

Note that you don't have to create this outlet; you only have to connect it. The NSWindowController class already comes with a window outlet and, in fact, can't perform many of its duties without your connecting this outlet.

▼

6. Now that we have created an empty shell for what will become our preferences window, we need to modify the application menu so it will launch this window on demand. To do this, open `MainWindow.xib` and select the Main Menu object. This will make the application's main menu appear on the top of the design surface.

7. Click the Hour12 menu item on the far left and then select the Preferences menu item.

8. Activate the assistant editor and make sure that it opens the `Hour12AppDelegate.h` file.

9. Drag the mouse from the empty connection "plug" for the selector under Sent Actions for the Preferences menu item into an empty space in the bottom of the `Hour12AppDelegate.h` file.

10. Choose to create a new action called **`preferencesClicked:`**. Xcode should then create the appropriate code in the header file, the implementation file, and the corresponding connection in the `MainWindow.xib` file.

11. Add the following code to the `Hour12AppDelegate.m` file to replace the stub implementation of `preferencesClicked:` that Xcode generated for you:

```
- (IBAction)preferencesClicked:(id)sender {
    if (prefController == nil)
    {
        prefController = [[PreferencesWindowController alloc]

                        initWithWindowNibName:@"Hour12PreferencesWindow"];
    }
    [prefController showWindow:self];
}
```

12. Note in the preceding code that there is a member variable called `prefController`. We need to declare that, so add the following line of code inside the interface portion of the `Hour12AppDelegate.h` file:

```
PreferencesWindowController *prefController;
```

Did You Know?

If you try to compile now, Xcode will tell you that `PreferencesWindowController` is an unknown class. Don't forget to add an `#import` directive at the top of the file for the `PreferencesWindowController.h` file to allow one class to know about another.

▼

13. If you run the application now, you should see an empty window appear. When you click the Hour12 menu item and then click Preferences, the empty preferences window should appear. You should be able to close and reopen the preferences window as many times as you like.

14. Add a toolbar from the object library to the preferences window (make sure you're editing `Hour12PreferencesWindow.xib`, not `MainWindow.xib`).

15. This toolbar should come with a couple of default toolbar items, such as Print and Colors. Delete those.

16. Add a tab view to the window. Expand the tab view so that it fills nearly all of the window below the toolbar. The blue guidelines in the designer should help you size it appropriately.

17. Set the tab view's style to Tables.

18. Set the label for the first tab view item to SuperSettings. Inside this tab, drag a label and text field. Change the text of the label to **Favorite Color:**.

19. Set the label for the second tab view item to **BoringSettings**. Inside this tab drag a label and text field *with number formatter*. Change the text of the label to **Favorite Number:**.

20. Using what you learned in the previous section, bind the text field on the first tab to a *shared user defaults* property called `favoriteColor`.

21. Bind the text field on the second tab to a shared user defaults property called `favoriteNumber`.

22. Add an image toolbar item to the toolbar called **Super Settings**. Feel free to set the image to anything you like. I chose the `NSComputer` icon. Make sure this toolbar item has the `selectable` check box checked.

Did You Know?

> To add a toolbar item, you might find it easier to select the toolbar to expand the toolbar designer and then drag the new toolbar item into the Allowed Toolbar Items section, as shown in Figure 12.3.

23. Add another toolbar item to the toolbar called **Boring Settings**. Again, you can set the image to anything you like. I chose the `NSInfo` icon. This toolbar item must also have its `selectable` check box checked.

▼

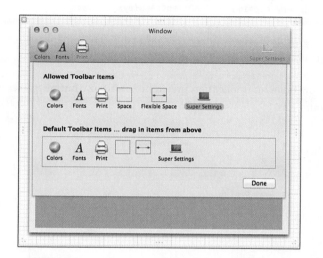

FIGURE 12.3
Configuring
toolbar items
in Xcode.

24. Create an action from the Super Settings toolbar item to the File's Owner object using the assistant editor. Call the action **superClicked:**. The code for this new method should look like this:

```
- (IBAction)superClicked:(id)sender {
    [tabView selectTabViewItemAtIndex:0];
}
```

25. Create an action from the Boring Settings toolbar item to the File's Owner object using the assistant editor. Call the action **boringClicked:**. The code for this new method should look like this:

```
- (IBAction)boringClicked:(id)sender {
    [tabView selectTabViewItemAtIndex:1];
}
```

26. At this point your preferences window should toggle between categories (boring and super) whenever the user clicks the appropriate button in the toolbar. The preferences window should appear when the user clicks the Preferences menu item in the application menu bar. Finally, the Favorite Color and Favorite Number fields should be bound to the user defaults. To make sure these bound fields have a value the first time the application starts, add the following code to the applicationDidFinishLaunching: method in the Hour12AppDelegate.m file:

▼
```
[[NSUserDefaults standardUserDefaults] registerDefaults:
 [NSDictionary dictionaryWithObjectsAndKeys:
     [NSNumber numberWithInt:42], @"favoriteNumber",
     @"gold", @"coinPreference",
     @"blue", @"favoriteColor",
 nil]];
```

You should now have an application preferences window that resembles the one shown in Figure 12.4.

FIGURE 12.4
A completed application preferences window.

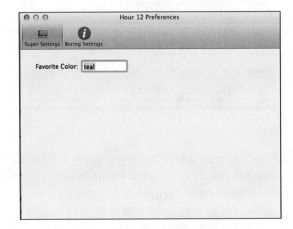

> By the
> Way
>
> The use of a toolbar to control the currently selected tab view in a "tabless tab view" is a pretty common pattern among Mac application developers. You will see this kind of technique used to create preferences windows and windows that present categories of related information in Mac applications everywhere. This is just one of many hundreds of really useful techniques Mac developers learn as their skills grow.

Summary

In this hour, we started exploring the first of many hours involving the storage and retrieval of data. The storage and retrieval of user defaults to enable users to configure their applications is essential to providing a compelling user experience, which is one of the things Apple insists on for all applications submitted to the Mac App Store.

In this hour you learned how the user defaults system works, where user defaults are stored, and how to read and write user defaults both programmatically and through bindings. As you explored the user defaults system, you also learned how to create a very native-looking preferences window for your application.

Being able to add a preference window to your application is another technique in your tool belt of techniques that can be used to create a rich, compelling experience for your users.

Q&A

Q. *Is there any reason why I shouldn't create a system preference pane for my application?*

A. If you want to distribute your application through the Mac App Store, you will not be able to use a preference pane because it makes low-level changes to the user's operating system, something that App Store applications cannot do.

Q. *Is there a limit to the amount of information I can store in user defaults?*

A. You should try and keep the size of this information to a minimum. You should not use user defaults to store data created by your users like documents, it should only be used to store user preferences and configuration related to your application.

Q. *When should I use the user defaults controller versus accessing defaults programmatically?*

A. The defaults controller is designed specifically to work with Cocoa bindings and should be used when you are displaying or allowing a user to edit defaults. If you just need to access the defaults in order to perform some application function, then you can just query the defaults manually without the defaults controller.

HOUR 13

Working with Core Data

What you'll learn in this hour:

▶ Overview of Core Data
▶ Creating Data Models
▶ Querying and Manipulating Data
▶ Binding UI Elements to Core Data Entities

So far, as you've progressed through this book, you have learned how to bind user interfaces to in-memory data structures like arrays of strings or instances of custom classes. You have also learned how to store and query user preferences that can be stored on disk.

In this hour you will continue your exploration of data-driven applications on the Mac by learning about Core Data, a powerful Cocoa framework that does far more than read and write data files. You will learn what Core Data is, how to build entity data models, how to query and manipulate data with those models, and how to bind your UI to Core Data-backed controllers.

Introducing Core Data

Core Data is a general framework that provides support and automation around the use of data models. When developers need to use data extensively in their applications, there are often a lot of tasks that must be done for each application of this type. With the release of Core Data, Apple wrapped many of these tasks with the Core Data framework and the APIs contained within.

The sample data models that we've used so far in this book have been very simplistic, but real-world data models for larger applications can be incredibly complex. These models often need to be able to deal with things like complex memory management, managing the relationships between objects, and detecting whether an object has been modified, and, if so, what changes have been made. Developers used to have to write their own code to manage all these tasks independently, and that was before they ever got around to tackling the problem of persistence, of reading and writing object hierarchies to and from some storage mechanism like a file on disk.

The Core Data framework takes a long, hard look at the tasks common to most data-driven applications and automates them, including the following:

▶ **Change tracking, including undo.**

▶ **Relationships**—Allowing objects to be related to each other, including fetching related objects.

▶ **Lazy loading**—Core Data is smart enough to know when objects do or do not need to be loaded into memory, and it can optimize object access so that they aren't loaded into memory until absolutely necessary.

▶ **Validation**—Based on the entity model configuration, Core Data will automatically validate properties based on data type and other constraints.

▶ **Grouping, filtering, and sorting.**

▶ **Compiled queries**—Developers can configure queries that are then optimized and cached, allowing developers to write easier-to-read queries instead of building SQL statements.

As you progress through the rest of this hour, you'll learn about how you can use Core Data to build data models, how to query and manipulate data, and, ultimately, how to build a complete data-driven application without writing a single line of code.

Creating Data Models

Before you can read or write your application's data, you'll need to know *what* you're writing. In other words, before you can start worrying about data model persistence, you need a data model.

In this section, we're going to go through the process of building a data model using Xcode and the built-in Core Data model designer. As mentioned earlier, a data model consists of entities, the attributes that belong to those entities, and the relationships that exist between the entities.

When developers think about data models with relationships, they often think in terms of primary keys and foreign keys, two common relational database topics. Core Data can deal with keys for you under the hood, but, as a developer, you don't need to worry about creating a key shared by two entities.

As antiquated and analog as it might seem, you may find it easier to start sketching out your data model on a piece of paper before you start using a tool like Xcode to design it.

The result of your initial sketching often results in a list of entities and their attributes, along with some arrows indicating relationships. As a sample, let's say that we're building an application that automates the task of matching socks. We've all been there, sitting in front of a mountain of unmatched socks. This (obviously fictitious) application allows you to enter the characteristics of each sock you find. As you pull a sock from the wash basket, it checks to see if you've previously found any socks that match those criteria.

A (contrived) example of a data model that might support this application could include two main entities:

▶ **Person**—This entity, as its name implies, represents a single person. People can be the owners of multiple socks.

▶ **Sock**—This entity represents a single sock. Socks have multiple attributes that enable the application to do matching against other socks.

The `Person` entity can be simple and contain a string attribute such as name, whereas the `Sock` entity might contain attributes to contain the various colors, stripes, and other identifying characteristics.

To see this in action, we can create a new Cocoa application and make sure the Use Core Data check box is checked (making sure we don't check the Document-Based application because we're reserving that for the next hour). When we create a Core Data-enabled application, we will get an empty data model file in our project that is in the form `(Project Name).xcdatamodel`, where `(Project Name)` is the name of the product that we entered into the new project wizard.

When we click this data model, we'll see a design surface that is split into two parts: the left side containing the entities, fetch requests, and configurations, and the right side containing attributes, relationships, and fetched properties for the entity selected on the left.

To create a new entity, we simply click the Add Entity button at the bottom left. We type a new name for the entity (such as Person or Sock), keeping in mind that entities need to follow a classlike naming convention, and as such, need to start with capital letters.

To add an attribute to the new entity, we click the plus (+) button under the Attributes group and supply a name and data type for the attribute. Our Person entity needs a name attribute, and the Sock entity has the following attributes, as shown in Table 13.1

TABLE 13.1   Sock Attributes

Attribute	Data Type	Description
heelColor	String	Color of the sock's heel
numberOfStripes	Integer 16	Number of stripes on the sock
primaryColor	String	Sock's primary color
stripeColor	String	Color of sock's stripes
toeColor	String	Color of sock's toe

Note the use of the initial lowercase letters at the beginning of the attribute names.

Figure 13.1 shows what the Sock entity looks like in the default designer for this sample data model.

FIGURE 13.1
The Sock entity.

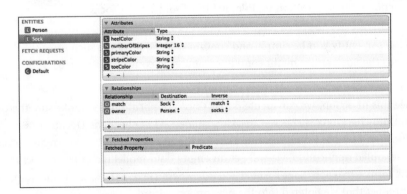

After creating both the Sock and the Person entities, we can create a relationship between the two. To do this, we select the Person entity and create a new relationship called socks, configuring that to be a "to-many" relationship with a target entity of Sock. We can then select the Sock entity and create an owner relationship, a singular relationship with a target entity of Person (because a sock can be owned only by a single person). You can see these relationships in the bottom half of Figure 13.1.

We aren't limited to creating relationships between two *different* entities. We can create a relationship where both sides of the relationship are Sock entities. This is how we can model a matched pair of socks.

If we want to see these relationships and entities laid out in diagram style, we can just click the diagram (it looks like a tree of boxes) button in the bottom-right corner of the design surface right above the words Editor Style.

Figure 13.2 shows what the designer looks like in this mode.

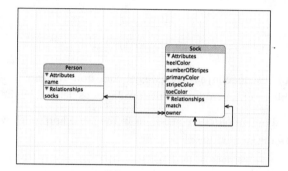

FIGURE 13.2
The graphical entity designer.

With this data model complete, we're ready to start writing code against it to read and write from the model.

Querying and Manipulating Data

Core Data gives you an abstraction layer over the underlying data supporting your model. This means that you interact with what is called a *managed object context*, which acts as a proxy between you and your model. Whenever you want to create a new entity, you do so through the context. To query a list of entities, you do so through the context. When you need to save changes, you guessed it; you do so through the context.

> In some more advanced Core Data scenarios, developers often find themselves working with multiple Managed Object Contexts (often abbreviated MOCs) at the same time. If you find yourself in one of those situations, you can find entire books dedicated to Core Data that you can use as a reference, such as *Core Data: Apple's API for Persisting Data on Mac OS*, from the Pragmatic Programmers.

By the Way

When you create a Core Data application, your application delegate is automatically given a property called `managedObjectContext`, which initializes your data model when you first access that property.

You can use a convenience method of the `NSEntityDescription` class to create a new entity, as shown next:

```
// Create a test sock
NSManagedObject *newSock = [NSEntityDescription
         insertNewObjectForEntityForName:@"Sock"
         inManagedObjectContext:[self managedObjectContext]];
[newSock setValue:@"Blue" forKey:@"primaryColor"];
[newSock setValue:@"Purple" forKey:@"heelColor"];
[newSock setValue:[NSNumber numberWithInt:3]
     forKey:@"numberOfStripes"];

NSLog(@"New sock, %@, created with %@ stripes",
    [newSock valueForKey:@"primaryColor"],
    [newSock valueForKey:@"numberOfStripes"]);
```

The instance of `NSManagedObject` that we get back from the convenience method is an entity on which we can read and write attributes as defined by the model.

After we've found an entity (or created it, as in the preceding code), we can modify it, or we can ask the context to delete it for us:

```
// delete it when we're done with it
[[self managedObjectContext] deleteObject:newSock];
```

Being able to create and update entities is only a small part of the tasks common to a data-driven application. Suppose we want to query the Sock entities for all blue socks, and we want them sorted by the number of stripes in ascending order. Fortunately, this is just as easy as creating or modifying entities:

```
NSEntityDescription *socksDescription =
    [NSEntityDescription entityForName:@"Sock"
       inManagedObjectContext:self.managedObjectContext];
    NSFetchRequest *blueSocksRequest =
[[[NSFetchRequest alloc] init] autorelease];
    [blueSocksRequest setEntity:socksDescription];
    NSPredicate *bluePredicate = [NSPredicate predicateWithFormat:
                          @"primaryColor = 'Blue'"];
    [blueSocksRequest setPredicate:bluePredicate];
    NSSortDescriptor *sortDescriptor = [[NSSortDescriptor alloc]
       initWithKey:@"numberOfStripes" ascending:YES];
    [blueSocksRequest
setSortDescriptors:[NSArray arrayWithObject:sortDescriptor]];
    [sortDescriptor release];
    NSError *error = nil;
    NSArray *blueSocks = [self.managedObjectContext
       executeFetchRequest:blueSocksRequest error:&error];
    for (NSManagedObject *sock in blueSocks)
```

```
    {
        NSLog(@"found sock %@ with %@ stripes",
[sock valueForKey:@"primaryColor"],
            [sock valueForKey:@"numberOfStripes"]);
    }
```

Essentially, everything starts with a fetch request, an instance of the NSFetchRequest class. To this class you can add predicates in the form of instances of the NSPredicate class. Predicates allow you to filter the results of the query so that only data matching your criteria will be included. In addition to defining the entity you are fetching and the predicate, you can also control how the results are sorted by adding an instance of the NSSortDescriptor class to your fetch request.

When you are done configuring your fetch request, as with everything else relating to your model, you go through the managed object context to execute the request. After it executes, you can check whether an error occurred and, if everything went well, you can examine the results that come back in the form of an array of NSManagedObject instances.

Creating NSManagedObject Subclasses

Although we can build an entire application that works exclusively with the NSManagedObject class where we call setValue:forKey: to modify the object and valueForKey: to read attributes, there is an easier way.

We can create a subclass of the NSManagedObject class that contains strongly typed properties for all the attributes. This allows us to set object properties directly and to not have to use the verbose key-value coding syntax.

To do this, open up the Core Data model in Xcode and select the entities for which we can create subclasses. After you've made selections, click the Editor menu and then choose Create NSManagedObject Subclass....

Figure 13.3 shows the dialog that appears as a result of clicking that menu option.

In the case of the sock-matching application, this action creates a Sock.m file and its corresponding header file, as well as a Person.m file and its corresponding header.

Listings 13.1 and 13.2 show the contents of Sock.h and Sock.m, respectively.

FIGURE 13.3
Creating
NSManaged
Object
subclasses.

LISTING 13.1   Sock.h

```
#import <Foundation/Foundation.h>
#import <CoreData/CoreData.h>

@class Sock;

@interface Sock : NSManagedObject {
@private
}
@property (nonatomic, retain) NSString * primaryColor;
@property (nonatomic, retain) NSString * toeColor;
@property (nonatomic, retain) NSString * heelColor;
@property (nonatomic, retain) NSNumber * numberOfStripes;
@property (nonatomic, retain) NSString * stripeColor;
@property (nonatomic, retain) Sock *match;
@property (nonatomic, retain) NSManagedObject *owner;

@end
```

LISTING 13.2   Sock.m

```
#import "Sock.h"
#import "Sock.h"


@implementation Sock
@dynamic primaryColor;
@dynamic toeColor;
@dynamic heelColor;
@dynamic numberOfStripes;
@dynamic stripeColor;
```

```
@dynamic match;
@dynamic owner;

@end
```

The dynamic keyword used in the Sock.m file indicates that the implementation of those properties is going to be supplied at runtime rather than at compile time. This allows the Core Data framework to dynamically inject all the necessary code into those properties at runtime without cluttering up your NSManagedObject subclass.

With these subclasses created, we can now modify our previous code for creating an NSManagedObject to be strongly typed and use the new Sock subclass, as follows:

```
Sock *newSock = [NSEntityDescription
        insertNewObjectForEntityForName:@"Sock"
        inManagedObjectContext:self.managedObjectContext];
newSock.primaryColor = @"Blue";
newSock.heelColor = @"Purple";
newSock.numberOfStripes = [NSNumber numberWithInt:100];
NSLog(@"New sock, %@, created with %@ stripes",
     newSock.primaryColor,
     newSock.numberOfStripes);
```

Not only is this version easier to read and maintain, the fact that the properties have strong data types will prevent us from accidentally trying to store inappropriate data at compile time, rather than forcing us to wait until we're running the application to find those types of errors.

Try It Yourself ▼

Connecting Views to Core Data

So far this hour, you've been introduced to the basic mechanics of building a Core Data model and how to write the code that will read and write entities within that model.

In this next section, you'll put that knowledge to use and combine it with the knowledge you already have of how to build user interfaces that take advantage of Cocoa bindings. This application will allow users to add, edit, and delete entities and modify their attributes. It will also allow users to see all the entities in the system as well as view and edit a single entity at a time. Finally, this application will not require you to write a single line of code—we can accomplish everything with the Core Data framework, a Core Data model, and Cocoa bindings.

The sample application you'll be building is a Zombie tracker; it keeps track of sightings of different types of zombies, including a picture of the zombie and where the

▼

zombie was last seen. This type of application could come in quite handy in case of a zombie apocalypse.

First, let's define the core data model for this application. This application has a single entity called Zombie. Table 13.2 shows the attributes for the Zombie entity.

TABLE 13.2   Zombie Attributes

Attribute	Data Type	Description
lastSeenAt	String	The location of the zombie's last recorded sighting.
lastSeenDate	Date	The date the zombie was last spotted.
name	String	The name of the zombie.
picture	Transformable	The picture of the zombie (don't worry about this data type yet; it will be explained later).
powerRating	Integer 16	A numeric rating of how powerful this zombie is.

Use the following steps to build a data-driven application that provides a user interface to the data model shown in Table 13.2.

1. Create a new Cocoa application, making sure you check the Use Core Data check box (do *not* check the Document-Based Application check box). Call the application **Hour13** (I've been using com.stylion as an application ID prefix, but you can choose whichever you like).

2. Open up the Hour13.xcdatamodel file and create the entity and attributes indicated in Table 13.2. Don't worry about the Transformable data type; you'll see how that works later.

3. Open up the MainMenu.xib file so that you can start creating a user interface.

4. Select the Window object, which should give you a standard empty window you can use to start building your GUI.

5. Change the title of the main window to **Zombie Spotter**.

6. Add a table view to the top half of the window.

7. Create two columns in the table view with these titles: **Name** and **Last Seen At**. Don't worry about data bindings yet.

8. Add two buttons to the bottom left of the table view. These buttons should be **Add** and **Delete** buttons, respectively, and you can set their images to NSAddTemplate and NSRemoveTemplate.

9. Add a box to the window and size it so that the box takes up the bottom half of the window.

10. Inside the box, drag in an image well that takes up most of the left side of the box.

11. Add a label to the right of the image well with the text `Zombie Name:`.

12. Add a text view to the right of the label from step 11.

13. Add a `Last Seen On` label below the one from step 11.

14. Add a date picker to the right of the label from step 13.

15. Add a `Last Seen At` label below the one from step 13.

16. Add a text view to the right of the label from step 15.

17. Add a `Power Rating` label below the one from step 15.

18. Add a level indicator control to the right of the label from step 17 and set the control type to "rating." Set the minimum to 0 and maximum to 10. Make sure you check the Editable check box.

19. Take a look at your window and compare it with the one shown in Figure 13.4. Compensating for personal taste, preferences, and design, your window should have the same basic elements as the one in the figure.

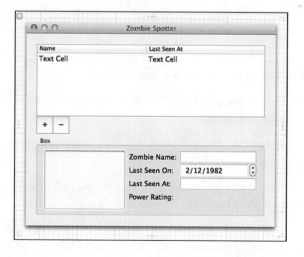

FIGURE 13.4
Designing the Zombie Spotter UI.

20. Now it's time to start binding the UI to your core data model. The first thing you need is an array controller that serves up instances of the `Zombie` entity.

▼

Add an array controller to the `MainMenu.xib` file and give it a descriptive Xcode label (I called mine **Zombies Array Controller**).

21. Set the array controller to Entity Name mode, with the entity name being **Zombie**. Make sure Prepares Content and Editable are both checked.

22. Bind the first column of the table view to the `name` property of the `arrangedObjects` key of the zombies array controller, as shown in Figure 13.5. For reference, you can flip back to previous hours for information on how to bind to array controllers.

FIGURE 13.5
Binding to the Zombies array controller.

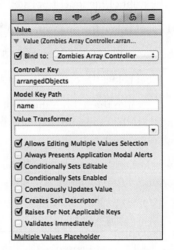

23. Bind the second (Last Seen At) column to the `lastSeenAt` property of the zombie entities being presented by the array controller.

24. Control-drag from the plus (+) button to the array controller and link the action with the `add:` method.

25. Control-drag from the minus (–) button to the array controller and link the action with the `remove:` method.

26. Bind the `enabled` property of the minus (–) button to the `canRemove` property of the zombies array controller.

27. Bind the value of the "zombie name" text view to the `name` model key path of the zombie array controller's `selection` controller key. This will bind this text view to the name of the *currently selected* row (zombie).

28. Bind the date picker to the `lastSeenDate` property of the currently selected zombie of the array controller.

▼

29. Bind the next text view to the `lastSeenAt` property of the currently selected zombie.

30. Bind the value of the level indicator to the `powerRating` property of the currently selected zombie.

> Make sure that when you're binding, you're working with the level indicator and *not* a level indicator *cell*. If you bind the cell (which is a child of the level indicator) instead of the level indicator, your application will throw an exception at runtime. Switch to the identity inspector to make sure you're binding the correct object's value.

31. Bind the `picture` property of the currently selected zombie to the image well's `Value` property. Believe it or not, you don't need to do anything else here. In classic Apple fashion, *this just works*.

32. Bind the `Title` property of the box to the `name` property of the currently selected zombie.

33. At this point you're ready to run the application. Run it and click the plus (+) button to create a new row. Double-click each column of the new row in the table view to edit the values. Note how the values below the table view change accordingly when you tab out of the column.

34. Find an image you like and drag it into the image well. You'll see a green plus sign appear. When you let go, the image well displays the picture you dragged.

35. Quit the application normally (quit the app, don't stop debugging from within Xcode). When you restart the application, notice that the data you previously created is still there, *even the pictures*. To prove that the application has its own private copy of the picture, you can delete or rename the pictures you used as source images and verify that the application still works as it should.

Figure 13.6 shows this completed application running with two rows of data.

At this point, you have a running application that allows a user to create, edit, and delete zombie sightings. If that wasn't enough, the application lets users drag images onto the application window to set pictures of the zombie sightings. All this data is persisted to disk and reloaded by the application when it starts up again.

If you want to explore how some of this happens, take a look at the code in `Hour13AppDelegate.m`. This code is responsible for initializing a managed object context, storing data to disk, and loading data from disk.

FIGURE 13.6
The Zombie
Spotter
application.

The following lines of code, which can be found in the Hour13AppDelegate.m file, are responsible for initializing a Core Data store that persists data in an XML format:

```
if (![__persistentStoreCoordinator
    addPersistentStoreWithType:NSXMLStoreType
    configuration:nil URL:url options:nil error:&error]) {
        [[NSApplication sharedApplication] presentError:error];
        [__persistentStoreCoordinator release];
         __persistentStoreCoordinator = nil;
        return nil;
    }
```

If you want to use a SQLite database instead of XML, you can replace the preceding code with the following:

```
if (![__persistentStoreCoordinator
    addPersistentStoreWithType:NSSQLiteStoreType
    configuration:nil URL:url options:nil error:&error]) {
        [[NSApplication sharedApplication] presentError:error];
        [__persistentStoreCoordinator release], __persistentStoreCoordinator = nil;
        return nil;
    }
```

Core Data is an incredibly powerful framework, and we've only barely scratched the surface of its power and flexibility in this hour.

Summary

In this hour you learned about Core Data and how to use this powerful framework to create data models. These data models not only provide an in-memory interface for developers to create, update, query, and delete entities, but Core Data can also handle the persistence of these entities on disk in multiple formats (binary, SQLite, or XML).

You put this knowledge to use by creating a Core Data application that provided a data-bound user interface that lets users add and remove rows, edit those rows, and even store image data. You did all this without writing a single line of code.

At this point we are starting to uncover the true power of using Cocoa and Objective-C to build Mac OS X Lion applications. In the next few hours, we'll dive even deeper into building data-driven applications for Mac OS X Lion.

Q&A

Q. *Can I have multiple Core Data models in one application?*

A. Yes and you can actually have multiple core data contexts as well, allowing your application to migrate a user's data after they install a new version of your application. As mentioned earlier, Core Data is a topic big enough for a book all its own.

Q. *Are there advantages or disadvantages to the different types of Core Data files?*

A. The XML files are easier to change over time but tend to be bigger and slower to read and write while the SQLite files require more effort for developers to migrate between versions but they are smaller and generally perform faster. The SQLite files are also easy for developers to open in the sqlite3 terminal application and query directly to troubleshoot their applications.

HOUR 14

Working with Documents, Versions, and Autosave

What you'll learn in this hour:

▶ How to Build Document-Based Applications
▶ Creating Core Data Documents
▶ Using Versions
▶ Understanding Autosave

Up to this point in the book, you have learned quite a bit about building Cocoa applications for Mac OS X Lion. You've explored the creation of robust user interfaces and learned how to bind those interfaces to different kinds of data sources.

In the preceding hour, you learned about Core Data and how to create data-driven applications that can read and write their persistent data from a SQLite database, a binary file, or an XML file.

In this hour, you'll learn about how to create document-based applications. Rather than the application communicating with a single file for all its data, a document-based application revolves around a document paradigm. In this hour you'll not only see the benefits of documents and document-based applications, but you'll learn how to create them and use some of Mac OS X Lion's most compelling new features: autosaving and versions.

Building Document-Based Applications

Whether or not we think about it, every time we use our computers, most of us are generally familiar with the paradigm of a document-oriented or document-based application.

When we think about documents, most of us tend to think of these collections of words, sentences, and paragraphs that we can store in files using tools like Pages or Microsoft

Word. This is just the beginning—audio/video presentations are documents; home movies that we edit on our computer are documents; music files that we download or purchase are documents; and even grocery lists, to-do lists, and sticky notes can be considered documents.

Many developers make the mistake of ignoring documents when designing their applications because they aren't building a word processor. There is a limitless supply of possible uses for documents, and in this hour we'll go through the process of building document-based applications for Mac OS X Lion.

What Is a Document?

Those of us who started using computers back in the days of DOS tend to think of simple text files when we think about documents. For others, their thoughts tend to gravitate toward Microsoft Word, Excel, or Apple's Pages, Keynote, or Numbers when thinking of documents.

Most of us familiar with modern computer interfaces feel confident that when we double-click a document, the computer will automatically launch whatever application knows how to display and manipulate the contents of that document.

If you double-click an Excel file, you should expect a spreadsheet to appear on your screen shortly thereafter. We think of these files as documents, but we rarely spend much time thinking about what a document really is or what might actually be contained within.

The point here is that documents are a physical container for information. Within this container can be something as simple as text or a robust, complex multimedia presentation you might find in Keynote or a home movie or an MP3 file. Documents are what you, the application's creator, choose. In this hour we're going to deal exclusively with Core Data documents. If you are interested in building more complicated documents that contain embedded files, images, folders, and more, there are APIs available within Cocoa that you can research for this purpose.

By the Way

> For more information on building applications that support more robust document types, check out the NSFileWrapper class and look closely at a concept within the Cocoa documentation called document packages (also called bundles). Documentation can be found here: http://developer.apple.com/library/mac/ #documentation/Cocoa/Reference/ApplicationKit/Classes/NSFileWrapper_Class/ Reference/Reference.html

Introducing Core Data Document-Based Applications

As you go through the exercise in the next section, you'll find out only a few small differences exist between a standard Core Data application and a document-based Core Data application.

The key difference is that whereas a standard Core Data application works with a single file, a document-based Core Data application allows the user to create new files, open multiple files at once, and edit and save those files.

The MainWindow.xib file that you are familiar with is replaced with a .xib file that represents an instance of a document window. This UI could be the UI for a task-tracking application, a word processing file, a presentation, a home video, or anything else. In a document-based application, the File's Owner object that you find in each .xib file corresponds to a subclass of the NSDocument class. In the case of a Core Data document-based application, the file's owner is a subclass of NSPersistentDocument, a class that takes care of a tremendous amount of busy-work on behalf of the developer.

> As you'll see in Hour 15, the NSPersistentDocument class even has built-in awareness of Apple's new iCloud system, making it easy for your application users to synchronize their documents in the cloud.

The best way to see how Core Data document-based applications work is to create one yourself.

Try It Yourself

Creating a Core Data Document-Based Application

In this exercise, you'll put to use your knowledge of building data-driven Core Data applications and create a document-based Core Data application. This application will be a simple tool that manages a list of tasks, due dates, and their current progress.

The main difference between an application like this and the one you built in the previous hour is that this application will allow the user to view, edit, and maintain multiple files, each containing their own logically related set of tasks. For example, you might want to have a file called Work that manages a to-do list of work-related items, a Household file that contains all your home maintenance tasks, and a Hobby

▼

file that you use to keep track of tasks related to your hobby. As you'll see, a document-based application provides the framework for supporting multiple open files at once without you having to write any extra code.

Use the following steps to build a Core Data document-based application:

1. Create a new Cocoa application and call it **ToDo**, as shown in Figure 14.1. Make sure to check *both* the document-based check box *and* the Core Data check box.

FIGURE 14.1
Creating a document-based application.

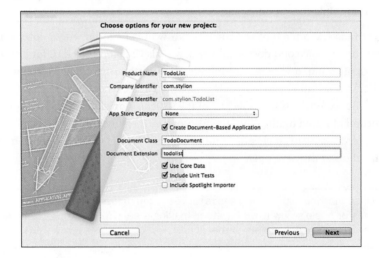

2. Take note that there are now *two* .xib files in the project: MainMenu.xib and TodoDocument.xib. The first of these files contains the application's main menu, and the second contains the user interface for an instance of the application's document window.

3. Click the TodoDocument.xdatamodel file to create the Core Data model for the application's document.

4. Create a new entity called **Task**. This entity should have a string attribute called name, a date attribute called dueDate, and a 16-bit integer attribute called pctComplete.

5. Make sure you set a default value for the dueDate field. Core Data is relatively forgiving when dealing with bound values and newly created entities, but if you don't set the default value of this field, a bound date picker control will fail to properly display the current value.

▼

You can enter a string like "now" into the default value of a date attribute, and newly created entities will set the value of that attribute to the current clock time.

6. **A**s you did in the previous hour, add an array controller, set its type to **Entity Name**, and set the entity name to **Task**. Make sure you add this array controller to the TodoDocument.xib file and *not* the MainMenu.xib file.

7. Under the Parameters section of the array controller's bindings tab, set the Managed Object Context of the array controller to the managed object context of the File's Owner object, as shown in Figure 14.2.

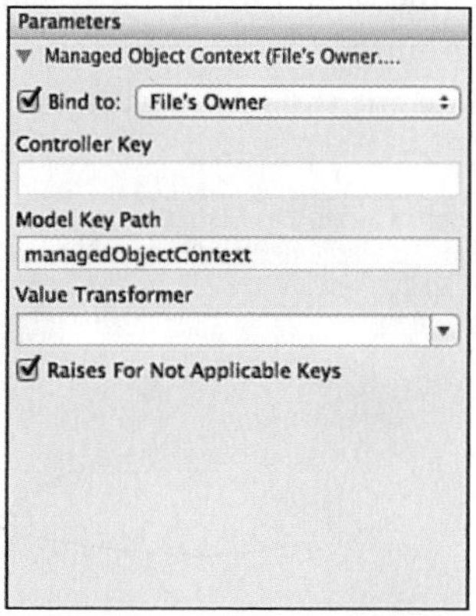

Parameters

▼ Managed Object Context (File's Owner....

☑ Bind to: File's Owner   ÷

Controller Key

Model Key Path

managedObjectContext

Value Transformer

▼

☑ Raises For Not Applicable Keys

FIGURE 14.2
Binding an array controller's managed object context.

8. Add a table view to the window and give it two columns. The first column should be titled **Task Name** and the second cell should be titled **% Complete**.

9. Add a plus (+) and minus (–) button to the bottom of the window below the table view, using the NSAddTemplate and NSRemoveTemplate stock images, respectively.

10. Control-drag from the plus (+) button to connect it to the add: method on the array controller.

11. Control-drag from the minus (–) button to connect it to the remove: method on the array controller. While you're there, bind the enabled property of the minus (–) button to the canRemove property of the array controller.

12. Add a label to the area below the table view with the text of **Current Task Due Date:**.

13. Add a date picker immediately to the right of the label in step 12.

▼

14. Scroll through the object library until you find the Level Indicator Cell (make sure you're not using a regular level indicator, it must be a *cell*). Drag this cell into the second column of the table view. You'll see the column change from a text column to one with a level indicator. Set the level indicator cell's style to Continuous and check the Editable box. Set the minimum value to 0 and maximum value to 100.

Did You Know?

Don't underestimate the power of what you've just done here. The ability to swap out different types of controls within table view cells is immensely powerful and can take you from stock interfaces to rich, amazing UIs very quickly!

15. Without binding any of the UI controls to the underlying attributes of Core Data entities, the design surface in Xcode for the `TodoDocument.xib` file should look similar to the one shown in Figure 14.3.

FIGURE 14.3
Building a
Core Data
document UI.

16. Bind the Task Name table view column to the model key path name of the array controller's `arrangedObjects` key.

17. Bind the % Complete table view column to the `pctComplete` property of the arranged objects of the array controller.

18. Bind the value of the date picker to the `dueDate` property of the *currently selected* item of the array controller.

At this point you've managed to build a user interface that has a lot of the same elements as the one you built in the previous hour. Next, we're going to deal with the document-based nature of the application.

▼

19. Click the `TodoList` project in the far-left project navigator and select the `TodoList` target. Now click the Info tab on the right.

20. Below the regular target properties, you should see a section called Document Types. Make sure this section is expanded. There should be three document types already there.

21. Click the X at the top right of the Binary and XML document types because we're going to be dealing only with the SQLite type (SQLite is the type of data file you used in the previous hour). Figure 14.4 shows what a few of the default document types look like.

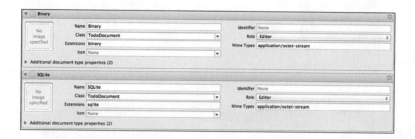

FIGURE 14.4
The Binary and SQLite Core Data document types.

22. Change the properties of the remaining (SQLite) document type so that the name is **TodoList** and the extensions field is **todolist**.

23. Drag any small icon you have on your hard drive into the image icon area. A green plus sign will appear, and you will see a dialog that looks like Figure 14.5, prompting you to add the file to your project. When prompted, choose to copy the file to the project folder rather than just creating a reference to it.

24. If Xcode doesn't do it for you automatically, change the value of the Icon drop-down list to the new icon you just dragged into the project.

25. When you're done modifying the document type properties and the icon, your document type editor should look very similar to the one shown in Figure 14.6 (although your picture will probably be different).

26. You should now be able to run your application. Notice how the title of the document window is Untitled. Go ahead and make changes, add rows, edit rows, and play with the UI. When you're done, quit the application normally (from the application's menu bar or via hot key, not by stopping the Xcode debugger).

FIGURE 14.5
Copying an
image to the
project folder.

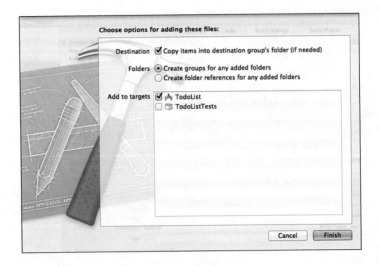

FIGURE 14.6
Configuring doc-
ument type
properties.

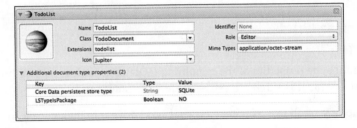

27. Restart the application and notice that the Untitled window reappears exactly
where you left it, and the data you entered previously is still there. Your document window might look something like Figure 14.7.

FIGURE 14.7
The TodoList
document
window.

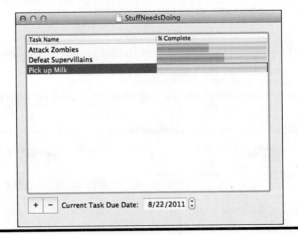

In the next section, we'll discuss more about what's going on here and how, without your having written any code, your application already supports versions, visual version comparisons and restoration, and autosaving.

Using Versions and Autosave

As you saw when you ran the TodoList application from the preceding section, the application automatically created a new document called Untitled (actually, the file is called Untitled.todolist but the OS defaults to hiding the extension).

At this point, you should play around with your new application. With the application running, click the File menu and then click Save a Version. If you've been using Macs for a while, this menu item might seem strange. Typically, people expect to see either a Save As or a Save option.

Mac OS X Lion introduces the concept of versions. The first time a file is saved to disk, that creates the first *version* of that file. Every time a new version is saved, it is stored on disk. The beauty of this new system is that the history of changes made to your file is not lost.

If you've ever been working on a critical document, deleted some important piece of data, and then accidentally saved the file, you know the kind of frustration file management can cause the average Mac user. Now add to that frustration the stress that can be caused by quitting an application without making sure you saved the latest changes, and things can get ugly quickly.

Mac OS X Lion endeavors to make the act of managing your files smooth, seamless, and worry-free. It does this by replacing the manual task of saving multiple copies of the same file under different filenames by giving you the native ability to save multiple versions of the same file without having to change the filename *and* without having to use the Time Machine application.

To really appreciate how much better this new version paradigm is than the traditional multiple-file paradigm, you need to experience it for yourself.

Using the application you built this hour, create a new document and save a version on your desktop. Add a couple rows to it and save another version. Delete a few rows, change a few tasks and due dates and then save another version.

This is where it gets really exciting. Click the application's File menu and then choose Revert to Saved. The desktop background will smoothly slide out of the way and a familiar Time Machine-like interface will appear. Your current document window appears on the left, and the next most recent version appears on the right. You can use the timeline interface to scroll backward and forward through time, comparing the current version against old ones. If you find a previous version to which you want to revert, just choose that one (click the Restore button) and you're all set. This screen is shown in Figure 14.8.

FIGURE 14.8
Comparing doc-
ument versions.

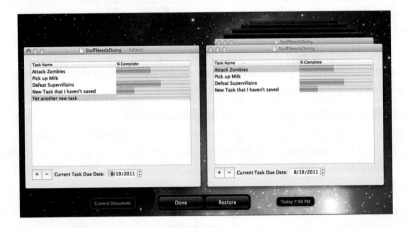

By default, your document is configured to automatically save pending changes at timed intervals. This allows users to stop worrying about when they save, how often they save, and coming up with elaborate naming and numbering schemes to deal with versions and avoid accidentally overwriting data.

You can override this behavior and prevent automatic autosaving if you choose by changing the return value of the autosavesInPlace method that is implemented by the TodoDocument class in the TodoDocument.m file.

Summary

In this hour you learned about the difference between window-based applications and document-based applications. These document-based applications allow users to create files, open and edit multiple files at once, and even view and compare file version history.

You created a Core Data document application that lets users manage multiple lists of tasks, and you saw how you can do all of that without writing a single line of code. Although production-ready applications will certainly involve more coding than this, the ability to create fully functioning applications like this using just Core Data and Cocoa bindings truly empowers Mac OS X Lion developers.

Q&A

Q. *Is there any limit to the number of versions of a document my application can keep?*

A. The versions kept around by OS X Lion are entirely up to the amount of free disk space available to the user at the time.

Q. *Can I access the version history of a file without displaying the "time machine" interface?*

A. Yes, there are methods you can call to gain access to the version history of a document if you need finer-grained control of document revisions than what comes with the OS by default.

HOUR 15

Working with Apple's iCloud

In this hour we'll discuss a service that Apple released shortly after the initial release of Mac OS X Lion: iCloud. iCloud gives developers the ability to create applications that can store information and documents in the cloud without worrying about the infrastructure required to support it.

In this hour, you'll learn about iCloud, when to use it, and how to write code that uses iCloud to store and retrieve data and documents.

Introduction to iCloud

With the release of Mac OS X Lion 10.7.2 and iOS 5.0, Apple made the iCloud service available. This service allows applications to store data in the cloud, making their data and documents ubiquitous and available from all the user's devices.

The phrase *the cloud* is often misleading. When Apple says that user data is stored in the cloud, they actually mean that it is stored somewhere within Apple's data centers. This could mean that a document might be stored in California, New York, Europe, or wherever else might be appropriate. The key benefit here is that as the programmer, you do not need to be concerned with how Apple stores the data or where. All you need to know is that ubiquitous user data and documents are available via Apple's iCloud APIs.

iCloud can also do more than store application data. For example, iCloud supplies the plumbing for new iTunes services that allow your music to flow freely among all your devices without you ever having to tether any of them.

If that wasn't enough, iCloud can also be used to synchronize contacts across all your devices and even comes with a mail service. Mac and iPhone users who used to subscribe to the MobileMe service can upgrade their MobileMe accounts to iCloud accounts, and then their iCloud disk space quota will be increased to reflect that they are paying customers (iCloud is a free service for the stock features).

Users who take advantage of the iCloud service not only gain the convenience of having their data and documents be ubiquitous, but they also gain added security and confidence knowing that even if a device should fail, their documents remain safe in the cloud.

By the Way

> *Ubiquitous* is a term that Apple uses throughout its documentation to refer to data or documents that are *available everywhere*. When a document is sent to the iCloud service, it is made ubiquitous. Conversely, when a document is removed from iCloud, it is no longer ubiquitous.

Ideal Scenarios for Using iCloud

Word processing applications like Pages and Microsoft Word are obvious examples of applications that can add value for their users by embracing cloud storage like iCloud. When users create documents in applications like this with iCloud support, they no longer have to deal with the headaches of copying files to USB drives (or worse, emailing files to themselves for use on another machine). Their files simply follow them no matter what device they're using.

Apple's iWork suite, which includes Pages, Numbers, and Keynote, supports iCloud on iOS and on Mac OS X Lion, allowing you to store your spreadsheets, presentations, and word processing documents in the cloud.

One huge benefit to iCloud isn't just that you can share files between your laptop and your desktop, but that it is also possible to share files between your laptop, desktop, iPhone, and iPad.

Suppose that you're on your laptop using a recipe creation and cataloging application. With a few recipes in mind for the week, you might go to the store to pick up the ingredients. Without iCloud (or some other type of cloud-based sharing service—Apple is not the only cloud provider), you might have to resort to unwieldy printouts, emailing yourself copies of the recipes, and so on. With iCloud and an application written to take advantage of it, you can pull up your recipes on your phone without having to do any extra work.

Another excellent use for iCloud is for backing up important data. iOS, for example, can be configured to automatically back up all your application data in iCloud so that if you replace the device or get a new one, all your apps and data will still be available.

Storing Key-Value Data in the Cloud

If you want to store small amounts of data without the overhead of having to store an entire document, you can take advantage of the `NSUbiquitousKeyValueStore` class. This class is used to synchronize *small* amounts of data between different devices owned by the same user. This class should be used to store noncritical data. In other words, you should not write your application in such a way that it relies on data stored in iCloud in order to perform its intended function.

> Each key in the key-value store must not exceed 64 bytes using UTF8 encoding. Additionally, the maximum amount your application can store is 64KB.

Watch Out!

It may help to think of the `NSUbiquitousKeyValueStore` class as a cloud-based replacement for (or supplement to) the `NSUserDefaults` class, as described in Hour 13, "Working with Core Data."

Changes that you make to the data in the ubiquitous key-value store are made immediately in memory and then are written to disk and eventually propagated to iCloud. If you want to force this synchronization to occur, you can use the `synchronize:` method of this class.

Your application can also react to when a value in the ubiquitous key-value store changes by registering for a notification with the name `NSUbiquitousKeyValue StoreDidChangeExternallyNotification`. This class follows the very common *singleton* pattern where there is a single shared instance rather than allowing you to create multiple instances.

To access the shared instance of the ubiquitous key value store, you can obtain a reference to it using code like this:

```
NSUbiquitousKeyValueStore *kvs = [NSUbiquitousKeyValueStore defaultStore];
```

Registering your class instance to receive notifications when the store values change externally (for example, someone on your iPhone application changes data and you want it to appear on the Mac) involves the use of the `NSNotificationCenter` class, as such:

```
[[NSNotificationCenter defaultCenter] addObserver:self
    selector:@selector(ubiqStoreUpdated:)
    name:NSUbiquitousKeyValueStoreDidChangeExternallyNotification
    object:kvs];
```

You read and write values with the store in a fashion that is very similar to the way in which you interact with an `NSMutableDictionary` instance. For example, to read and write a string value, you might use code like this:

```
NSUbiquitousKeyValueStore *kvs = [NSUbiquitousKeyValueStore defaultStore];
[kvs setString:@"hello world" forKey:@"myappsample"];
NSString *test = [kvs stringForKey:@"myappsample"];
NSLog(@"test from ubiq kvs: %@", test);
```

If you want a read-only dictionary that contains the current values for all keys in the store, you can get it using the `dictionaryRepresentation` method.

Your application will not be able to use the ubiquitous key-value store until you have enabled the iCloud entitlements and created a proper provisioning profile, which is discussed later in this hour.

Storing Documents in the Cloud

Storing documents in the cloud is a little more complicated than storing key-value pairs, but fortunately, the iCloud document storage APIs still keep things fairly simple for developers, especially when compared to the alternative of hosting your own cloud server to support document sharing in your application.

To create a document in iCloud, you must first create a document locally on the disk of the device on which your app is running. After you have a physical file on disk, you can move that file into iCloud by making it ubiquitous. This moves the file from its original location to a special folder on your computer (probably in a location like `/Users/(user)/Library/Mobile Documents/(iCloud container ID)`). From there, a special synchronization daemon pulls changes to that document from iCloud and makes those changes to the document. Additionally, changes to that local document are propagated to iCloud by this same daemon.

Figure 15.1, an image from Apple's documentation on the subject, illustrates this process.

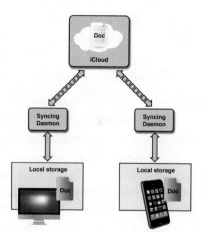

FIGURE 15.1
Synchronizing
documents with
iCloud from mul-
tiple devices.

To avoid conflicts where files are being overwritten all the time by multiple changes
from local and cloud sources, "file coordinators" mediate all file changes. Although
there are classes for file coordination, in this hour we'll mainly be using the
NSDocument class, which has file coordination built in.

Using a document-based Cocoa application, you can make a file ubiquitous with
code that looks like the following:

```
- (void)windowControllerDidLoadNib:(NSWindowController *)aController
{
    [super windowControllerDidLoadNib:aController];

    self.ubiquityURL =
        [[NSFileManager defaultManager]
URLForUbiquityContainerIdentifier:@"(YOURTEAMID).com.stylion.todoicloud"];
    self.ubiquityURL =
[[self.ubiquityURL URLByAppendingPathComponent:@"Documents"]
    URLByAppendingPathComponent:[self.fileURL lastPathComponent]];

    NSLog(@"ubiq url: %@", self.ubiquityURL);
    NSLog(@"current URL: %@", [self fileURL]);
    if ([self.ubiquityURL isEqualToURL:self.fileURL]) {
        // we're in iCloud
        NSLog(@"current URL is in iCloud");
    } else {
        // we are NOT in iCloud
        NSLog(@"current URL is not in iCloud");
        NSError *error;
        NSURL *baseURL =
[self.ubiquityURL URLByAppendingPathComponent:@"Documents"];
        NSURL *targetURL =
[baseURL URLByAppendingPathComponent:[self.fileURL lastPathComponent]];
        [[NSFileManager defaultManager] setUbiquitous:YES
                itemAtURL:self.fileURL
```

```
                    destinationURL:targetURL
                    error:&error];
          if (error != nil) {
              NSLog(@"failed to set ubiquitous: %@", error);
          }
      }
  }
```

In the preceding code, the window controller checks to see if the file being managed by the current window is ubiquitous. It is ubiquitous if its ubiquity URL is the same as the file's current URL. If the file is not ubiquitous (not currently stored in iCloud), the appropriate method is called to place the file in iCloud. Note that the file is placed in a subdirectory called `Documents`. Files contained in this folder in iCloud are visible when users look at the contents of their iCloud document store, as shown in Figure 15.2.

FIGURE 15.2
Displaying a list of iCloud documents.

Also note that in the preceding code the file manager asks for the ubiquity URL of an iCloud container. Here, you must use your Team ID or your individual member ID (if you do not belong to a team) followed by a unique name for your container. These container IDs are up to you but are autogenerated when you enable entitlements and iCloud support in your application, as shown in Figure 15.3.

Also in the preceding code, I used a little shortcut method called `isEqualToURL` that encapsulates some additional logic to ensure that two URLs are equivalent.

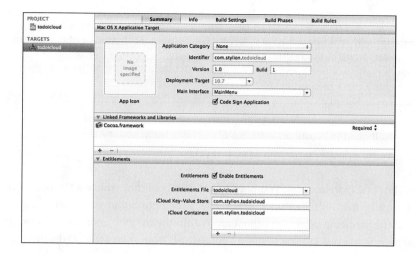

FIGURE 15.3
Enabling iCloud
in an Xcode
project.

> You cannot rely on the fact that the NSURL class will return YES when you compare it to another instance of NSURL with the == operator. Two NSURL instances are considered equal when their absoluteURL properties are equivalent or, if the URLs are file URLs, their path properties are equivalent.

When you call setUbiquitous:itemAtURL:destinationURL:error: for a particular file, that file is moved to the special staging area on your disk, as shown in Figure 15.1. From there, the synchronization daemon is responsible for getting that file into iCloud. Additionally, once in that directory, changes made to that file from other devices connected to iCloud will be propagated back to the local device. File coordinators watching the file in that folder will be notified that changes occurred and can then allow your application to respond to that change accordingly.

Querying the Contents of an iCloud Container

In the preceding section you saw how an individual document could tell whether it is being managed in iCloud by comparing its file URL to its ubiquitous URL. This is great for an individual document, but what if you want to query the list of all documents stored in iCloud for your application for the current user?

To accomplish this, you'll need to make use of the NSMetadataQuery class. This class can be used to perform any number of query tasks and is extremely flexible and powerful. Using this class to query all ubiquitous documents is quite simple.

> The NSMetadataQuery class has been around since before iCloud and was upgraded with the release of Mac OS X 10.7.2 to support queries of the iCloud document store. A thorough coverage of this class is beyond the scope of this book, but you will find good coverage in any of Aaron Hillegass's Big Nerd Ranch Guides to Cocoa programming.

First, you'll need to create an instance of the NSMetadataQuery class:

```
self.query = [[NSMetadataQuery alloc] init];
```

Now that you have a query, you need to define a *predicate*, which is the condition that must be met for potential search results to be returned in your query. In other words, the predicate determines the items within the target container that you *want* to appear in the results. The following code shows how to create a predicate to pull all ubiquitous documents within your application's iCloud container:

```
self.query.predicate = [NSPredicate predicateWithFormat:@"%K == YES",
                            NSMetadataItemIsUbiquitousKey];
self.query.searchScopes =
    [NSArray arrayWithObject:NSMetadataQueryUbiquitousDocumentsScope];
```

> Keep in mind that your application will never have to do any manual exclusion of iCloud documents that don't belong to your app. This is because it is *impossible* for your app to see iCloud documents that reside within another app's iCloud container. This basic fact is essential to ensuring that users feel secure and comfortable storing their documents in the cloud.

Metadata queries start asynchronously and then use the delegate pattern to report results back. To start a query, invoke its startQuery method:

```
[self.query startQuery];
```

Mac OS X Lion will post notifications to your application when your metadata query completes or when it has updated. You can use code like the following to register methods to be invoked when such events occur:

```
[[NSNotificationCenter defaultCenter] addObserver:self
    selector:@selector(updateUbiquitousDocuments:)
    name:NSMetadataQueryDidFinishGatheringNotification
    object:nil];
[[NSNotificationCenter defaultCenter] addObserver:self
    selector:@selector(updateUbiquitousDocuments:)
    name:NSMetadataQueryDidUpdateNotification
    object:nil];
```

The preceding code registers the updateUbiquitousDocuments: method to be called whenever the query updates (that is, has retrieved some portion of the results) or when the query has finished gathering data. You can use a method like this to update a data-bound NSArrayController that is then used to present your application users with a list of files stored in iCloud, as shown next (the cloudFilesArrayController variable is an array controller outlet that has been bound to a table view, as you've done in previous hours):

```
- (void)updateUbiquitousDocuments:(NSNotification *)notification
{
    NSLog(@"ubiq query came back: %@", notification);
    NSLog(@"query results: %lu", self.query.results.count);
    [[self.cloudFilesArrayController content] removeAllObjects];
    for (NSMetadataItem *mdItem in self.query.results) {
        NSLog(@"received mdItem: %@", mdItem);
        NSURL *url = [mdItem valueForAttribute:NSMetadataItemURLKey];
        NSMutableDictionary *cloudFile = [[NSMutableDictionary alloc] init];
        [cloudFile setValue:[url lastPathComponent] forKey:@"displayName"];
        [cloudFile setValue:url forKey:@"fileUrl"];
        [self.cloudFilesArrayController addObject:cloudFile];
    }
}
```

Here we are adding instances of an NSMutableDictionary to the array controller. This dictionary contains two keys: displayName and fileUrl. The displayName key is used for the table view binding to display just the filename (the user should never have to see the ubiquitous URL), and the fileUrl can be used for other code that might allow users to open files or move them out of iCloud and back into their local Documents folder.

Figure 15.4 shows a panel window that exists independently of all the application's document windows. This panel window has a table view that is bound to the array controller in the preceding code snippet.

Handling Document Conflicts in the Cloud

One of the biggest advantages to iCloud is that it allows a document to be viewed and edited in multiple locations on multiple devices at the same time. Unfortunately, this can turn out to be a headache for developers if left unchecked.

Consider the following scenario: You are on your laptop working diligently at modifying the directions for a recipe that your family is planning to prepare. Meanwhile, at the store, someone else in your family using your iCloud account on an iPhone has also made changes to the same recipe. iCloud will take changes from both your laptop and the iPhone and attempt to reconcile them. As the developer of this application, it is entirely up to you to enable the resolution of any conflicts that arise. For example, if one person modifies the ingredients and another modifies the instructions, your application should be able to handle this without complaint. However, if two people modify the same piece of data, your application needs to provide some kind of UI that allows for manual conflict resolution.

FIGURE 15.4
A floating panel containing an iCloud documents list.

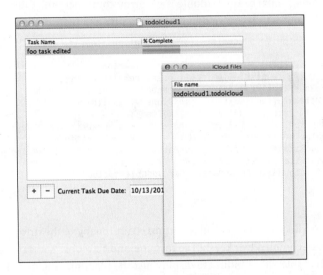

This kind of conflict resolution involves manual intervention with the iCloud store, file presenters, file managers, and a lot of effort and code that is beyond the scope of this book. However, any decent Mac OS X reference book (perhaps an *Unleashed* title) that covers iCloud will contain sample code to illustrate conflict resolution.

Conflicts can happen in more cases than you might think, even if only one person is using your iCloud account. Suppose that you are using the same recipe application on your laptop, but the laptop is not currently connected to the Internet. You make several changes while not in contact with iCloud. Then you make other changes from your iPhone while you are out traveling. Those changes do make it to iCloud via your cellular data network. Finally, you turn on your Mac laptop in an area with public Wi-Fi. At this point, the changes previously made on the laptop will be sent to iCloud, while changes made on the phone will be sent to your laptop, potentially creating conflicts even though only one person used the iCloud storage container. Again, it will be up to you as the application developer to provide your users with the ability to cope with these kinds of conflicts.

Enabling Mac OS X Lion Applications for iCloud

In the preceding section (especially in Figure 15.3) you saw how you could turn on application entitlements and how to specify container identifiers for iCloud Documents and key-value storage. If you attempt to run an application with just those entitlements, you will probably see that the application runs and is then immediately terminated with no error messages displayed in the Xcode debug log. The only way to find out why the application terminated is to check the Mac OS X console log (found in Applications, Utilities, Console), where you might see errors that look like this:

```
10/13/11 6:58:27.733 PM taskgated: killed com.stylion.todoicloud[pid 1987]
➥because its use of the com.apple.developer.ubiquity-container-identifiers
➥entitlement is not allowed
```

The reason for this is that an application's entitlements, including the entitlements claiming the right to communicate with iCloud, are validated by the presence of a *provisioning profile*. This provisioning profile is a digitally signed statement granting a specific application (identified by a UTI code like `com.stylion.todoicloud`) the ability to execute on a specific machine. In addition to the ability to execute, an application with entitlement declarations is granted the ability to perform the activities indicated by those entitlements, such as accessing the file system, communicating with the network, accessing a user's pictures folder, and so on. Figure 15.3 shows two of those entitlements as they relate to iCloud: the iCloud key-value store identifier and an array of iCloud containers.

For more information on provisioning profiles and how to create and download them to enable your iCloud applications, you can consult Apple's iCloud documentation, or you can read through Hours 23 and 24. The final two hours of this book focus specifically on issues like certificates, code signing, provisioning profiles, and enabling various application abilities through Apple's iTunes Connect portal website.

Feel free to skip ahead and read through those hours, or you can proceed with the rest of the book, read through Hours 23 and 24, and then come back to this hour.

Summary

Apple has released a ton of new features with iOS 5, and especially with Mac OS X Lion. As of Mac OS X Lion 10.7.2 and iOS 5, iCloud is available to users of Macs, iPhones, and iPads everywhere.

iCloud gives you the ability to create applications that afford users the convenience of ubiquitous document and data storage and the peace of mind knowing that no matter what device they use to edit documents, those documents are stored safely in the cloud.

In this hour, you learned about how to take a document-based application and enable it for iCloud, using the iCloud Storage APIs to make documents ubiquitous and perform metadata queries to locate ubiquitous documents.

Q&A

Q. *Is iCloud free?*

A. For the features discussed in this chapter yes, iCloud is free of charge. There is an optional music match service through iTunes that uses iCloud for which Apple charges a subscription fee.

Q. *Is there a limit to the amount of documents I can store in iCloud?*

A. Yes. By default, new iCloud accounts are given a certain quota of disk space usage in the cloud. You can pay an additional fee to extend this quota and expand your maximum usage. Keep in mind that there are other services and applications that can all fill up your iCloud disk quota, so your application shouldn't use it wastefully.

Q. *Do files sync with iCloud immediately?*

A. No. There is a background process responsible for checking iCloud to see if new files need to be copied from the cloud to the local disk and from the local disk out to the cloud. It can take anywhere from a few seconds to a few minutes for updates to propagate through the cloud to your other devices.

HOUR 16

Using Alert Panels and Sheets

What you'll learn in this hour:

▶ Using Alert Panels
▶ Using Sheets

This hour is all about informing the user of important events and prompting the user for additional information and to perform additional actions. Often, developers learning a new platform will do things the hard way, without knowing that an easier way exists.

In this hour, you'll learn about the multitude of situations where you can use the easy alert panel and sheet APIs to quickly and easily prompt users for data and action—all without having to create complicated data entry forms and view controllers. You'll learn about alert panels and sheets, how to use them, and, most importantly, *when* to use them.

Using Alert Panels

Alert dialogs are used to inform the user about important events and typically prompt the user for some course of action. You're probably familiar with one of the most common types of alert panels: the *error dialog*. In this all-too-frequent scenario, something goes completely haywire with the application and, as a last resort, it decides to pop up a dialog box explaining to you that something terrible happened. Sometimes you might be given the option to cancel or abort whatever caused the problem, and other times, your only option might be the OK button that you click just before the application shuts down.

As you'll see in this section, it takes very little code to create and display alerts, as well as customize them to look how you like and prompt for more detailed information from your users.

Creating and Displaying Alerts

The NSAlert class provides you with an easy way of creating and displaying alert dialogs. For example, suppose your application monitors the level of nearby zombies. When this level reaches a certain threshold, it needs to know whether you intend to attack or retreat.

The following code will create a new alert and display it:

```
NSAlert *alert = [[NSAlert alloc] init];
[alert addButtonWithTitle:@"Attack"];
[alert addButtonWithTitle:@"Retreat"];
[alert setMessageText:@"Zombies are invading!"];
[alert setInformativeText:@"Choose how you respond to the invading
➥zombies."];
[alert setAlertStyle:NSWarningAlertStyle];

if ([alert runModal] == NSAlertFirstButtonReturn) {
    NSLog(@"You decided to attack the zombies.");
}

[alert release];
```

There are three main steps to displaying an alert dialog:

1. Create an instance of the NSAlert class.

2. Configure the NSAlert instance by setting properties, adding buttons, and so on.

3. Call the runModal method and react to the return value.

A very important point here is that buttons are added to the alert dialog from *right to left*. This means that when you test for a value like NSAlertFirstButtonReturn, you are actually checking if the *rightmost* button was clicked.

You can also check for NSAlertSecondButtonReturn (second from right) or NSAlertThirdButtonReturn. If you need more buttons, add that number to NSAlertThirdButtonReturn and test for that value.

Figure 16.1 shows a sample of what this alert dialog looks like when displayed via the runModal method.

Using Accessory Views

Sometimes you may have an alert that you want to display to a user that contains more information than what the NSAlert class comes with by default.

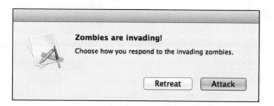

FIGURE 16.1
Displaying an
alert.

You might need to display a custom text view containing a detailed description of the error that occurred, or you might want some custom graphics and a clickable email address or phone number to initiate contact between your user and your product support team. This is often where developers think that the NSAlert class is insufficient, and they think they should create their own custom window.

Before you go that route, see if you can get the job done with an *accessory view*. Accessory views are very common throughout Cocoa for the Mac and are used even more frequently in iOS. They provide a visual extension point for existing controls. In short, accessory views allow you to extend built-in functionality without requiring you to write your own custom controls and views.

The NSAlert class has a simple property called accessoryView. If this property is set to an instance of a view when the runModal method is called, that view will be displayed between the alert view's buttons and the alert message.

You can use this alert view to display text, to display images, or even to offer additional interactive controls. The easiest way to use an accessory view is to create one in a .xib file, allowing you to use Interface Builder to create an outlet from the code displaying the alert to the accessory view.

The following code will create and display an alert view that also contains an accessory view between the alert text and buttons:

```
- (IBAction)displayAlertWithAccessory:(id)sender {
    NSAlert *alert = [[NSAlert alloc] init];
    [alert addButtonWithTitle:@"Yes"];
    [alert addButtonWithTitle:@"No"];
    [alert setMessageText:@"Are you sure you want to?"];
    [alert setInformativeText:
@"Choose wisely. If you choose poorly, something terrible might happen."];
    [alert setAccessoryView:accessoryView];

    NSInteger result = [alert runModal];
    if (result == NSAlertFirstButtonReturn) {
        NSLog(@"Chose Yes");
    }
    else {
```

```
        NSLog(@"Chose No");
    }

    [alert release];
}
```

In the preceding code, a member of the class (an IBOutlet), accessoryView, is used to link the view to one that was created using Interface Builder. The setAccessoryView method sets the accessory view, and then the alert displays the alert text, caption, buttons, and the custom view, as shown in Figure 16.2.

FIGURE 16.2
An alert with an accessory view.

Using Suppression Buttons

The possibilities for customizing and extending alerts don't stop with custom accessory views. Many kinds of alerts can continue to pop up over and over, depending on the type of alert.

For example, an application could display an alert indicating that it failed to save information to a network host. If the application keeps trying to save this information over the network, and the network continues to fail, this alert dialog could begin to annoy the user.

Another scenario in which the user might want to stop receiving the same alert is when an application displays an alert to a user that has meaning only one time, such as an alert for the first launch of the application or tips and tricks that a user might learn over time. After users have learned the tip, they might want to indicate that they never want to see that tip again.

This is where *suppression buttons* come in. Suppression buttons give users the ability to indicate to the application that they do not want to receive that alert again. It is then up to the application how it handles that information.

The following code shows how to create and use an alert with a suppression check box. This code also shows how you can store and retrieve the user's suppression preference from the NSUserDefaults class, which you learned about earlier in this book.

```
- (IBAction)displayAlertWithSuppression:(id)sender {
    NSString *tipKey = @"ZombieKillTip";
    NSUserDefaults *defaults = [NSUserDefaults standardUserDefaults];
    if ([defaults boolForKey:tipKey])
    {
        NSLog(@"Wanted to display alert, but user suppressed it.");
    }
    else {
        NSAlert *alert = [[NSAlert alloc] init];
        [alert addButtonWithTitle:@"OK"];
        alert.messageText = @"Zombie Tip";
        alert.informativeText =
@"When killing zombies, make sure you always have spare ammunition.";
        alert.showsSuppressionButton = YES;

        [alert runModal];
        if (alert.suppressionButton.state == NSOnState) {
            [defaults setBool:YES forKey:tipKey];
        }
        [alert release];
    }
}
```

The preceding code produces a view with a suppression check box that looks similar to the one in Figure 16.3.

FIGURE 16.3
An alert view with a suppression check box.

Try It Yourself

Creating a Custom Alert Dialog

In this section you're going to combine what you've learned so far about creating and using alert views to create an application that displays an optionally suppressed alert view that uses a custom accessory view.

▼

Use the following steps to create this sample application:

1. Create a new Cocoa application called **Hour16Demo**. Make sure you do *not* check the Use Core Data and Document-Based check boxes. Check the Use Automatic Reference Counting check box. You can set the class prefix to anything you like, but I've used STY by convention.

2. Add a new push button labeled **Display Alert** to the application's main window.

3. Using the control-drag technique and the assistant editor, create an action for this new button called **displayAlert:**.

4. Drag a Custom View object somewhere onto the design surface (just not inside any other view).

5. Add whatever buttons, labels, or other controls you choose to this custom view. This will be your accessory view.

6. Control-drag from this new view into the STYAppDelegate.h file. (This file should be visible in the assistant editor.) Then create a new outlet called **accessoryView**.

7. Now add code to the displayAlert: method to query the user defaults option for whether the alert should be suppressed.

8. Add code so that if the alert should not be suppressed, a new alert is created and displayed via the runModal method.

9. Make sure to set the alert's accessoryView property to self.accessoryView.

10. Add code that stores a Boolean value in the user's preference based on the value of the alert's suppressionButton.state property.

11. When you've finished, you should see a dialog that looks similar (with variance for your configuration of the accessory view) to the one shown in Figure 16.4.

▲

FIGURE 16.4
A custom alert view with accessory view and suppression button.

Using Sheets

So far we've talked about the various ways you can use alerts to display modal pop-up dialog windows to users. These windows can be used to alert users about important information, errors, or prompt them to take action about something.

Sheets are a different type of alert, with a few exceptions. Probably the biggest difference between sheets and alerts is that you are responsible for displaying and dismissing sheets using your own code. Alerts are displayed via the runModal method and are dismissed automatically when the user clicks one of the buttons.

Sheets are also attached to a parent window. Although they can be positioned differently, they are *always* attached to the parent window. Custom sheets provide developers with a lot more flexibility than standard alerts, while still not requiring you to do all the work yourself.

Deciding When to Use Sheets

Sheets are often used with document windows to prompt users to take action before saving or deleting documents. They can also be used to display license and end-user agreements to which a user must agree before any action can take place in that window. You may have seen this type of sheet before while using iTunes.

Modal dialogs that belong to single-window applications such as the ones we've been building throughout this book are ideal candidates for sheets. Anytime you need a user to react to some alert before continuing, and you need that information to be more prominent or obscure the contents of the window below, a sheet is the right tool for the job.

Sheets are also typically larger and contain a more complex view hierarchy than alerts do. The small and simple nature of alert dialogs produced by the NSAlert class can be hard to see on a screen filled with multiple windows from multiple applications, whereas a sheet that unfurls across a user interface puts the alert right in front of the user where it can't be easily ignored or avoided.

Displaying a Sheet

To display a sheet, all you really need to do is create a window. The contents of this window will be displayed when the sheet drops down (or from wherever you have it positioned) from the top of the window.

As mentioned earlier, you are responsible for dismissing the sheet as well as displaying it. This means that you'll need to provide a button inside the window that closes the sheet.

> You must make sure that you *uncheck* the Visible at Launch check box for the window in the attributes inspector. Otherwise, the window will not be usable as a sheet, and things won't work properly.

To start the display of a sheet, you can invoke the beginSheet: method on the NSApp class:

```
- (IBAction)displaySheet:(id)sender {
    [NSApp beginSheet:self.customSheetWindow
        modalForWindow:self.window
         modalDelegate:self
        didEndSelector:@selector(didEndSheet:returnCode:contextInfo:)
           contextInfo:nil];
}
```

The @selector macro allows you to specify the name of a method that will be invoked when the sheet ends. This enables you to write code that can inspect values and react to whatever the user did in the window while it was open as a sheet.

> When specifying methods with the @selector command, you need to make sure you type the method name correctly and with proper capitalization. Incorrectly typed method names *will not* cause a build failure, but they can cause your application to crash at runtime when the code attempts to execute that selector!

As you may expect, we need to create a method called didEndSheet:returnCode: contextInfo: to properly handle the sheet completion:

```
- (void)didEndSheet:(NSWindow *)sheet
         returnCode:(NSInteger)returnCode
        contextInfo:(void *)contextInfo
{
    [sheet orderOut:self];

    // handle whatever the user did to the window
    // while it was open...
}
```

Calling `orderOut:` on the sheet removes it from the parent window. Without calling this, the sheet will never disappear, even though it has technically ended and is no longer receiving input.

When adding a button to the window you're using as a sheet, you'll need to make sure the button can close the sheet. The only requirement here is that the method you use to close the sheet needs to have a reference to the `NSWindow*` pointer, as in the following code:

```
- (IBAction)closeSheet:(id)sender {
    NSLog(@"About to close sheet...");
    [NSApp endSheet:self.customSheetWindow];
}
```

That's really all there is to it. To summarize, the use of a custom sheet involves the following steps:

1. Create a custom `NSWindow` in Interface Builder.

2. Link an Outlet to this new window so that it can be referenced programmatically.

3. Call `beginSheet:` passing your custom window as an argument.

4. Create an Action in the new window that closes the sheet.

5. Make sure you call `orderOut:` in your did-end selector to remove the sheet from the parent window.

When positioned in the default location, a sheet displayed over a window looks similar to Figure 16.5.

FIGURE 16.5
Displaying a
sheet.

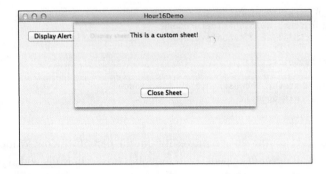

Positioning Sheets

You aren't limited to displaying a sheet attached to the top border of a window. You can override the default positioning behavior of a sheet with delegate methods.

Further, you can even control the animation of the appearance of the sheet. For example, if you set the initial height of the sheet's position rectangle, it will appear to explode out of the destination origin using a smooth, stock Apple animation.

Before you can override the positioning of a sheet for a given window, you need to identify a class as the window's delegate. To do this, connect the window's `delegate` property to the instance of your window delegate class. For simple applications, you can set the window's `delegate` property to the application delegate object.

For applications with multiple, complicated windows, you want to avoid using the AppDelegate as a window delegate and instead create multiple window controllers.

To override the starting position of a sheet, implement the `window:willPositionSheet:usingRect:` method:

```
- (NSRect)window:(NSWindow *)window
    willPositionSheet:(NSWindow *)sheet usingRect:(NSRect)rect
{
    NSRect buttonRect = [self.displaySheetButton frame];
    buttonRect.size.height = 0;
    return buttonRect;
}
```

The preceding sample will cause a sheet to explode out from underneath the button that triggered the sheet. You can use this technique to make modal sheets appear near or attached to the controls to which the sheet is related.

Figure 16.6 shows what a sheet might look like when positioned below a button rather than the default position.

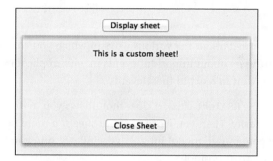

FIGURE 16.6
Changing a
sheet's
position.

Displaying a Series of Sheets

Apple's *Human Interface Guidelines* indicate that before a second sheet is displayed, the currently visible sheet must be closed. Another way of putting this is that you cannot have more than one sheet visible at a time.

It might seem like a difficult thing to do, but the situation occurs more often than you might think. One situation is where a developer presents a modal sheet below a control, and a button on that newly presented sheet also presents a sheet.

Do not try to present multiple sheets at the same time in order to display *help*. There are already built-in facilities in both the sheet and NSAlert APIs for providing help for currently displayed alerts.

While this situation is *technically* possible, it is a violation of Apple's *Human Interface Guidelines*. As you'll see later in the book, if you intend to submit your application to the Mac App Store, your application can't violate these guidelines.

If you need to present users with a series of prompts, and those prompts must all be modal, there are a couple of options. You could display a sheet, end it, gather up the information from the sheet, and then pass it to a subsequent sheet. You may find that this particular pattern can get unwieldy and difficult to maintain, especially as the number of successive sheets increases.

A technique that many developers use in this situation is to display a *single* window as a sheet, and then within that window, use an invisible tab control to give users the appearance of proceeding through a wizard. This way, only a single sheet is presented, the information gathered from this sheet is all in the same place, and the code is easy to write and maintain.

Summary

In this hour, you learned about the various ways in which you can use built-in Cocoa APIs to alert users about important events in your application and prompt them for how they want to react to those events.

You learned about the NSAlert class, a class that allows you to display modal dialog boxes quickly and easily. Then you learned about sheets, a more flexible and customizable way of popping up modal interactive windows, and you learned how to customize them and their positions.

Notifying users about important events and prompting them for action may happen quite often in the lifetime of an application, and Apple's built-in facilities supporting this make your job as a Mac developer much easier.

Q&A

Q. *Should I use sheets for non-alert purposes?*

A. As their name implies, alerts should be used for small bits of information, generally in response to an event the user needs to be aware of. Sheets are larger and more configurable. Apple's Human Interface Guidelines contains information on when to use the various forms of modal alerting.

Q. *Can you trigger an alert from a sheet and vice versa?*

A. While it is possible to trigger alerts from within alerts, you generally want to avoid doing this. Apple's guidelines specifically call out the chaining of multiple modal views as a bad practice.

Q. *Can I use sheets to gather input?*

A. Yes, sheets are just custom wrappers around views and provide a fairly efficient way for you to present a modal dialog into which your users can provide information. Just try and keep the input small and quick because the shorter period of time your alerts/sheets are visible the better.

HOUR 17

Working with Images

What you'll learn in this hour:

▶ Reading and Writing Images
▶ Displaying Collections of Images
▶ Manipulating Images with Core Image Filters

Throughout this book you have seen bits and pieces of Cocoa's ability to deal with images. In one hour you used Core Data to allow users to drag images into a box and save them. In other hours, you've seen how you can place images and icons throughout your user interface to create a richer, more interactive experience.

In this hour, we'll take that knowledge and extend it. Images can add tremendous power to your application and can dramatically enhance the overall user experience. In this hour, you'll learn how to display images read from disk and how to save them to disk. You'll also learn how to display collections of image thumbnails, and finally, you'll get a taste of the power of Apple's Core Image framework to perform incredible image manipulations.

Reading and Writing Images

There are many ways you can load images—from disk, from the Web, from resources embedded in your application, and many more. The NSImage class has several helper methods that allow you to create an instance of NSImage from some data source. In general, you load images from image sources into NSImage instances using object initializer methods, such as the following:

▶ initWithContentsOfFile—Loads an image from a file.

▶ initWithContentsOfURL—Loads an image from a file on the Web or on disk.

▶ `initWithData`—Creates an image from raw binary data that may have been obtained from some other source.

▶ `initWithPasteboard`—Loads an image from a paste board.

▶ `imageNamed`—A class method (not an object initializer) that loads an image from a resource embedded in the application bundle.

To create an instance of the `NSImage` class with the contents of a file, you might use code like this:

```
NSImage *myPicture = [[NSImage alloc]
    initWithContentsOfFile:@"/Users/me/Desktop/epic.png"];
```

Saving the contents of an image to disk is almost as easy. You need to decide which type of image representation you want (PNG, Bitmap, JPG, and so on) and then create that representation from your source image. There are a number of ways to obtain a representation, including asking for the best representation given a context, getting a TIFF representation directly, or selecting the representation from among an array:

```
NSImage *bobImage = [NSImage imageNamed:@"bobImage"];
NSArray *reps = [bobImage representations];
NSData *bitmapData =
    [NSBitmapImageRep representationOfImageRepsInArray:reps
     usingType:NSPNGFileType
     properties:nil];
[bitmapData
    writeToFile:
@"/Users/kevin/Desktop/output.png"
atomically:NO];
```

In the preceding example, we loaded an image as a bundle resource but, as we've already seen, myriad options exist for loading images from different sources. After we have that image, we get the available representations by accessing the `representations` array. From that array, we then pick the PNG representation by asking for the `NSPNGFileType` in the `NSBitmapImageRep`'s class method `representationOfImageRepsInArray:usingType:properties:`.

We could spend the entire hour covering the different ways you can read and write images. To keep things moving quickly, we are covering only a few of the options. The key thing to remember is that reading and writing (as well as converting in the middle!) images is a straightforward task for Mac OS X developers.

Displaying Collections of Images

Now that you're familiar with some of the techniques for loading images, and you know where to go to find more, you may be wondering how you can display those images in a user interface.

Up to this point, we've seen many ways for displaying images in the UI when you know ahead of time which images you're going to display, such as displaying icons from embedded bundle resources or Apple stock images.

What if you want to display a list of thumbnails of images that might be specified by the user at runtime? Fortunately, there's an extremely handy control available to Mac OS X developers—the Image Kit Image Browser, also known by its class name as the `IKImageBrowserView`.

Using the image browser view requires us to create one or more classes that implement the browser view's data source and delegate protocols. By now the concept of delegates and protocols should be somewhat familiar to you.

The image browser view's data source protocol, `IKImageBrowserDataSource`, has only two required methods:

► `numberOfItemsInImageBrowser:`—This method returns the number of images contained in the browser.

► `imageBrowser:itemAtIndex:`—This method returns an instance of an object that implements the image browser item protocol, `IKImageBrowserItem`.

Browser items are responsible for telling the browser view how to fetch the related image content, including the location and type of that content. Browser items must implement the following methods:

► `imageUID`—This is a unique string that identifies the image within the browser. Although the browser won't break if there are duplicate identifiers, it won't function properly either, so you should make sure that your items all have their own *unique* identifiers.

► `imageRepresentationType`—This tells the image browser what type of representation is being used: URL, raw data, object instance, and so on.

► `imageRepresentation`—This is the actual representation that corresponds to the representation type indicated by the item.

The following is a very crude data source class that always returns empty instances of a dummy browser item. Obviously, in a real-world scenario you might be fetching the data that supports this class from a directory, a database, a web service, or some other means.

LISTING 17.1   ImagesDataSource.m

```
#import "ImagesDataSource.h"
#import "ImageItem.h"
#import <Quartz/Quartz.h>

@implementation ImagesDataSource

- (NSUInteger)numberOfItemsInImageBrowser:
(IKImageBrowserView *)aBrowser
{
    return 5;
}

- (id)imageBrowser:(IKImageBrowserView *)aBrowser
itemAtIndex:(NSUInteger)index
{
    return [[ImageItem alloc] init];
}

@end
```

The image item class needs to supply the required methods of the informal protocol, although it can supply more methods for a richer image browsing experience. Listing 17.2 shows the code for a very contrived image item class that *always* tells the image browser to display the circular lion image from Apple's website (note that the UID for these images isn't unique—you shouldn't use constants for these objects):

LISTING 17.2   ImageItem.m

```
#import "ImageItem.h"
#import <Quartz/Quartz.h>

@implementation ImageItem

- (NSString *)imageRepresentationType {
    return IKImageBrowserNSURLRepresentationType;
}

- (NSString *)imageUID {
    return @"http://images.apple.com/macosx/images/overview_callout_osx.png";

}

- (id)imageRepresentation {
    return
    [NSURL URLWithString:
    @"http://images.apple.com/macosx/images/overview_callout_osx.png"];
}
```

Another thing that you'll need to do is manually call the reloadData method on the image browser before it will ask the data source for any information. Figure 17.2 shows a sample UI with an image browser that has its datasource outlet connected to an instance of the ImagesDataSource object from Listing 17.1.

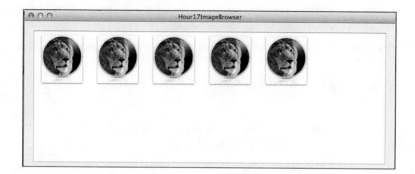

FIGURE 17.1
Using an IKImageBrowser View.

Manipulating Images with Core Image Filters

Core Image is an incredibly powerful image-processing framework for Mac OS X. Core Image can be found within the QuartzCore framework. Core Image allows developers to easily apply filters and effects to images, and these applications can be chained one after the other to create incredible experiences. Core Image can even be used to apply image-processing techniques to each frame of a high-resolution video.

One of the most amazing aspects of Core Image is that it's free! High-end image editing and manipulation tools can cost large sums of money, but all the effects that are part of Core Image are available on every Mac free of charge.

> Most of Core Image and all its intricacies are far beyond the scope of this book. If you find yourself still interested in Core Image after finishing this book, I suggest purchasing *Core Image: Advanced Image Processing for Mac OS X Developers* from Addison-Wesley, available in June of 2012.

Did You Know?

So far in this hour you've been dealing with images using the NSImage class. Images that you intend to manipulate at a lower level are represented within Core Image as instances of the CIImage class.

Another extremely powerful feature of Core Image is that, at any time, you can interrogate the user's system to figure out which transformations and effects are available. After you've decided on a filter, you can query that filter's attributes at runtime to get documentation on the filter's expected inputs and outputs.

For example, if you were using a filter to interleave two images, the runtime attributes for that filter would indicate that it requires two input images.

To display the list of filters available on the system, you can get an array of filters that belong to a certain category, as shown below:

```
NSArray *filterNames = [CIFilter filterNamesInCategory:kCICategoryColorEffect];
    for (NSString *filterName in filterNames)
    {
        NSLog(@"filter: %@", filterName);
    }
```

Before you can use any of the code that belongs to Core Image, you will need to add the `QuartzCore` framework to your application. Additionally, the preceding code won't work unless you #include a reference to the Quartz Core header file:

```
#import <QuartzCore/QuartzCore.h>
```

A number of different categories of image processing filters are available. Experiment on your own querying the list of filters that belong to each of these categories. The following list is not complete:

▶ Distortion Effects

▶ Geometry Adjustments

▶ Composite Operations (two images sources to produce one output)

▶ Halftone Effects

▶ Color Adjustment

▶ Color Effect

▶ Transitions

▶ Tile Effects

▶ Generators (pattern producers such as solid colors, checkerboards, and so on)

▶ Reductions

▶ Gradients

▶ Stylized (to make photos look sketched or painted, for example)

▶ Sharpen

▶ Blur

▶ Video

▶ Still Images

▶ Interlaced Image Effects

▶ Non-Square Pixels

▶ High Dynamic Range

After you've decided on the filter you want to use, it becomes a simple matter of supplying the appropriate inputs to the filter and then doing something with the output.

The following code sets the input parameters for the `CISepiaTone` filter and then stores the filtered output in a new `CIImage` object:

```
CIFilter *sepiaFilter;
sepiaFilter = [CIFilter filterWithName:@"CISepiaTone"];

CIContext *context =
  [CIContext contextWithCGContext:
  [[NSGraphicsContext currentContext] graphicsPort] options:nil];
NSString *imagepath = [[NSBundle mainBundle] pathForImageResource:@"palmtree"];
CIImage *sourceImage = [CIImage imageWithContentsOfURL:[NSURL
fileURLWithPath:imagepath]];

[sepiaFilter setDefaults];
[sepiaFilter setValue:sourceImage forKey:@"inputImage"];
CIImage *resultImage = [sepiaFilter valueForKey:@"outputImage"];
```

In the preceding code, we create an instance of the `CIImage` class by loading an image that has been added to the Xcode project as a resource and, as such, is available as a bundle resource.

Next, we configure the sepia filter object, set the input parameter, and then query the output value.

Core Image filters are dynamic and on-demand. As a result, the filter won't be applied until we ask for the value in the `outputImage` key.

Finally, we can choose to either save the image to disk as we've done earlier in this hour, or we can use the `drawRect:` method of a custom view and render the image directly to the user interface:

```
        CIContext *context = [CIContext contextWithCGContext:
            [[NSGraphicsContext currentContext] graphicsPort] options:nil];
        [context drawImage:resultImage inRect:NSMakeRect(0, 0, 640, 480)
    fromRect:NSMakeRect(0, 0, 640, 480)];
```

Don't worry too much about the details like CIContext and NSGraphicsContext; the important thing to take away from this section of the hour is just how much image-processing power is at your fingertips.

> The drawRect: method of a view is called every time the view needs to be displayed within a particular region. This is where custom drawing takes place that is beyond the scope of this hour. Any of the available Cocoa programming reference books, as well as Apple's documentation, have lengthy guides on creating custom views, including the documentation at http://developer.apple.com/library/mac/ #documentation/Cocoa/Conceptual/CocoaViewsGuide/SubclassingNSView/ SubclassingNSView.html

▼ Try It Yourself

Creating a Grayscale Image Converter

In this section, you'll put to use your new knowledge of reading, writing, and converting images. To do this, you'll create an application that loads an image of any kind using a file browser dialog. This image will then be converted to a grayscale image using a Core Image filter. Finally, the converted grayscale output will be saved to disk using code you've already seen this hour.

To build this application, use the following steps:

1. Create a new Cocoa application. This application is not document based, does not use Core Data, and *should* use Automatic Reference Counting. Call it anything you like.

2. Drag a single button onto the main window in the MainMenu.xib file. Label this button **Load Input Image**.

3. Create an action (control-dragging to the assistant editor) corresponding to that button called **loadInputImage:**.

4. Add the Quartz Core framework to your application. To do this, click to select the project in the project navigator and click the target. Click the plus sign (+) below the Linked Frameworks and Libraries and add QuartzCore.Framework to the project.

5. Add #import <QuartzCore/QuartzCore.h> to the top of your application
▼   delegate file.

6. Open an NSOpenPanel when the user clicks the button from step 2. The
NSOpenPanel opens a dialog that allows users to browse for files. Use the following stub code to configure and launch this open panel:

```
NSOpenPanel *openPanel = [NSOpenPanel openPanel];
openPanel.canChooseFiles = YES;
openPanel.canChooseDirectories = NO;
openPanel.canCreateDirectories = NO;
openPanel.allowedFileTypes =
    [NSArray arrayWithObjects:@"png", @"jpg", @"gif", nil];

if ([openPanel runModal] == NSOKButton) {
    NSLog(@"User selected %@", openPanel.URL);
    // Process the file...
}
```

7. Run your application. You should see a file browse dialog like the one in
Figure 17.2 when you click the Load Input Image button.

FIGURE 17.2
Loading files
using an
NSOpenPanel.

There are several other built-in panels that your application can use for additional
functionality, such as print dialogs. When you get a chance, look through the
Cocoa documentation to see what other kinds of prebuilt dialogs are available.

Did You Know?

8. After the user selects a file, add a line of code that creates a CIImage (remember this differs from the higher-level NSImage class) to the "Process the file..."
section from step 6:

```
CIImage *sourceImage = [CIImage imageWithContentsOfURL:openPanel.URL];
```

9. Now let's add some code that will process the file. To do this, you'll use the CIColorMonochrome filter. First, create an instance of this filter:

```
CIFilter *monoFilter;
monoFilter = [CIFilter filterWithName:@"CIColorMonochrome"];
[monoFilter setDefaults];
```

10. After you have an instance of a Core Data filter, you need to set the input parameters. For grayscale, we can leave all the defaults as is and just supply the filter with the input image:

```
[monoFilter setValue:sourceImage forKey:@"inputImage"];
```

11. As mentioned earlier, Core Image filters don't actually perform work until some piece of code requests the outputImage property. Let's add that code to obtain a pointer to the converted grayscale image:

```
CIImage *resultImage = [monoFilter valueForKey:@"outputImage"];
```

12. Finally, let's obtain an instance of a PNG representation of the converted, filtered output and save it on disk (change the path to something more appropriate to your computer):

```
NSBitmapImageRep *bitmapRep =
 [[NSBitmapImageRep alloc] initWithCIImage:resultImage];
NSData *pngData =
 [bitmapRep representationUsingType:NSPNGFileType properties:nil];
BOOL result =
 [pngData writeToFile:@"/Users/kevin/Desktop/converted.png" atomically:NO];
if (!result)
{
    NSLog(@"Failed to write output to disk.");
}
```

13. Now run your application. Click the Load Input Image button and select a reasonably small image. When the application is done, find the output image and verify that it has been converted into a grayscale image.

Reader Challenge

If you get the image converter sample done in less than an hour, and you feel like you want some more practice extending Cocoa applications, see if you can add the following features to the application you just finished:

▶ Using the skills you learned in the previous hour, display an informative dialog box letting the user know that the file has been converted. Include the filename of the newly created output file in the information displayed to the user.

▶ After the user has selected a source image, present the user with a sheet. This sheet should prompt the user for which effect to run on the source image. Allow the user to choose between grayscale and Sepia.

The Sepia filter is called `CISepiaTone` and can be applied using almost the same code you use to perform a grayscale filter.

Summary

In this hour you learned how to perform some basic image tasks, such as reading and writing image files and displaying images in a collection in a user interface. Additionally, you learned how to perform incredibly powerful and complex image effects and filters with very little code by leveraging the Core Image framework. Finally, in this hour you built an application that reads in normal image files and saves their grayscale counterparts to disk, further illustrating how simple and accessible image processing power is on Mac OS X Lion.

Q&A

Q. Are there memory concerns when working with images?

A. Yes, even on today's modern computers with large amounts of memory. Images take up a lot of space in memory and when you perform various effects on them, you could consume even more. While you shouldn't shy away from performing visual effects, you should also keep in mind that they do make your application work harder and use more memory.

Q. Do I really need to create custom views to do a lot of this stuff?

A. Yes, to control some of the lower level behaviors of a view you will need to create your own custom views. The upside is that this is a relatively easy task, as shown in this hour.

HOUR 18
Using Popovers

What you'll learn in this hour:

▶ Introduction to Popovers
▶ When to Use Popovers
▶ Creating Popovers
▶ Customizing Popovers
▶ Creating Detachable Popovers

Popovers are an Apple technology that first appeared on the iPad. They provided an advanced user interface that allowed developers to "pop over" additional views that appeared to be contextually attached to some piece of the main interface.

In this hour, you'll learn what Popovers are, when they should be used, and how to create them. You'll also learn advanced techniques to customize Popovers and even create Popovers that can be detached from their contextual source just by dragging the window.

Introducing Popovers

The NSPopover class provides a way to display additional content related to existing content already on screen. Popovers are positioned relative to the content to which they apply with a subtle arrow pointing toward the related content.

Many of us have seen simple popovers when using thumbtacks on maps, whether these maps are on our mobile phones or desktops. Typically, landmarks or search results will appear on a map as a thumbtack or some other icon. When we tap or click that icon, additional content *pops up* that provides more detail and possibly some interactive content related to the thumbtack we just clicked.

For example, in an application that allows us to read and provide reviews for restaurants, we might tap the restaurant's thumbtack to bring up reviews and enter our own rating and review text. In a real-time strategy game, we might click a tank that is moving across the battlefield to see the tank's health, fuel, and current orders. The number of uses for popovers is limited only by our creativity and, thanks to the iPad, most Mac OS X Lion users are already familiar with interacting with Popovers.

When to Use Popovers

As mentioned, there are numerous ways you can use Popovers, but the trick is figuring out when to use them and how to use them in a way that enhances the experience of your application rather than detracts from it.

Did You Know?

> If you are familiar with Popovers on the iPad, or if you have written iOS code that uses popover controllers, you'll need to try to avoid using them on the Mac for the same reasons you use them on the iPad. Macs have far more screen real estate, they are capable of right-clicking, *and* they support multitouch gestures. Don't use a popover just because it might have been a good idea on the iPad version of a similar app.

The first rule when using popovers is to never launch a popover from within another popover. This follows the same guideline we learned in the previous hour about not having two alerts or sheets open at the same time.

The second rule is that Popovers should be smaller than the window containing the contextually related content. One of the main purposes of a popover is to deliver contextually related content in a *quick*, *small*, and *easy to access* fashion. If you find your popover is growing to the size of another full window, perhaps you should consider a different way of displaying the popover content (such as using a new tab, a wizard-style approach, or having two open windows).

Finally, ask yourself whether the presence of your popover provides the user with a *simpler* or *easier* experience than if the content of that popover was delivered through some other medium. Popovers should never be an inconvenience. One increasingly common use of popovers is to deliver details when a user clicks an icon, such as the icon of a notification in a social networking app that, when clicked, displays a popover containing that user's profile.

Creating Popovers

Now that we're acquainted with what popovers are and when we should use them, let's get into the details of how to create a popover. Popovers are created using the NSPopover class.

You can use two kinds of popover behaviors—transient or semitransient. If a user interacts with any user interface, whether or not it belongs to the source application, a transient popover will be automatically closed. A semitransient popover will be automatically closed when a user clicks somewhere in the window that launched the popover, but not if a user clicks within another application. If you don't want to use either of these automatic behaviors, you can opt for application-defined transience, where you are responsible for manually closing the popover when you see fit.

A popover is easily displayed with the showRelativeToRect:ofView:preferredEdge: method. This method will display a popover relative to the NSRect (a definition of a rectangle somewhere within a container view) specified. In addition to the relative rectangle (which controls where the popover's anchor points), you also specify the view in which the rectangle exists and the preferred edge where you want the popover to appear.

This means that you can choose to have the popover appear above, below, to the left, or to the right of the anchor rectangle.

Did You Know?

Pay special note to the word "preferred" in the edge selection. As its name implies, this is only your preference. If the popover cannot be displayed on the preferred edge, the next best edge will be chosen automatically. The system will do whatever it can to honor your preference, but it won't hide or obscure the popover window to do so.

Up to this point in this book, we have been taking quite a few liberties by putting outlets and actions in the application delegate class. This is actually not a very good practice. It is recommended that a controller class accompany each window, and a view controller should also accompany each view that has its own functionality.

Now that you are familiar with creating user interfaces, working with Cocoa bindings, and working within Xcode and design surfaces within .xib files, you are ready to start using controllers in ways you might find in real, commercial applications.

The following code will display a popover with its anchor pointing upward at a button, with the view being the view in which the button resides. You might find a method like this within a *view controller* or *window controller* far more often than you would find it in an application delegate class:

```
- (IBAction)buttonClicked:(id)sender {
    [self.myPopover
        showRelativeToRect:[myButton bounds]
        ofView:sender
        preferredEdge:NSMaxYEdge];
}
```

Popovers are made possible by combining a Popover object (an instance of the NSPopover class) and a Popover view controller (a regular instance of NSViewController). Fortunately, you can drag this combined pair right out of the object library and onto your Interface Builder design surface.

The popover object and the controller give you the capability to display content inside a popover. The trick, of course, is telling the popover *which* content you want to display.

The simplest way to do this is to drag a custom view object out of the object library onto your design surface and then connect the view outlet of the Popover view controller object to this new view.

> The more you force yourself to use smaller, more task-oriented classes like individual view and window controllers, the better. Getting out of the habit of dumping everything into the application delegate will make things easier for you in the future.

If you're not using the application delegate as a catchall for outlets and actions, the simplest thing you can do is create a new window controller for your main window.

To do this, you can add a new file to your project and instead of inheriting from NSObject, choose to inherit from NSWindowController, as shown in Figure 18.1.

The first thing you'll need after you have a window controller is an outlet for your NSPopover object. Additionally, you'll need an outlet for whatever object you want to use as your Popover's anchor so you can get its bounding rectangle. For example, if you want to anchor a Popover to a button, you'll need an outlet for that button as well. Finally, you'll need an action inside this controller to react to the button press that activates the popover using the showRelativeToRect:ofView:preferredEdge: method.

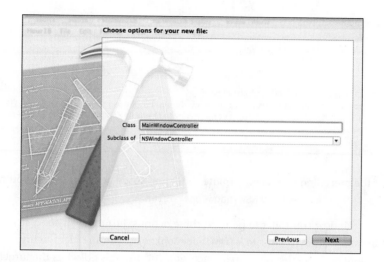

FIGURE 18.1
Creating a window controller.

Assuming you've made the appropriate attachments in Interface Builder, a simple window controller to launch a popover might look like the code in Listing 18.1 and Listing 18.2, respectively.

LISTING 18.1   MainWindowController.h

```objc
#import <Cocoa/Cocoa.h>

@interface MainWindowController : NSWindowController
- (IBAction)popoverClicked:(id)sender;
@property (weak) IBOutlet NSPopover *myPopover;
@property (weak) IBOutlet NSButton *popoverButton;

@end
```

LISTING 18.2   MainWindowController.m

```objc
#import "MainWindowController.h"

@implementation MainWindowController
@synthesize myPopover;
@synthesize popoverButton;

- (id)initWithWindow:(NSWindow *)window
{
    self = [super initWithWindow:window];
    if (self) {
        // Initialization code here.
    }

    return self;
}
```

```
- (void)windowDidLoad
{
    [super windowDidLoad];

}

- (IBAction)popoverClicked:(id)sender {
    [myPopover showRelativeToRect:[popoverButton bounds]
                    ofView:sender preferredEdge:NSMaxYEdge];
}
@end
```

Most of the preceding code is boilerplate code that Xcode generates when you create a new class that derives from `NSWindowController`.

To get this window controller to perform these actions, just drag an *object* from the object library and set its class to `MainWindowController` in the identity inspector panel. After you have this object reference, you can use this object as the target for connections and outlets.

As mentioned previously, the easiest way to provide content for a Popover is to create a connection between the popover view controller's `view` outlet and a custom view you dragged onto the design surface. An example of a Popover in action that was launched using a window controller like the one in Listings 18.1 and 18.2 is shown in Figure 18.2.

FIGURE 18.2
Launching a
Popover.

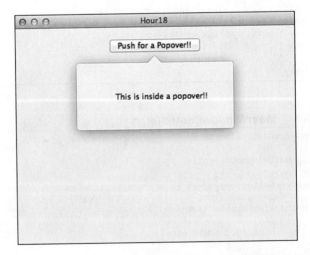

Figure 18.3 shows what that same Popover looks like when the preferred edge is changed from `NSMaxYEdge` to `NSMinXEdge`, anchoring it to the left side of the button.

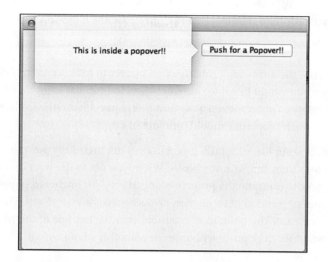

FIGURE 18.3
Displaying a
Popover with an
NSMinXEdge
anchor.

Remember that the view managed by the Popover controller is just like any other Cocoa view. This means the UI elements within it can be bound to data just like elements in the main window. This gives us tremendous power and flexibility to use Popovers to solve all kinds of interesting problems.

Customizing Popovers

You already know that can control the transient nature of popovers, but you can change several other aspects of the popover, including its appearance.

In recent versions of Mac OS X, Apple has introduced the use of the "HUD" style window. These windows are used, as their name implies, for quick "heads-up display" purposes. If you think that your Popover window should be displayed as a HUD window rather than a regular gray window, you can change the appearance of that window.

> Consult Apple's *Human Interface Guidelines* for guidance as to when you should use HUD windows versus using regular windows.

You can change the appearance of the Popover by picking the appearance from a drop-down list in Interface Builder, or programmatically as shown in this line of code:

```
myPopover.appearance = NSPopoverAppearanceHUD;
```

To set the appearance to minimal (default gray), use the following code:

```
myPopover.appearance = NSPopoverAppearanceMinimal;
```

You can also use the `animates` property of a Popover to indicate to the OS as a *preference* that you would like it to animate when the content view changes size or when the window position moves. Note that this is just a *hint*—the OS has the final decision over which properties should animate, if any.

Popovers might seem like nice little toys, but they are incredibly powerful and have many more uses than simple static boxes. When you get to the hour on animation, you'll learn how to animate the properties of controls. An anchored popover will respect the current position of its anchor, *even when that anchor moves*. This means that you can animate the position of a button from the left side of the window to the right, and the attached popover will animate smoothly along with it.

> Just for fun, in the code download for this hour, there is a block of code you can uncomment to see a Popover animate along with a moving button.

Creating Detachable Popovers

Another powerful thing you can do with Popovers is give users the ability to upgrade a small, anchored, contextual window to a full-blown detached window.

Suppose you're building an application that displays a list of contacts. If you click a contact's picture, you might get a Popover that displays a contact card for that person.

If users decide they want even more information, they have a couple options. They could dismiss the little popover window and then go back to the main window and figure out how to get more details on a contact. They could also click and drag the popover and pull it away from the anchor. After the popover is far enough away from its anchor, the Popover will be converted into a full window. This provides a very elegant, meaningful transition from small amounts of contextual information to a full window containing more information.

Detachable Popover windows are a little tricky but well worth the effort. A window delegate can expose a method called `detachableWindowForPopover:`. If this method is defined on a window's delegate (which should be a window controller, if we're following best practices) the Popover will automatically become detachable. The window will resize itself and morph from the anchored Popover into the full window you provide as a return value from the `detachableWindowForPopover:` method.

Try It Yourself

Building a Popover-Enabled Window

In this exercise, you'll get a chance to build a window that has a detachable popover. This Popover will share the same content and view controller class as the detachable window, creating a nice seamless experience.

We are building a client application for a fictitious social networking site called *Blither*. This client will show individual messages from users (called *Blits*). When a user clicks the profile icon or avatar from one of these Blits, a Popover appears, displaying the user's profile. This Popover can then be dragged away from its anchor to convert it into a full window.

We will be doing a few things we've never done before, such as creating a second xib file and using window and view controllers, but these are things that should be fairly easy if you've been building the code samples from previous hours.

Use the following steps to build the *Blither* client application:

1. Create a new Cocoa application called **Blither**. This is not a document-based application, doesn't use Core Data, and *should* use Automatic Reference Counting.

2. Add a box, some images, and whatever text you like. This is a simulated application and doesn't actually do anything, so feel free to get creative. The only requirement is that you place a button somewhere in the application window. Figure 18.4 shows a design surface for this window; note how one of the user profile images is a square button with an image.

3. Add a window controller. To do this, add a new file to the project called **MainWindowController**, making sure it inherits from NSWindowController.

4. Add a view controller to the project, but not from the object library. Instead, create a new file and have it inherit from NSViewController. Name the new file **PopoverViewController**. After this you should notice three new files added to your project: PopoverViewController.h, PopoverViewController.m, and PopoverViewController.xib.

5. Select the MainMenu.xib file.

6. From the object library, drag an *object* into the object tray. Using the identity inspector, set the class type of the object to MainWindowController.

7. Using the assistant editor, connect the delegate outlet of the main window object to the MainWindowController object.

▼

FIGURE 18.4
Designing the
Blither window.

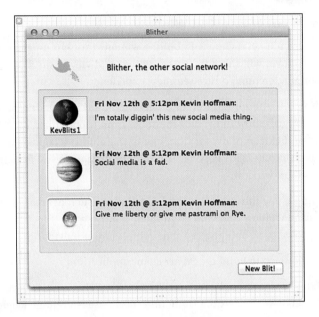

8. Drag a Popover and View Controller object from the object library into the object tray. You should see that it has created two objects: a Popover View Controller and a Popover object.

9. Examine the connections inspector for the Popover object and note that the `contentViewController` outlet is already connected to the Popover view controller that was automatically created.

10. Still in the connections inspector, connect the `delegate` connection to the `MainWindowController` object.

11. At this point, the Popover view controller doesn't have a view associated with it. To associate it with the view contained in the `PopoverViewController.xib` file, view the identity inspector for the Popover view controller. For the Nib Name property, use the drop-down box to select "PopoverViewController." This will *automatically* set the view within that `.xib` as the view for this controller.

By the Way

Using multiple xib files and linking controllers to views contained within them is a fairly complicated topic that is usually covered by more in-depth reference books. For now, it should be enough to know that if there is only one view contained in a xib file, and a view controller links into that file, a connection is created between that controller and that view without your having to manually create the link.

▼

12. Using the assistant editor again, create a connection between the button you created for launching the Popover and the `MainWindowController` class. Call the method **earthClicked**. (I named it this because I used the Earth image for the button.)

13. Add an outlet from the `MainWindowController` class referencing the button you just linked in step 12 and call it **earthImage**.

14. Add the following code to the earthClicked: method:

```
[self.profilePopover
 showRelativeToRect:[earthImage bounds]
 ofView:sender
 preferredEdge:NSMaxYEdge];
```

15. Make sure the behavior of the Popover object is set to Transient and the appearance is set to HUD. This will make the Popover appear with a dark gray background. Also check the Animates box.

16. Run the application. You should be able to click the button and see an empty view appear with the Popover anchor. Click elsewhere to see the Popover fade away because of its transient behavior.

17. Now let's make the Popover detachable. First, add a window object to the `MainWindow.xib` file. You can provide whatever Xcode label you like for it.

18. Add an outlet for the window you created in step 17 to the `MainWindowController` class called detachedWindow.

19. Add the following code to the `MainWindowController.m` file, telling the Popover which window should be used when the user wants to detach:

```
- (NSWindow *)detachableWindowForPopover:(NSPopover *)popover
{
    return self.detachedWindow;
}
```

20. This is enough to allow the application to provide a window into which the Popover will morph when detached. However, we want to make it so that both the Popover window and the detached window have the same content and behave the same way.

21. Add a View Controller object to the `MainWindow.xib` file. Use the identity inspector to change the title to **Detached View Controller** and set the Nib Name to **PopoverViewController**.

For reasons beyond the scope of this book, we need to have *two different instances of the same view controller*, one for the Popover and one for the detached window. The trick here is that both instances of the view controller will have the same view, allowing us to share content between the detached window and the Popover window.

22. The `awakeFromNib:` method is called whenever an object is pulled out of a `xib` file and provides a great spot for one-time initialization. To make both the Popover controller and the detached window share the same content, add the following `awakeFromNib:` method to the `MainWindowController.m` file:

```
- (void)awakeFromNib
{
    self.detachedWindow.contentView =
        self.detachedViewController.view;
}
```

23. For this to work properly, the detached window needs to be configured properly. Go to the attributes inspector for the window object and set the style to HUD Panel. Set the only control to Close, and make sure that Release When Closed and Visible at Launch are both *unchecked.*

24. Now when you run the application, you should be able to pull the popover window away from the anchor, and the Popover will morph into the detached window.

Figure 18.5 shows a sample *Blither* window with a detached Popover HUD.

Figure 18.6 shows the same application without detaching the Popover. Note that the content of the Popover window is identical to the content of the detached window from Figure 18.5.

If you find that you have trouble setting up this sample, you can always use the `Blither` example in the source code download for this hour as a reference.

Do not skip to the `Blither` example without actually following the steps. Following the steps in this hour is essential to learning some of the more intricate patterns of dealing with multiple `xib` files, view controllers, and window controllers.

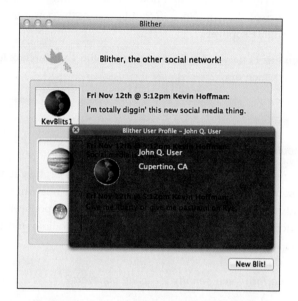

FIGURE 18.5
Using detached Popover windows.

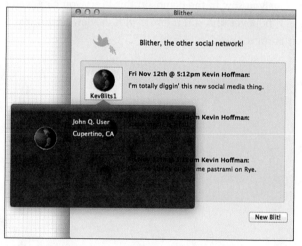

FIGURE 18.6
Using Popover windows in the Blither application.

Summary

In this hour, you learned about one of the powerful new user interface features of Mac OS X Lion, the Popover. Popovers provide a means for displaying contextual content anchored to the related content in another view. This provides a wide assortment of possibilities for creating compelling applications as well as something familiar to users of iPad applications that also use Popovers.

You learned how to create Popovers and how to control, configure, and customize them. Finally, you created an application that harnesses the power of Popovers and you created detachable Popovers.

After completing this hour, you have yet another tool in your toolbox for building amazing Mac OS X Lion applications.

Q&A

Q. *When should I use popovers versus sheets or alerts?*

A. Popovers aren't merely for alerting or notifying the user; they are for presenting an interactive control surface that is contextually relevant to some portion of the main view. If you need examples of when to use popovers, find some iPad applications that make extensive use of the paradigm and see how you might adapt that to your application.

Q. *Is there a performance penalty for using popovers?*

A. No, in fact, as you saw in the demos in this hour, you can even animate the location of a popover and still interact with its view as it moves with very little impact on performance.

HOUR 19

Building Animated User Interfaces

What you'll learn in this hour:

▶ Introduction to Core Animation
▶ Animating Views
▶ Advanced Animation Techniques
▶ Knowing When to Use Animation

Users of modern operating systems from Mac OS X Lion to iOS are accustomed to seeing user interface transitions occur over time. Effects like the "Genie" that pulls applications out of Mac OS X's Dock to warps, blends, twists, curls, rotations, and everything else are becoming increasingly more commonplace.

In this hour you'll learn about Apple's Core Animation framework and how to use the APIs within it to create visually appealing, animated applications that provide users with animated feedback and smooth transitions. You'll also get some guidance with regard to when animations are appropriate and when they aren't. The only thing worse than an application without animations is an application with *too many* animations.

Introduction to Core Animation

As human beings, we are accustomed to the way the real world reacts to our presence. When we open a door, it swings wide. When we open a window, it slides open. When we slowly depress the gas pedal in our cars, they steadily gain speed.

Unfortunately, as users of computer software, we have been subjected to experiences that are unnatural and uncomfortable to the human eye. Although it might be perfectly acceptable for a window to move from the left side of the screen to the right side of the screen in less time than it takes the human eye to blink, this kind of movement is jarring and uncomfortable for people. Even if it takes less than 1 second, our eyes (and minds!) much prefer seeing a visual transition from one position to the other.

Lately, as computing power, graphics cards, and animation libraries have become more ubiquitous, we have been treated to a growth of natural interfaces that react to our presence. Changes are made gradually and visually in a way that is pleasing and doesn't cause eyestrain over time.

This is what Core Animation is all about. It is a framework that makes it easy for you to animate various aspects of views over time. It doesn't just let us gradually change the position of views, but we can animate all kinds of things, such as size, position, rotation, colors, and much more.

Core Animation provides classes that facilitate smooth, animated, composited user interfaces that fall into four categories: layer classes, animation and timing classes, layout classes, and a transaction class. Although you don't have to know all the details of the plumbing that supports Core Animation, knowing a little bit about how it all works will make it easier for you to craft an application with an animated user interface.

Layer Classes

Layers are the foundation of Core Animation. Similar to the view hierarchy you've learned about throughout this book, there is also a layer hierarchy where the layers are displayed from the bottom up. Unlike views, layers have tremendous compositing capabilities that allow them to perform very powerful compositions and animations.

Layer functionality is provided by the CALayer class and by the classes that derive from this common parent. You'll see more about layers and manipulating them later in this hour.

Animation and Timing Classes

Building on the foundation of layers, a concept many designers and artists with experience in Photoshop will be familiar with, there are classes that facilitate animation and perform timing operations.

Many animations can be performed simply by *animating a property value*. This means that rather than immediately forcing a view's property to a new value, the property's value is gradually changed from its current value to the target value. These classes can do everything from moving rectangles and changing points to performing complex animations that animate values along curves. For example, instead of having a view move the same speed throughout the duration of its animation, you can have the view start and finish slowly and move quickly in the middle. This type of animation is often called an *ease-in* or *ease-out* animation. Thanks to Core Animations animation and timing classes, you don't have to worry about manually writing any of that code.

Animations start with the CABasicAnimation class. You can perform more complicated *key frame* style animations using the CAKeyFrameAnimation class. Other classes, like CAAnimationGroup, allow you to group animation effects into a single animation batch; The CATransition class can animate a transition between two entire views (or rather, the Core Animation layers that correspond to those views).

A key frame animation is one where rather than specifying that a value must change by a certain amount over a certain period of time, you require that a property have *specific* values at *specific*, *key* points during the animation. Hence the name, *key frame* animation.

The Transaction Class

Every modification that is made to an animatable property of a Core Animation layer takes place within the context of a transaction, represented by an instance of the CATransaction class. If you don't explicitly create a transaction for your animation, one will be created for you. Don't worry too much about transactions for now, because their use is beyond the scope of this hour.

For more details on the CATransaction class and an in-depth coverage of how Core Animation works, both for Mac OS X and iOS, check out the Pragmatic Programmers' book, *Core Animation for Mac OS X and iPhone* or the O'Reilly book, *Graphics and Animation on iOS*.

By the Way

Animating Views

Now that we've been through some background on the classes and plumbing that support Core Animation, we can go through some examples of how animation can be done in Mac OS X Lion applications.

You can animate properties in your application in a number of ways. Which method you choose will typically depend on how much control you want to have over the animation.

If you just want to change some visual aspect of a control, and you'd like it to be animated, but you just want the animation to look and feel like a stock Apple animation, you might want to use the *animator proxy*, which we'll talk about shortly. If you want a little more control over the animation, such as duration, you might want to use implicit animations by setting properties on a layer. Finally, you can control even more aspects of the animation by using explicit animations by creating instances of specific animation classes.

Using the Animator Proxy

The quickest and easiest way to enable animations in your application is to use the animator proxy. Every object that contains animatable properties also contains a *proxy* that you can reference by sending the object the `animator` message. The `animator` acts exactly like the original object, but it intercepts calls to property changes and makes those changes animated by having the changes take place over a period of time. By default, the period of time is very short but long enough that the user knows an animated transition between values took place.

To see this in action, you can create an application with a single button on the main window. When you click the button, execute the following code:

```
NSRect startRect = moveMeButton.frame;
[moveMeButton
    setFrame:NSMakeRect(startRect.origin.x, 0,
    startRect.size.width, startRect.size.height)];
```

When you run this code, the button moves to its new location at the bottom of the window as fast as it possibly can. This creates a jarring effect where something has moved faster than the human eye can comfortably track the movement.

To quickly and easily make this movement smooth, animated, and less disturbing to your users, you can send the `setFrame:` message to the `animator` proxy rather than the original class:

```
[[moveMeButton animator]
    setFrame:NSMakeRect(startRect.origin.x, 0,
                        startRect.size.width,
                        startRect.size.height)];
```

Now when you run the same application, the button takes about .75 seconds to get from its original location to the new position. If all you need to do is change a few simple properties of objects and you are fine with letting the OS control all the other parameters of the animation, using the `animator` proxy is the way to go.

Using Implicit Animations

The next level of control you can have over animations is by interacting directly with a view's Core Animation layer (an instance of CALayer). After you have this layer, every time you change a visual aspect of that layer, that change will occur in an animated fashion without requiring you to use a proxy.

For example, to get a button's layer and then make the button fade away, you might write the following code:

```
CALayer *buttonLayer = moveMeButton.layer;
[buttonLayer setOpacity:0.0];
```

By setting the opacity to 0.0, the button will take about .75 of a second to fade away. If we set the opacity of the button itself rather than its animator proxy or the CA layer, the button would disappear and the user would have no visual feedback regarding what happened.

> Note that Core Animation layers are more expensive than regular views. If you know that you're going to be interacting with a control's animation layer, you can call the setWantsLayer method on that control and pass YES as a value. Anytime after this method call, the control will have an active core animation layer that you can play with.

By the Way

As mentioned before, Core Animation is also a composition engine. This means that when you slowly fade something out, whatever happens to be underneath is gradually phased in. Core Animation takes care of figuring out how much of the foreground and background should be blended at any given time to give you great fade, dissolve, and wipe effects.

Using Explicit Animations

If you still need finer-grained control over your animation, you can use explicit animations. Explicit animations allow you to control some of the aspects of an animation that are normally left to default values, such as the duration. You can also control things such as whether the animation reverses automatically, how many times it continues running, and so on. These values are available only when you explicitly control animations.

The following code will take a subview and move it from its current location to the bottom left of its parent view, and do so over a period of 4 seconds. It will then autoreverse and animate its path back to its original location.

```
NSPoint originalPoint = customView.frame.origin;
CALayer *layer = customView.layer;
CABasicAnimation *mover = [CABasicAnimation
    animationWithKeyPath:@"position"];

mover.duration = 4.0;
mover.repeatCount = 1;
mover.autoreverses = YES;
mover.delegate = self;
mover.fromValue = [NSValue valueWithPoint:originalPoint];
mover.toValue = [NSValue valueWithPoint:NSMakePoint(0, 0)];

[layer addAnimation:mover forKey:@"animatePosition"];
```

As soon as the animation has been added to the layer, it will be processed and executed. The real power of this technique comes from the ability to control the duration, the autoreverse option, and the ability to add multiple animations and
animation groups to a single layer.

When we run this code we'll see whatever view we're animating move slowly from
its starting point to the end point and back again. It will have a *constant* velocity
from start to finish. If we want to give it a more natural feeling where the view
speeds up at first, then moves at a constant rate, then slows down, we can set the
timing function of the animation:

```
mover.timingFunction = [CAMediaTimingFunction
    functionWithName: kCAMediaTimingFunctionEaseInEaseOut];
```

There are a number of built-in timing functions, including ease-in, ease-in/ease-out,
and linear. If you're feeling adventurous, you can even write your own timing
function.

Advanced Animation Techniques

Before we get to building our own animation sample application, we should cover a
couple of other ways of performing animations: the animation context and using
whole-view transitions.

Using the Animation Context

Ideally, you should only have to drop down to the CALayer level when there is no
other way to accomplish the type of animation you're looking for. Fortunately, a nice
middle ground exists between directly manipulating CABasicAnimation and
CALayer instances and using the animator proxy. That middle ground is the animation context. The animation context works in conjunction with the animator proxy

to override the default values used by the proxy, such as duration and timing functions.

The following code shows how we can use the animation context to change the default duration used by the animator proxy:

```
NSRect originalRect = [fadeButton frame];
[[NSAnimationContext currentContext] setDuration:4.0];
[[targetButton animator] setFrame:
    NSMakeRect(0, 0, originalRect.size.width, originalRect.size.height)];
```

Waiting for Animations to Finish

Many times your application will need to perform some action when an animation completes, rather than when the animation starts. For example, if you click a button to perform an action, and you have an animation that moves a file icon from the source folder to the target folder, you might want to start some action when the animation finishes.

To do this using the animation context, you can set a *block* to be executed when the animation completes. A *block* is a piece of Objective-C code that can be passed around like it was data. As you'll see in this piece of code that follows, you can pass blocks around as parameters to other methods:

```
[[NSAnimationContext currentContext] setCompletionHandler:^{
    NSLog(@"finished frame change.");
}];
```

This technique comes in very handy if you want to cascade animations. For instance, if you want to start one animation when another completes, you can start the second animation inside the completion handler *block* of the first animation.

Animating View Transitions

Next to animating simple properties, one of the most common animation tasks that developers perform is transitioning from one view to another. You see this type of transition when an application allows you to move forward and backward through wizard-style interfaces or when the application transitions from a master view to a detail view. This type of master-to-detail *push* or *slide* transition is extremely prevalent on iOS and is gaining in popularity on Mac OS X.

Before you see how we can animate the transition from one view to another, you need to know how to do it without animations. Every view has a parent view, except for the application or document window, which have no parent views. To swap one view for another, you need to do so *within a container view*.

Suppose your application has a content region and a Next Page button. When users click the Next Page button, you want the current page to slide out of the way to make room for the next page. This is a classic view transition that requires a container view.

The hierarchy for such a scenario involves a container view that can be (and often is) just a plain, unmodified NSView instance. Within the container view, the application starts with the first page view showing. When the user clicks Next Page, the *container view* swaps out the first page for the second page, using an animated transition.

Without animation, a container view can swap one subview for another using the following method:

```
[transitionContainerView
    replaceSubview:firstView
    with:secondView];
```

This will immediately swap views with no visible transition; the secondView object will instantly appear, possibly creating a jarring experience for the user.

In keeping with the patterns Apple uses throughout Cocoa, you might expect that sending the animator proxy the replaceSubview:with: method would perform a subtle, default animation to transition the views:

```
[[transitionContainerView animator]
    replaceSubview:transitionFirstView
    with:transitionSecondView];
```

This will use the default view transition animation, which is a fade. The fade takes a little under a second and gives you a nice default for when you need to transition from one view to another within a container view.

If you want full control over the view transitions, you can create an instance of the CATransition class and add that object to the container view's animation collection.

The following awakeFromNib: method configures a CATransition for the transition container view that will *push* the old view out while the new view slides in from the top. Additionally, an *easing* animation will be used to give this push a more pleasing look:

```
[transitionContainerView setWantsLayer:YES];
[transitionContainerView addSubview:transitionFirstView];
CATransition *transition = [CATransition animation];
[transition setType:kCATransitionPush];
[transition setSubtype:kCATransitionFromTop];
transition.timingFunction =
    [CAMediaTimingFunction
        functionWithName:kCAMediaTimingFunctionEaseInEaseOut];
```

```
[transition setDuration:1.5];
[[transitionContainerView layer]
    addAnimation:transition forKey:kCATransitionPush];
[transitionContainerView
    setAnimations:
    [NSDictionary dictionaryWithObject:transition
      forKey:@"subviews"]];
```

In this code sample, there is a parent (or container) view referenced by the `transitionContainerView` outlet. The application starts up with `transitionFirst View` as the only subview of the parent container. The `CATransition` object is configured to create a *push* transition that comes in from the top and uses an easing function for timing. The transition will take 1.5 seconds to complete, and we set the animations of the container view to a dictionary containing the `CATransition` object.

It is *extremely* important that the key in the dictionary for the transition is called "subviews". This is the animation that is referenced when the `replaceSubview: with:` method is called on a view.

Try It Yourself

Creating an Animated Application

In this sample application, you'll explore the `NSAnimationContext` class and how each time you give it something to do, it adds to a *stack* of animation actions. You'll see what happens to an animating object that is then acted on by another animation—what are called *in-flight* changes to an animating object.

To see all this in action, you'll create an application with a button in each corner of the window. Every time you click a corner button, a new animation will be added to the stack to move the center object toward that button. Experiment with the finished application by clicking multiple buttons in a row before the object reaches its final destination.

To create this application, perform the following steps:

1. Create a new Cocoa application called Hour19. This application is not document based, doesn't use Core Data, and *does* use Automatic Reference Counting.

2. We'll reinforce our skills with window controllers now to create a new window controller called `MainWindowController`. Remember that this is done by creating a new file and inheriting from `NSWindowController`.

▼

3. Drag an *object* out of the object library and set its custom class to `MainWindowController` using the identity inspector.

4. Set the delegate of the main window in `MainMenu.xib` to the newly created window controller object.

5. Add four buttons to the main window, one for each corner. Label each one of these buttons `Go Here`.

6. Ctrl-drag using the assistant editor to create four outlets, one for each of the buttons. Call them `topLeftButton`, `bottomLeftButton`, `topRightButton`, and `bottomRightButton`, respectively.

Make sure you create the outlets inside the `MainWindowController` class and *not* inside the `Hour19AppDelegate` class! The assistant editor doesn't always know which class you want to use for creating outlets and connections.

7. Ctrl-drag using the assistant editor to create four actions, one for each button. Call these actions `topLeftClicked:`, `bottomLeftClicked:`, `topRightClicked:`, and `bottomRightClicked:`, respectively.

8. Drag a custom view object from the object library into the middle of the new window.

9. Ctrl-drag using the assistant editor to create an outlet for this new view called `gearView`.

10. Drag an image well into the middle of the custom view you created in step 9.

11. Set the image for the image well to `NSAdvanced`, which should show up as a gear.

12. Add a label below the gear image and set the text to `No Finished Animation`. At this point, your design surface should look something like the one in Figure 19.1.

13. Add the `QuartzCore` framework to your application. To do this, click the project in the project navigator and then under Linked Frameworks and Libraries on the Summary tab, click the plus (+) sign. Locate the `QuartzCore` framework and add it.

14. Add an `#import` statement to the top of `MainWindowController.m` that references `<QuartzCore/QuartzCore.h>`. This import is necessary for doing lower-level Core Animation tasks like transitions. You'll need this if you decide to try to enhance this application when you're done with these steps.

▼

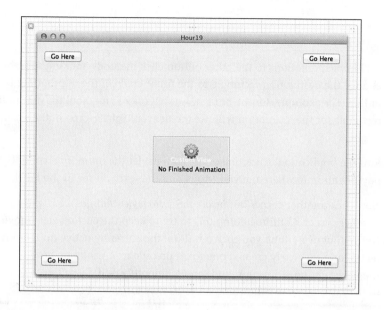

FIGURE 19.1
Creating an animated user interface.

15. We're going to use a shortcut method on the NSAnimationContext class called runAnimationGroup that takes two code blocks as parameters: the code to execute to configure the animations and the code to execute when the animations are completed or cancelled.

> Note that using just the NSAnimationContext, you can't tell the difference between a successfully completed animation and an animation that was cancelled because another animation took precedence. If you need that level of detail, you'll need to create your own CABasicAnimation object and set your controller as the animation object's delegate.

By the Way

Set the implementation of the topLeftClicked: method to the following code:

```
- (IBAction)topLeftClicked:(id)sender {
    [NSAnimationContext runAnimationGroup:^(NSAnimationContext *context) {
        [context setDuration:2.5];
        [context setTimingFunction:
            [CAMediaTimingFunction
functionWithName:kCAMediaTimingFunctionEaseInEaseOut]];
        [[gearView animator]
setFrame:NSMakeRect(topLeftButton.frame.origin.x,

topLeftButton.frame.origin.y,

                                        gearView.frame.size.width,
                                        gearView.frame.size.height)];

    }
```

▼
```
    completionHandler:^{
        messageLabel.stringValue = @"Top Left Finished.";
    }];
}
```

16. Add implementations to the other button click methods, making sure that you change the destination rectangle to the *frame origin* of the appropriate target button. For example, for the `bottomRightClicked:` method, the destination rectangle for the animation will use the `bottomRightButton` outlet's frame origin.

17. Run the application. Click one of the corners, let the animation complete, and pay attention to where the view stops and the text you see in the label.

18. Now click another corner but *before the custom view finishes moving*, click another corner. Continue doing this to try to keep the custom view moving. Notice that every time you click a button, the currently active animation completes, and the newly created one takes precedence. Also note, however, that the object changes direction and targets smoothly and doesn't need to go back to the middle before continuing on to its new target.

▲

If you are enjoying animation programming, experiment with some of the other techniques shown earlier in this hour. For example, try to combine the moving animations done on the custom view with a transition so that while the custom view is moving toward its target, the contents of the view are being swapped with alternate contents. If you get this working, experiment with differing durations so you can see how smoothly Core Animation can handle multiple animations on multiple timelines without any jitter or awkwardness.

Summary

Reactive and interactive user experiences often separate the popular applications from ones that nobody remembers. Users of modern operating systems like iOS and Mac OS X Lion have come to expect that when changes occur in their user interface, those changes will occur visually and in a way that provides meaningful feedback to the user about the purpose of those changes.

In this hour, you learned several techniques to provide animated, rich user interfaces to the users of your applications. You learned about Core Animation layers, the animator proxy, the animation context, and even how to use transition effects to swap between views.

At this point we are starting to explore some of the most powerful aspects of Mac OS X Lion programming; hopefully, you have been getting lots of ideas for ways in which you can incorporate these techniques into your application development.

Q&A

Q. *What happens when you set the value of an animatable property within an animation context?*

A. The new value is used as the target value of that property and the value of the property changes from its current value to the target value over time and according to the easing curve that you've chosen. This allows you to animate everything from color to size to position and rotation.

Q. *What happens when two different animations act on a view at the same time?*

A. The animation system handles this and aggregates the animations acting on a view. This way, if you animate a view toward one corner and then something else makes it go toward another, it won't "rubber band" back to its starting point, it will just drop what it's doing mid-flight and move toward the new target.

Q. *Just because you can animate something, does it mean you should?*

A. Not necessarily. Animations should be used to provide users with meaningful context about things taking place in your application and to draw their eye toward important things. Finally, animations are also used to transition views from one state to another to avoid a jarring experience. Animations shouldn't be used just because they are available. Apple's Human Interface Guidelines can also help in deciding when and how to use animations.

HOUR 20

Consuming Web Services

Modern applications are becoming increasingly intertwined with the Web. Some applications allow you to store files in "the Cloud," other applications pull weather, news, stock quotes, maps, and thousands of other kinds of data from the Web. Whether applications are running on phones, tablets, laptops, or desktops, chances are that many of these applications will be taking advantage of services on the Internet in some way.

In this hour you'll learn about the concept behind web services, what that means to you as an application developer, and how you can increase the power and reach of your application by taking advantage of services on the Web.

Introducing Web Services

The Web originally started as a means by which scientists and researchers could publish interconnected and linked documents, and it has grown into something far more expansive today. Today, people do everything from find babysitters, restaurants, and shopping deals to booking hotels, doing research, and even publishing documents.

Although the Web, as most people know it, might seem like a repository for content, programmers know that it can also be a repository for *data*, or *structured* content. The Web, whether public or within a company's enterprise, provides developers with the means to accomplish many things.

A *web service* is just a name for some discrete unit of work or data that is accessible via web protocols, such as HTTP. Web services are used within and without organizations to allow disparate systems to communicate with each other using standard protocols such as HTTP and standard data representation formats such as XML and SOAP.

Common Web Service Scenarios

Web services can be used to expose business logic and functionality for a nearly infinite number of uses. You might expose a private web service (one that only certain people can access) to allow client applications to query your data. For example, a shipping company might expose web services that allow e-commerce companies (like Amazon.com) to query the in-stock status and shipping time for individual products.

A media company might expose web services that allow people to execute queries against music catalogs, search lyrics, search for actors in movies or TV shows, and much more.

Amazon already exposes web services that allow Amazon partners to query its product catalog. This extends Amazon's reach and provides added value for partner sites.

All of these scenarios expose structured data over the Web using simple HTTP requests. The same transport that transports a video of kittens playing the piano to your computer can also be used to transport raw data, which can then be skinned, repurposed, and retooled in whatever fashion the client application sees fit.

More than just content, the Web is an interconnected collection of *resources*, ready to be tapped by your application. In the next few sections, we'll take a look at the two most common ways in which data and functionality are exposed as web services.

Introducing SOAP Services

SOAP is an acronym that stands for *Simple Object Access Protocol*. SOAP is a structured dialect of XML that was designed specifically to facilitate remote communication with services by transporting object representations and invoking methods.

SOAP comes in two varieties, the *Remote Procedure Call* variety that acts to support remote method invocation over HTTP, and the *document* variety, which acts to facilitate transporting messages (documents that conform to a schema) between endpoints over HTTP.

SOAP services typically expose something called WSDL, or *Web Service Description Language*. This information, again a dialect of XML, provides metadata about the service itself. It contains a list of methods that the service exposes as well as the parameters for those methods. The WSDL for a service can be used by client frameworks to generate client access code.

For example, a shipping company might expose a SOAP service that exposes the following methods:

- ▶ CheckInventory(string SKU)
- ▶ GetShippingTime(string SKU, string zipCode)

These methods allow client applications to query the remaining quantity of a particular SKU and to query the length of time it takes to ship an item to a given ZIP Code.

The developer may not know all of this information ahead of time, and the people exposing the service certainly wouldn't want to make the developer guess as to how to talk to the service.

This is where the WSDL comes in. Using the WSDL document, the developer can create a client *proxy* that can invoke these services. For example, if the developer created an Objective-C proxy, messages might be sent using code that looks like this:

```
int quantityLeft = [stockService checkInventory:@"FRIDGE101"];
int shippingDays = [stockService getShippingTime:@"FRIDGE101" toZip:@"90210"];
```

These objects are local and in-memory, and you can send them messages, but these objects forward those messages out over HTTP, encoding the parameters in SOAP (remember, SOAP is just a special type of XML for describing objects in a platform-neutral manner). These objects perform the grunt work of talking over HTTP, encoding parameters, decoding the response, and giving the calling application back platform-native objects.

Recently the Internet has been buzzing with debate over whether SOAP (and its counterpart, WSDL) is the right way to expose and consume web services. Some argue that it is ideal for exposing services within an organization but that different standards should be used for public, consumer-facing services. The goal of this book isn't to take a stance in this argument, but to let you know that such an argument exists. As you research web services on your own, you are likely to run into varying opinions.

There are many repositories of public web services; one such repository can be found at http://www.service-repository.com.

Introducing RESTful Web Services

Those who argue against the use of SOAP-style services might argue in favor of RESTful services. The acronym REST stands for *Representational State Transfer.* The idea behind REST is that everything on the Web is a *resource.*

What we typically consume in the form of individual web pages are all resources. However, the list of customers that belongs to a customer relations application might belong to a resource called `customers`. The important thing about resources in a REST architecture is that every resource is identifiable with a unique URI. So, the resource for all customers within a sample application might be found at a URL like this:

http://www.mycompany.com/myapp/customers

The *state transfer* part of REST comes in when we request the `customers` resource with the HTTP GET method. When we hit this URL, we are asking for a *representation* of the current state of the customers resource. This representation might be a blob of XML, it might be an HTML page displaying a list of customers—it could be anything.

If we want to query the state of a single customer, we can ask for a representation of the current state of a child resource, such as the following:

http://www.mycompany.com/myapp/customers/45

This will give us a view of a customer with an ID of 45. There's no formal protocol that says this is how things work, but this is an expected behavior within a RESTful architecture.

With an implicit knowledge of how we can interact with public resources, we can easily expose powerful APIs and functionality using nothing more than the simple methods that HTTP already contains, such as GET, PUT, POST, and DELETE.

In a typical RESTful architecture, sending a representation of a resource to a resource URL with the HTTP PUT method will perform an update. An HTTP POST implies object creation, and HTTP DELETE implies object deletion.

There is an elegant simplicity to be found in well-designed RESTful web services. Additionally, the nature of RESTful architectures makes it so that the *shape* of the state representation isn't all that important. Often RESTful web services expose data in multiple formats, including XML, JSON (JavaScript Object Notation), or even in news-feed formats like Atom and RSS.

The simple, easy-to-use nature of RESTful APIs coupled with the flexible state format makes them ideal for exposing services to multiple platforms that can be used by multiple languages, rather than forcing both client and server to agree on a particular version of SOAP.

As with proponents and detractors of SOAP, there are also proponents and detractors of REST. The truth is that ideal situations may exist where each type of service can thrive, and if you find yourself in a situation where you need to decide which type of service to expose, it may be a difficult decision—and one that is certainly beyond the scope of this book.

Making Web Service Calls

Now that we've talked a little bit about the types of things people use web services for, and two of the most common web service architectures, it's time to talk about the technical details involved in communicating with web services.

Using the NSURLConnection and NSURLRequest Classes

Before we talk about how to send and receive structured data with a web service, we need to learn how to do the basics: sending and receiving raw data from the Web. This can be accomplished in a couple of different ways, but we'll cover the use of two classes, NSURLRequest and NSURLConnection, here because these classes are also available to iOS applications.

Using these two classes requires the use of a *delegate*. We've seen bits and pieces of delegates throughout this book, but this is the first time we're going to implement a full suite of delegate methods. A delegate is just an instance of an object that responds to some well-known set of methods. In the case of NSURLConnection, the connection delegate is what receives notifications about data that is downloaded, connection success, and connection failure.

The NSURLConnection request provides an abstraction around the connection between your application and a remote server over HTTP (or HTTPS). The NSURLRequest is used to tell the connection where to go and how to get there, such as the target URL, parameters to be passed in the body of the message, credentials used for authenticated requests, and so on.

The following code (Listing 20.1) shows an example of pulling the HTML from Apple's home page using these two classes. The startAppleDownload: method creates a new request and a new connection, whereas the other methods are delegate methods that will be called by the connection as needed.

LISTING 20.1   Downloading Raw HTML

```
- (void)startAppleDownload
{
    responseData = [NSMutabl-eData data];
    NSURLRequest *request = [NSURLRequest requestWithURL:
                             [NSURL URLWithString:@"http://www.apple.com"]];
    [[NSURLConnection alloc] initWithRequest:request delegate:self];
}
- (void)connectionDidFinishLoading:(NSURLConnection *)connection {
    // Do something with the data...
        NSString *result = [[NSString alloc] initWithData:responseData
encoding:NSUTF8StringEncoding];
}
- (void)connection:(NSURLConnection *)connection
➥didReceiveResponse:(NSURLResponse *)response  {
    [responseData setLength:0];
}

- (void)connection:(NSURLConnection *)connection didReceiveData:(NSData *)data {
    [responseData appendData:data];
}

- (void)connection:(NSURLConnection *)connection didFailWithError:(NSError
➥*)error {
    NSLog(@"Connection failed: %@", error);
}
```

In the preceding code, `responseData` is a member variable that is a pointer to
`NSData`. `NSData` is a class used for representing binary data of unspecified format,
such as the raw bytes downloaded from a website or read from an image file.

Data may come back from the connection in multiple chunks, so each time we get
more data from the remote website, we append it to the `responseData` object using
the `appendData:` method. Another benefit of working with the `NSData` class is that it
comes equipped with all the methods you might expect to need when working with
large chunks of binary data.

If you were to examine the `result` variable, you would see the contents of Apple's
home page as raw HTML. Note that we're not performing actual web browser
actions, so we didn't download any script files or images or anything else.

Consuming RESTful Services

The great thing about RESTful services is that if you know how to download raw
data from a website (like the one in Listing 20.1) then you already know how to
obtain data from a service.

To manipulate data on the service, we change the HTTP method on the request from GET to something else such as PUT, POST, or DELETE. Where and how you format the data for these requests is entirely dependent on which service you're consuming.

If you're working with a simple service, you may be able to make a simple request like the one in Listing 20.1 to obtain structured data. For example, at geonames.org, a web service API allows your application to perform reverse geocoding requests. These requests can convert latitude and longitude, such as the information obtained from a GPS device, into a street address.

Opening a web browser (or your client application) to the following URL will return an XML document that describes the street address closest to the supplied latitude and longitude:

http://api.geonames.org/findNearestAddress?lat=37.451&lng=-122.18&username=demo

The XML returned from this API looks like this:

```
<?xml version="1.0" encoding="UTF-8" standalone="no"?>
<geonames>
<address>
<street>Roble Ave</street>
<mtfcc>S1400</mtfcc>
<streetNumber>651</streetNumber>
<lat>37.45127</lat>
<lng>-122.18032</lng>
<distance>0.04</distance>
<postalcode>94025</postalcode>
<placename>Menlo Park</placename>
<adminCode2>081</adminCode2>
<adminName2>San Mateo</adminName2>
<adminCode1>CA</adminCode1>
<adminName1>California</adminName1>
<countryCode>US</countryCode>
</address>
</geonames>
```

The web is positively overflowing with web services that can give us data on just about anything we're looking for. Netflix has even exposed its data catalog in an industry standard XML "feed" format called OData.

If you point your browser at the following URL:

http://odata.netflix.com/v2/Catalog/Titles

Your browser might recognize the feed format and give you a news-feed type view over the data, as shown in Figure 20.1. Keeping in mind that this feed is XML data that can be easily parsed by your application, we start to realize some of the power at our fingertips when consuming web services.

FIGURE 20.1
Browsing the
Netflix catalog
as a feed.

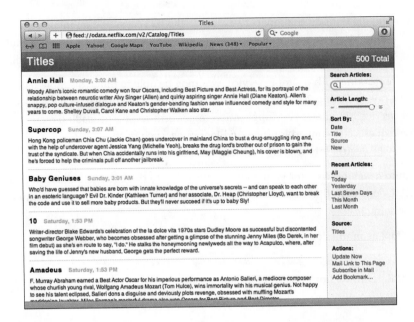

The possibilities for integrating external data with your application via web services are nearly limitless.

Working with JSON Data

In the preceding sample, you saw the data retrieved from the web service formatted as XML. Although XML makes for a great format for cross-platform interchange over the web, there are other ways of representing data.

Once such alternate representation is JSON (JavaScript Object Notation). JSON provides for a tighter, more compact data representation and so can often save on bandwidth costs. However, often more important to developers than saving bandwidth is that JSON is a format naturally understood by JavaScript, which makes it ideal for use in integrating web service data directly into HTML pages with JavaScript.

To see what JSON looks like, you can ask for the same reverse geocoding service data in JSON format using this URL:

http://api.geonames.org/findNearestAddressJSON?lat=37.451&lng=-122.18&username=demo

The JSON produced from the preceding URL looks as follows:

```
{
"address":{
"postalcode":"94025",
"adminCode2":"081",
"adminCode1":"CA",
"street":"Roble Ave",
"countryCode":"US",
"lng":"-122.18032",
"placename":"Menlo Park",
"adminName2":"San Mateo",
"distance":"0.04",
"streetNumber":"651",
"mtfcc":"S1400",
"lat":"37.45127",
"adminName1":"California"}
}
```

Thankfully, Mac OS Lion comes with a class that can convert between JSON strings and Objective-C objects, and back again. This makes it incredibly easy for our applications to pull JSON data off the Internet from web services and convert that data into objects that we can work with in our code.

The key-value pairs that you see in the preceding JSON string are converted into instances of NSDictionary, and repeated elements in collection-type objects are converted into NSArray objects. There is virtually no limit on the number of times dictionaries and arrays can be nested within each other in a JSON-serialized object, other than available memory and processing power.

To convert from a JSON string that we either created ourselves or downloaded from a web service, we can use simple code like this:

```
NSError *error;
NSDictionary *resultDict =
  (NSDictionary *)[NSJSONSerialization JSONObjectWithData:responseData
    options:NSJSONReadingMutableContainers error:&error];
```

In this code, responseData is the NSData* object that we downloaded using the NSURLConnection delegate methods. We can initialize JSON objects with either strings or data objects, whichever happens to be more convenient.

Try It Yourself ▼

Creating a Web Service Consumer

Now that we've had some exposure to web services and learned, specifically how we can communicate with web servers using Objective-C classes, let's put that knowledge to use and create a fully functioning web service consumer application.

▼

This application will make use of a weather service provided by Weather Underground to provide current weather conditions for whatever ZIP Code the user enters.

To create this application, use the following steps:

1. Create a new Cocoa application called **WeatherApp**. This application is not document based, doesn't use Core Data, and *should* use Automatic Reference Counting.

2. Add a new class to the project called **WeatherWindowController**. This class inherits from NSWindowController.

3. Add an object to the MainMenu.xib file that is of type WeatherWindowController.

4. Set the main window's delegate to the newly created WeatherWindowController object.

5. Add a 50×50 image well to the top-left corner of the window.

6. Add a slightly larger, bold label to the right of the image well. Set the placeholder label text to **Some City, ST**.

7. Add an italicized label underneath the preceding label and set the placeholder label to **Current conditions**.

8. Add labels below the image well labeled **Current Temperature:**, **Relative Humidity:**, and **Wind:**, respectively.

9. Add three labels to the right of the ones you created in the previous step. Leave the default Label placeholder text.

10. Add a text field below the labels and set the placeholder text to **Enter ZIP Code.**

11. Add a button to the right of this text field labeled **Query**.

12. I added the Weather Underground image on the bottom right of the form; this step is optional if you don't feel like doing it.

13. Your window, as shown in Interface Builder, should look something like the one shown in Figure 20.2.

14. Create *properties* (not outlets—do not use Interface Builder to create these) in MainWindowController called **currentTemp**, **currentHumidity**, **currentWind**, **currentZipCode**, **currentCity**, **currentIcon**, and **currentWeatherDescription**. These properties are all synthesized and are all of type NSString* except for currentIcon, which is of type NSImage*.

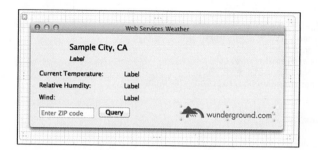

FIGURE 20.2
Designing the weather application.

15. Bind the value of each of the labels on the window to these newly created properties. For example, bind the value of the current city label to the `currentCity` *model path* of the `WeatherWindowController` object.

16. Bind the value of the text field to the `currentZipCode` property.

17. Bind the value of the image cell within the image well to the `currentIcon` property.

18. Set the code of your `WeatherWindowController.m` file to the code shown in Listing 20.2. There's a lot going on in this class, so it may be easier for you to type the code in or copy it from this hour's code downloads.

LISTING 20.2   `WeatherWindowController.m`

```
//
//  WeatherWindowController.m
//  WeatherApp
//
//  Created by Kevin Hoffman on 9/20/11.
//  Copyright (c) 2011 __MyCompanyName__. All rights reserved.
//

#import "WeatherWindowController.h"

#define kApiKey @"—YOU HAVE TO GET YOUR OWN-"

@implementation WeatherWindowController
@synthesize currentTemp, currentWind, currentZipCode,
currentHumidity, currentCity, currentIcon,currentWeatherDescription;


NSMutableData *responseData;

- (id)initWithWindow:(NSWindow *)window
{
    self = [super initWithWindow:window];
    if (self) {
        // Initialization code here.
    }
```

```objc
        return self;
}

- (void)awakeFromNib {
    self.currentCity = @"Nowhere, US";
    self.currentWind = @"";
    self.currentTemp = @"0F";
    self.currentHumidity = @"0%";
    self.currentWeatherDescription = @"Unknown";
}

- (void)windowDidLoad
{
    [super windowDidLoad];
}

- (IBAction)performWeatherLookup:(id)sender {
    NSLog(@"About to perform lookup on zip code %@", currentZipCode);
    responseData = [NSMutableData data];

    NSString *targetUrlString =
    [NSString
     stringWithFormat:
     @"http://api.wunderground.com/api/%@/geolookup/conditions/q/%@.json",
        kApiKey, currentZipCode];
    NSMutableURLRequest *request =
    [NSMutableURLRequest requestWithURL: [NSURL URLWithString:targetUrlString]];


    [request setValue:@"application/json" forHTTPHeaderField:@"Accept"];
    [request setValue:@"application/json" forHTTPHeaderField:@"Content-Type"];
    [request setValue:@"STYOSXLionBookDemo" forHTTPHeaderField:@"User-Agent"];
    //    [request setValue:@"application/json" forKey:@"Content-Type"];
    [[NSURLConnection alloc] initWithRequest:request delegate:self];
}

- (void)connectionDidFinishLoading:(NSURLConnection *)connection {
    NSString *result = [[NSString alloc] initWithData:responseData
encoding:NSUTF8StringEncoding];
    NSError *error;
    NSDictionary *resultDict = (NSDictionary *)
    [NSJSONSerialization
     JSONObjectWithData:responseData options:NSJSONReadingMutableContainers
     error:&error];

    NSLog(@"results: %@", resultDict);
    NSDictionary *current_observation =
      [resultDict objectForKey:@"current_observation"];
    NSDictionary *current_location = [resultDict objectForKey:@"location"];

    // Set values
    self.currentCity = [NSString stringWithFormat:@"%@, %@",
                          (NSString *)[current_location objectForKey:@"city"],
                          (NSString *)[current_location objectForKey:@"state"]];
    NSNumber * tempF = [current_observation objectForKey:@"temp_f"];
    self.currentTemp = [NSString stringWithFormat:@"%@ F", [tempF stringValue]];
```

```
NSString *icon_url =
    (NSString *)[current_observation objectForKey:@"icon_url"];
self.currentIcon =
    [[NSImage alloc] initWithContentsOfURL:[NSURL URLWithString:icon_url]];
self.currentHumidity =
    (NSString *)[current_observation objectForKey:@"relative_humidity"];
self.currentWind =
    (NSString *)[current_observation objectForKey:@"wind_string"];
self.currentWeatherDescription =
    (NSString *)[current_observation objectForKey:@"weather"];
}

- (void)connection:(NSURLConnection *)connection
    didReceiveResponse:(NSURLResponse *)response   {
    [responseData setLength:0];
}

- (void)connection:(NSURLConnection *)connection
didReceiveData:(NSData *)data {
    [responseData appendData:data];
}

- (void)connection:(NSURLConnection *)connection
didFailWithError:(NSError *)error {
    NSLog(@"Connection failed: %@", error);
}
@end
```

19. Now you should be able to build and run the application. When you run the application and supply a valid ZIP Code, it will download the appropriate image for the weather and extract the current weather conditions from the JSON object downloaded from the web service, as shown in Figure 20.3

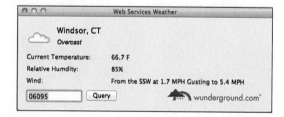

FIGURE 20.3
The completed weather application.

Summary

In this hour you learned about the power that accessing *data* and *information* over the Web, rather than just content, provides our applications. We can pull all kinds of information—data from astronomical charts to geocoding to weather conditions and everything in between. There are unit conversion services, e-commerce services, media and entertainment services, and everything else we can think of.

By giving our applications the capability to consume these services, we can add tremendous value to these applications and provide users with the amazing experience they've come to expect from Mac OS X applications.

Q&A

Q. *What is a RESTful Web Service?*

A. A RESTful Web Service is a piece of functionality exposed as a web service that follows a particular architectural style called REST. These services are lauded for their ease of use, simplicity, and platform-agnostic capabilities.

Q. *What's the difference between REST and SOAP?*

A. REST is all about the exchange of resource representations or messages between resources, in other words, sending raw XML or JSON to a web service. SOAP is more geared toward providing RPC (Remote Procedure Call)-like functionality by encoding method names and arguments into an XML envelope.

Q. *What is JSON?*

A. JSON stands for JavaScript Object Notation and is a compact, efficient way of representing simple data over the wire, especially when talking to web servers via HTTP. This has been gaining popularity for use in building dynamic, interactive websites as well as a preferred format for communicating with Web Services.

HOUR 21

Building Full-Screen Applications

What you'll learn in this hour:

▶ Overview of Full-Screen Applications on Mac OS X Lion
▶ Knowing When Full Screen Is Appropriate
▶ Adding Full-Screen Support to an Application

Mac OS X Lion introduces the ability for applications to provide full-screen, immersive experiences. In this hour, you'll learn about the capabilities of full-screen applications, how to develop applications that use those capabilities, and, more importantly, when it is appropriate to provide full-screen experiences.

Overview of Full-Screen Applications

Full-screen applications in Mac OS X Lion give developers the ability to provide users with an immersive, distraction-free experience. This experience allows your users to focus exclusively on the task at hand within your application and gives you additional screen real estate to further enhance that experience.

In this section, you'll learn about how to enable full-screen window support and how to programmatically control and respond to full-screen events.

Enabling Full-Screen Support in an Application

You can perform a number of steps of increasing complexity that will enable full-screen support in an application. The first step is the easiest; it places the full-screen icon in the top-right corner of your application window and provides the default behavior.

To enable your application's main window for full-screen support, select the window object in Interface Builder, and then on the attributes inspector, choose Primary Window as the option for the Full Screen option.

As soon as you do this, the full-screen toggle icon appears in the top-right corner of the window, as shown in Figure 21.1.

FIGURE 21.1
Enabling a window for full screen.

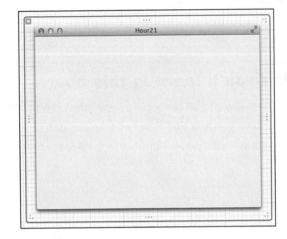

If you create a second window and set its full-screen option to Auxiliary Window and make sure the first window's full-screen support is set to Primary Window, you can create some very interesting effects.

When the primary window's full-screen button is clicked, that window will morph into full-screen mode and the auxiliary window will be carried along with it, sitting on top of the full-screen window. This kind of behavior comes in handy when you want free-floating control panels to be available to the user while the main window is in full-screen mode.

Figure 21.2 shows what this layout looks like in Interface Builder, with the main window having the full-screen icon and the auxiliary window being configured to display as a white-on-black HUD (Heads-Up Display) window.

At any point, your application can query the current presentation options using the following code:

```
NSApplicationPresentationOptions presOptions =
    [[NSApplicationsharedApplication] currentSystemPresentationOptions];

NSLog(@"pres options: %lu", presOptions);
```

Presentation options can be combined and queried using bitwise operators just like many other Cocoa enumerated types.

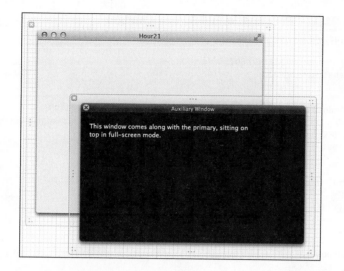

FIGURE 21.2
Displaying a
HUD window on
top of a full-
screen window.

Building Full-Screen Windows

In addition to being able to set the full-screen behavior of a window in Interface
Builder on the design surface, you can control this behavior programmatically.

Assuming you have a controller with outlets pointing at your main and auxiliary
windows, you can write code like this to control the full-screen behavior of the windows:

```
self.window.collectionBehavior =
NSWindowCollectionBehaviorFullScreenPrimary;
self.auxWindow.collectionBehavior =
NSWindowCollectionBehaviorFullScreenAuxiliary;
```

This will accomplish *exactly* the same thing as having chosen the window behaviors
on the design surface. Like the presentation options,
NSWindowCollectionBehaviorXXX enumerations can be combined with bitwise
operators.

If you need to write code that executes when your window transitions to or from full-
screen mode, we can use delegate methods for this that are part of the
NSWindowDelegate protocol.

To see this in action, we can create a window controller the way we have in previous
hours and then provide the code shown in Listing 21.1, which changes the text of a
label based on the full-screen status of the window:

LISTING 21.1   Reacting to Full-Screen Changes

```
- (void)windowWillEnterFullScreen:(NSNotification *)notification
{
    NSLog(@"windowWillEnterFullScreen");
    mainLabel.stringValue = @"before entering full screen";
}

- (void)windowDidEnterFullScreen:(NSNotification *)notification
{
    NSLog(@"windowDidEnterFullScreen");
    mainLabel.stringValue = @"done entering full screen";
}

- (void)windowWillExitFullScreen:(NSNotification *)notification
{
    NSLog(@"windowWillExitFullScreen");
    mainLabel.stringValue = @"before leaving full screen";
}

- (void)windowDidExitFullScreen:(NSNotification *)notification
{
    NSLog(@"windowDidExitFullScreen");
    mainLabel.stringValue = @"done exiting full screen";
}
```

If you run an application with code like this, you can examine the debug log output to see the order in which the methods are invoked when you click the full-screen button and when you exit full-screen mode via the Escape key or via gestures.

There are several other delegate methods that you can implement to control a window's full-screen behavior:

▶ `window:willUseFullScreenContentSize:`—Lets the delegate modify the full-screen content size.

▶ `window:willUseFullScreenPresentationOptions:`—Lets the delegate indicate the presentation options to be used when switching to full-screen mode.

▶ `customWindowsToEnterFullScreenForWindow:`—Lets the delegate provide an array of windows to be used in the animation to transition between regular and full-screen mode.

▶ `window:startCustomAnimationToEnterFullScreenWithDuration:`—Lets the delegate provide a custom animation for transitioning to full-screen mode.

▶ `windowDidFailToEnterFullScreen:`—This method is called when a window fails to transition to full-screen mode for some reason.

▶ `customWindowsToExitFullScreenForWindow:`—Allows the delegate to control the animated transition back to regular mode from full screen.

▶ `window:startCustomAnimationToExitFullScreenWithDuration:`—Allows the delegate to control a custom animation to be used when exiting full-screen mode.

▶ `windowDidFailToExitFullScreen:`—This method is invoked if the window fails to exit full-screen mode.

Finally, if you want to programmatically switch your window in and out of full-screen mode without relying on the default button that appears on windows with the `NSWindowCollectionBehaviorFullScreenPrimary` option, you need to invoke the `toggleFullScreen:` method on the window.

Knowing When Full Screen Is Appropriate

When one of your application windows is enabled to support full-screen mode, it gives the application the ability to provide a rich, immersive, cinematic experience.

Full-screen mode can provide an experience that gives users better access to their data. When the menu bar is hidden and there is no title bar on a window, users don't see anything except your application window. This frees them from distraction and allows them to concentrate exclusively on that one window, which has become a *space*.

Spaces have been available in Mac OS X for some time, but Lion takes them one step further. Every window that becomes a full-screen window is given its own space.

Not all applications, however, should be run in full-screen mode. For example, users are unlikely to need a full-screen calculator, because typically the calculator is used to figure out something *related to another window or application*. When deciding whether you want your application to support full-screen mode, you should ask yourself whether the user might want to read from or input into your window while other windows are present.

A writer's word processor is an ideal candidate for full-screen mode, freeing writers from the distraction of other windows and clutter, allowing them to focus solely on the words in front of them.

Other applications that are ideal for full-screen operation are games, entertainment applications, and multimedia experience applications. Users watching movies, playing games, or interacting with rich visuals can definitely benefit from this new full-screen experience.

▼   **Try It Yourself**

Building a Full-Screen Application

In this section we'll be taking an application that we've already built and upgrading it so that it supports toggling between normal mode and full-screen mode.

Use the following steps to build your own application that supports full-screen mode.

1. Copy the `WeatherApp` application from Hour 20 into a new folder for Hour 21.

2. Select the `MainMenu.xib` file and set the Use Autolayout property to `true`. Accept the subsequent dialog box if one appears, warning you about deployment targets.

3. Make a small adjustment to the position of the image well so that it automatically creates constraints fastening it to the upper-left corner of the window.

4. Adjust the surrounding labels so that they also attach to the image and to the top of the window.

5. Adjust the temperature, humidity, and wind labels so that they attach to the left side of the window and to the bottom of the views above them.

6. To make sure everything is adjusting properly, expand and shrink the window design surface and verify that the image and surrounding labels stay in the upper-left corner of the window.

7. Make the Weather Underground logo stick to the bottom-right corner of the window.

8. Resize the window again to make sure that all the controls are sticking to the appropriate locations.

9. Add a button to the top-right corner (make sure it creates Autolayout constraints there). Label this button **Full Screen**.

10. Create an Action from this button to the `MainWindowController` class and name this method **toggleFullScreen:**.

11. Have the method created in step 10 execute the following code:

    ```
    [self.window toggleFullScreen:sender];
    ```

12. Add the following line of code to the bottom of the awakeFromNib: method:

```
self.window.collectionBehavior =
    NSWindowCollectionBehaviorFullScreenPrimary;
```

▼

13. Now when you run the application and click the Full Screen button, the window will perform an animated transition to full-screen mode. Clicking that same button will switch the window back to normal. Observe how the autolayout constraints control the relative positions of the window's contents.

14. As a challenge if you have extra time this hour—create a second window and second window controller. Make this second window a HUD window that has a collection behavior of `NSWindowCollectionBehaviorAuxiliary`. Move the ZIP Code text field and query button to the HUD window and verify that the application still works as it did before.

Summary

In this hour you learned about one of Mac OS X Lion's striking new features, full-screen applications. You learned how you can rapidly enable support for this feature in your application windows and how to programmatically control and respond to full-screen events. Then you put this knowledge to work by adding full-screen support to the weather application from the previous hour.

With the ability to build full-screen applications under your belt, you are rapidly growing your skill set as a Mac OS X Lion developer.

Q&A

Q. *What is the easiest thing you can do to enable full-screen support in your application?*

A. Simply modify the main window properties in Interface Builder and choose an enabled option for the Full-Screen window behavior.

Q. *What are some of the methods on the NSWindowDelegate protocol that pertain to full-screen windows?*

A. `windowWillEnterFullScreen`, `windowDidEnterFullScreen`, `windowWillExitFullScreen`, `windowDidExitFullScreen`.

HOUR 22

Supporting Drag-and-Drop Behavior

What you'll learn in this hour:

▶ Common Uses for Drag-and-Drop

▶ How to Create Drag-and-Drop Sources and Destinations

▶ Building Your Own Drag-and-Drop Application

We have been able to use our mice to pick things up and drag them around desktops, windows, and other virtual environments for so long now that we take this ability for granted. As we gain more control over our virtual environments with touch screens, track pads, stylus inputs, and more, we become even more accustomed to being able to drag and drop everything from files to web pages to virtual tanks in a video game.

In this hour, we explore the various aspects of drag-and-drop programming on Mac OS X Lion, including when and where it's applicable and how to write code to implement drag and drop in your own application.

Introduction to Drag-and-Drop

Drag and drop is one of those behaviors that users take for granted. If it looks like they can pick up an object in your user interface, users will try to drag it. Users have been trained to do this by years of exposure to mice, window-based operating systems, and more recently, touch screens and trackpads.

In this section you'll learn some of the terminology that Apple uses when it talks about Cocoa's drag-and-drop support and the vocabulary you'll see as you write code to support drag and drop. Additionally, we'll talk about when you should and perhaps should not implement drag and drop.

Learning Drag-and-Drop Terminology

It is important to remember that there are multiple aspects to a drag-and-drop operation; as we start writing code for drag and drop, we need to be clear on the vocabulary used by Cocoa.

The first aspect of drag and drop, and the one that users are most aware of, is the visual aspect. This involves users initiating a drag operation via clicking, holding, and then moving while hovering over a *drag source*. Typically, a small iconographic representation of the operation about to take place is attached to the mouse cursor. This lets users know they are dragging. Finally, when users are done moving the mouse cursor, they "let go" and the item is "dropped" onto a *drag destination*.

All of that is a visual representation of something far more low-level occurring. Underneath the visual representation of the operation, a drag source provides some data to a *pasteboard*. This pasteboard is essentially a clipboard for programs. The *drag destination* can then peel the information off of the pasteboard so that it can determine what is being dropped and *how* the item should be handled. A typical dragged item can be moved, copied, or linked.

To recap, here is the vocabulary we'll need before continuing with the rest of the hour:

- ▶ **Drag Source**—This is something that occupies a portion of the screen (therefore a view or a window) *from which* a drag operation can begin. Sources define the type of operations they support.

- ▶ **Drag Destination**—This is a portion of the screen (again, a view or a window) *to which* something can be dragged. Destinations define the type of objects that can be dragged onto them.

- ▶ **Drag Operation**—A drag operation is the *completion* of the user's intent to move, copy, or link some piece of data from a source to a destination.

- ▶ **Pasteboard**—The pasteboard is a shared piece of memory where drag sources and drag destinations can read and write the data necessary to complete drag-and drop-operations.

Figure 22.1 shows all of the moving parts in a drag operation, using a file copy operation as an example.

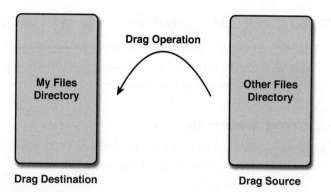

FIGURE 22.1
Anatomy of a drag-and-drop operation.

Common Uses for Drag-and-Drop

As a Mac user, you have no doubt already seen countless examples of drag-and-drop behavior in both the operating system and within applications. You can drag a file from one folder to another, and you can choose whether this operation is a file copy or a file move. If you drag a file from a folder into Xcode, you get an extra dialog that prompts you for how you want to handle that file. When you launch many types of application installers, you drag the application icon into an icon representing your Applications folder. When this drag operation completes, the application installs itself.

In spreadsheet and data-intensive applications, you can drag a row of data up and it will change the order in which that row appears. If you drag it down, it also reorders it. Dragging a single cell in a grid can often allow you to move that cell to the new location. Dragging a block of text in a word processing application like Pages allows you to move that block to wherever your mouse is when you complete the drag operation.

In general, if the task you want a user to perform can be performed easily by giving the user something to click and hold as a representation of a source and then complete the operation by dropping that representation onto a target, the operation is a prime candidate for drag and drop. Most tasks suitable for drag and drop are those that can be categorized as *copy*, *move*, or *link* operations.

Keep in mind that just because you *can* do something doesn't mean you *should*. If users can accomplish something faster and easier with a button press or a gesture, you shouldn't force users to drag anything.

> The smaller your drag source and drag destinations are, the easier it is to frustrate your users with "drag misses." Keep this in mind when designing your drag-and-drop applications.

Did You Know?

Programming Drag-and-Drop Behavior

In this section, we'll cover the details of how you can create custom views that can act as drag sources and drag destinations. In addition, you'll learn how to use dragging sessions, pasteboards, drag items, and more.

Creating Drag Sources

Creating a dragging source involves creating a class that derives from NSView or NSWindow that implements the formal protocol NSDraggingSource.

> Beware when sifting through documentation and blog posts about drag and drop. As of Mac OS X 10.7, Apple has deprecated many methods. Make sure you check the latest documentation for the NSDraggingSource protocol to compare against any tutorials you find online.

The NSDraggingSource protocol includes the following delegate methods. There are others, but these are the ones most pertinent:

- ▶ **draggingSession:sourceOperationMaskForDraggingContext:**—This is a required method that gives your code the ability to provide the allowable NSDragOperation.

- ▶ **draggingSession:endedAtPoint:operation:**—This method is called on a dragging source when a session completes.

- ▶ **draggingSession:movedToPoint:**—While a drag session is active, this method is called every time the mouse cursor moves.

- ▶ **draggingSession:willBeginAtPoint:**—This method is called just before a dragging session is about to begin, giving your code the opportunity to perform any setup before the drag session begins.

Your code is responsible for starting the dragging session after it detects the user's intent to drag, typically in response to a mouseDragged: event.

When initiating the drag session, your drag source is responsible for putting whatever relevant data is necessary onto the shared pasteboard that will be used by the drag destination when the drag session completes.

The code in Listing 22.1 is a sample NSView subclass that implements the NSDraggingSource protocol.

LISTING 22.1   A Dragging Source

```
#import "DragSourceView.h"
#import "STYAppDelegate.h"

@implementation DragSourceView

- (id)initWithFrame:(NSRect)frame
{
    self = [superinitWithFrame:frame];
    if (self) {
        // Initialization code here.
    }

    returnself;
}

- (void)drawRect:(NSRect)dirtyRect
{
    // Drawing code here.
}

- (NSDragOperation)draggingSession:(NSDraggingSession *)session
          sourceOperationMaskForDraggingContext:(NSDraggingContext)context
{
    NSLog(@"draggingSession:sourceOperationMaskForDraggingContext");
    returnNSDragOperationMove ¦ NSDragOperationCopy;
}

- (void)draggingSession:(NSDraggingSession *)session
movedToPoint:(NSPoint)screenPoint
{
    NSLog(@"draggingSession:movedToPoint: %@", screenPoint);
}

- (void)mouseDragged:(NSEvent *)theEvent
{
    NSString *customData = @"this is custom data";

    NSPasteboardItem *pbItem = [[NSPasteboardItemalloc] init];
    [pbItem setData:[customData dataUsingEncoding:NSUTF8StringEncoding]
forType:kMyDragType];
    NSDraggingItem *item =
    [[NSDraggingItemalloc] initWithPasteboardWriter:pbItem];
    [item setDraggingFrame:
        NSMakeRect(10, 10, self.bounds.size.width-20,
        self.bounds.size.height-20)
        contents:[NSImageimageNamed:@"paperball.jpg"]];

    NSArray *dragItems = [NSArrayarrayWithObject:item];

    [selfbeginDraggingSessionWithItems:dragItems event:theEvent source:self];
}
```

Here is the header file for this same class. Note that unlike other scenarios where we implicitly implemented protocols, this time the implementation of the protocol is explicit and declared in the header file:

```
#import <Cocoa/Cocoa.h>

@interface DragSourceView : NSView<NSDraggingSource>

@end
```

When a `mouseDragged:` event occurs on the view, we create a string that we're going to store in the pasteboard (`customData`). Next, we create a pasteboard item and set its data to the custom string. The constant `kMyDragType` uniquely identifies data that came from this particular drag source. This is just a UTI string like `com.stylion.dragtype.garbage` or something similar. As you'll see in the next section, drag destinations *register* for these types so that they act as live drag destinations only when the data on the pasteboard comes from a registered source. This prevents our drag destinations from accepting data from unknown source types.

Next, we set the dragging frame and contents of the dragging item to be slightly smaller than the original view and to contain an image called `paperball.jpg`, which is a crumpled up piece of paper.

The actual dragging session is initiated by the call to the `NSView` method `beginDraggingSssionWithItems:event:source:`.

With a dragging source capable of initiating dragging sessions, we're ready to create a dragging destination.

Creating Drag Destinations

Dragging destinations work very much like dragging sources. To create a dragging destination, create a subclass of `NSView` or `NSWindow` and implement the `NSDraggingDestination` protocol.

This protocol includes the following delegate methods:

▶ **draggingEntered**—This method is called when a dragging item enters the bounds of the dragging destination. Implementing this method gives you a chance to change the appearance of your drag destination before the session completes.

▶ **wantsPeriodicDraggingUpdates**—Indicates whether the destination wants to be sent `draggingUpdated:` messages each time the dragging item moves within the destination's bounds.

▶ **draggingUpdated**—Called when a dragging item is updated while it is within the destination's boundaries.

▶ **draggingEnded**—Called when the dragging operation finishes *within another destination*. This method is *not* what you use when the user finishes a drop within your view.

▶ **draggingExited**—Called when the dragging item exits the destination's boundaries while still being dragged.

▶ **performDragOperation**—Called when the user drops the dragging item within your destination's boundaries. If your destination accepts the data, return YES; otherwise, return NO.

The code in Listing 22.2 shows a custom drag destination. This destination contains an image well where the image is bound to an outlet on the application delegate.

> A better practice would have been to bind the image to a window controller, but the goal was to keep this sample as small as possible.

By the Way

LISTING 22.2 A Custom Drag Destination

```
#import "DragDestinationView.h"
#import "STYAppDelegate.h"

@implementation DragDestinationView

- (id)initWithFrame:(NSRect)frame
{
    self = [superinitWithFrame:frame];
    if (self) {
        // Initialization code here.
    }

    returnself;
}

- (void)drawRect:(NSRect)dirtyRect
{
    // Drawing code here.
}

- (void)awakeFromNib
{
    NSLog(@"Registering for drag types...");
    [selfregisterForDraggedTypes:[NSArrayarrayWithObject:kMyDragType]];
}

-(NSDragOperation)draggingEntered:(id<NSDraggingInfo>)sender
```

```
{
    NSLog(@"dragging entered (destination)");
    NSPasteboard *pb;
    NSDragOperation sourceDragMask;

        sourceDragMask = [sender draggingSourceOperationMask];
        pb = [sender draggingPasteboard];


    STYAppDelegate *appDelegate =
    (STYAppDelegate *)[[NSApplicationsharedApplication] delegate];
    appDelegate.trashCanImage.image = [NSImageimageNamed:@"fullcan.png"];

    returnNSDragOperationCopy ¦ NSDragOperationMove;
}
- (void)draggingExited:(id<NSDraggingInfo>)sender
{
    STYAppDelegate *appDelegate =
    (STYAppDelegate *)[[NSApplicationsharedApplication] delegate];
    appDelegate.trashCanImage.image = [NSImageimageNamed:@"emptycan.png"];
}
- (BOOL)performDragOperation:(id<NSDraggingInfo>)sender
{
    STYAppDelegate *appDelegate =
    (STYAppDelegate *)[[NSApplicationsharedApplication] delegate];
        appDelegate.trashCanImage.image = [NSImageimageNamed:@"emptycan.png"];
        NSPasteboard *pb;
    NSDragOperation sourceDragMask;

        sourceDragMask = [sender draggingSourceOperationMask];
        pb = [sender draggingPasteboard];

    NSData *pbData = [pb dataForType:kMyDragType];
    NSString *customData = [[NSStringalloc] initWithData:pbData
    encoding:NSUTF8StringEncoding];
    NSLog(@"received a drag operation: %@", customData);

    returnYES;
}
```

The first thing this drag destination does is register for pasteboard data types. In this case, it is the same data type that the source uses when filling the pasteboard with data, kMyDragType, which is a #define'd string with a value of com.stylion. hour24.dragtype.

After the destination has registered for pasteboard types, it is active and ready to be used as a drop target, and it will receive NSDraggingDestination protocol messages.

The draggingEntered: method changes the image inside the dragging destination view to an open trash can. When the draggingExited: method is called, the image is changed to a closed trash can.

Finally, the `performDragOperation:` method pulls the data out of the dragging pasteboard and then changes the image to a closed trash can. This creates a nice effect where the dragging destination view changes its appearance as you move potential dragging items in and out of its bounds.

Try It Yourself ▼

Building a Drag-and-Drop Application

So far in this hour you've seen all the code necessary to build dragging sources and destinations. In this next section, we'll put that code to good use by creating the "trash can" sample. In this sample, we'll have a large drag destination view that contains an image of a trash can. To the right of this view, we will have three drag source views, each containing an image of a crumpled up piece of paper. In the application, we will be able to drag crumpled pieces of paper and drop them into the trash can.

Use the following steps to create this application:

1. Create a new Cocoa application. This application is not document based, does not use Core Data, but does use Automatic Reference Counting. Call the application **Hour22**.

2. In the main window in `MainMenu.xib`, drag a custom view object and resize it to fill most of the left side of the window.

3. Drag three more custom view objects onto the window and spread them out evenly, arranged vertically, to the right of the view from step 2.

4. Add a class to the application that derives from `NSView`. Name this class **DragSourceView**.

5. Using the identity inspector, change the custom class of each of the smaller custom view objects to `DragSourceView`.

6. Add a class to the application that derives from `NSView`. Name this class **DragDestinationView**.

7. Using the identity inspector, change the custom class of the larger custom view to `DragDestinationView`.

8. Find an image of a crumpled piece of paper (or use the one from the code download for the book) and add corresponding image wells as subviews to each of the `DragSourceView` objects. Figure 22.2 shows a sample of what your design surface might look like at this point.

▼

FIGURE 22.2
Laying out custom drag sources and destinations.

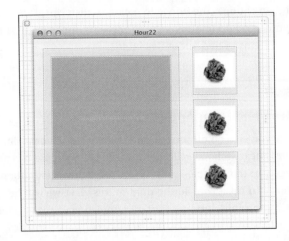

9. Add a property called `trashCanImage` to your application delegate. For this sample, I called the application delegate class `STYAppDelegate`.

10. The image should have a default value, so in `STYAppDelegate.m`, add the following line to the `applicationDidFinishLaunching:` method (feel free to find your own trash can image or use the one supplied with the book's sample code):

    ```
    self.trashCanImage.image = [NSImageimageNamed:@"emptycan.png"];
    ```

11. Add an image well as a subview to the `DragDestinationView` object.

12. Bind the value of this image well to the application delegate's `trashcanImage` property (again, in a real-world application you would probably be using separate window controllers).

13. Modify the `DragSourceView.h` file to indicate that the class implements the `NSDraggingSource` protocol (hint: the code for accomplishing this is shown earlier in the hour).

14. Modify the `DragSourceView.m` file so that it contains a `mouseDragged:` event handler. In this event handler, it should create some custom data, add that data to a pasteboard item, add that to a dragging item, and then call the `beginDraggingSessionWithItems:event:source:` method on the view.

15. Implement the `draggingSession:sourceOperationMaskForDragging Context:` method in the `DragSourceView` class.

16. Implement the `draggingSession:movedToPoint:` method in the `DragSourceView` class so that you use the `NSLog()` method to report the coordinates of moving drag items within a session.

17. Modify `DragDestinationView.h` so that it explicitly implements the
    `NSDraggingDestination` protocol.

    ▼

18. Create an `awakeFromNib:` method in `DragDestinationView` that registers for
    your drag type.

19. Implement the `draggingEntered:` method that changes the trash can image
    to `fullcan.jpg` and returns `NSDragOperationCopy | NSDragOperationMove`.

20. Implement the `draggingExited:` method that changes the trash can image
    back to `emptycan.jpg`.

21. Implement the `performDragOperation:` method. This method should pull the
    custom data from the pasteboard and log it using `NSLog()` and then change
    the current trash can image to `emptycan.jpg`.

    ▲

When you compile and run the application, you might see something that looks like
Figure 22.3, which depicts a drag operation in progress.

FIGURE 22.3
A drag session
in progress.

> This excellent trash can picture and the cute creature contained within was
> designed by Gert Jan Lodder, who can be found at http://www.gertjanlodder.com.

By the Way

Make sure you play around with this application. Watch the console log as you
move the mouse and drag items around. Let items drop outside your destination
bounds to see them smoothly slide back to their source.

This is just the tip of the iceberg—the number and type of compelling experiences
that you can create with simple drag-and-drop programming is nearly infinite.

Summary

In this hour you learned about the power and usefulness of the drag-and-drop concept. You learned how to harness this power by creating custom views that support dragging sessions, dragging sources, and dragging destinations. You put that knowledge to use by creating an application that simulates dragging items into a trash bin and implementing the drag-and-drop protocols.

Drag-and-drop is another tool in your toolbelt, giving you yet another operation to take what might otherwise be a bland application and make it more powerful and compelling.

Q&A

Q. *What are the three main components of drag & drop that a developer needs to be concerned with?*

A. The drag source, the drag destination, and the drag operation representing the act of dragging from the source to the destination.

Q. *How does a dragging source inform a dragging target about what is being dragged?*

A. This is done through the use of a Pasteboard. Pasteboards are blocks of memory that can contain arbitrary data. The drag destination looks up the Pasteboard that was used during the drag operation and can then extract all of the meaningful data.

HOUR 23

Building Apps for the Mac App Store

What you'll learn in this hour:

▶ Guidelines for Building Apps for the App Store
▶ How to Prepare your App for the Store
▶ Submitting Your Application to the Store

Throughout this book you have been learning how to build Cocoa applications for Mac OS X Lion. Now all those skills become essential as you reach the point where your application is ready to be sold in the Mac App Store.

In this hour, you'll learn the necessary prerequisites for participating in the Mac App Store. We'll cover everything from getting set up with iTunes Connect to using developer certificates, code signing, and the store submission process itself.

Getting Started with iTunes Connect

iTunes Connect is a web application that you use as your administration console and profile center for managing all your iOS and Mac applications. When you have completed your application and you're happy that it has been tested thoroughly and works properly, you will go through iTunes Connect to submit your application.

In addition to submitting applications, you can also use iTunes Connect to review your application sales trends, update contracts and tax information, download financial statements and reports, and manage additional users for iTunes Connect and In-App Purchase.

Developers who have submitted applications to the iOS or Mac App Store become very familiar with this application.

Creating an iTunes Connect Account

To get to iTunes Connect, first log in to the AppleDeveloperMemberCenter at http:/ /developer.apple.com/membercenter. The member center is a dashboard that provides links to the various developer centers (Mac, iOS, and Safari), the Developer Certificate Utility (which we'll discuss next), the iOS Provisioning Portal for mobile applications, and of course, iTunes Connect.

Click the iTunes Connect link from the MemberCenter to go there. The first time you go you will be asked to associate your Apple ID with an iTunes Connect account. Follow all the prompts and provide all the information accurately.

Be very careful when supplying personal and financial information to iTunes Connect. It is notoriously difficult to go back to change this information later, so double-check everything before you submit each form.

iTunes Connect is used to manage all your contracts. To charge money for applications in either the Mac or iOS App Store, you will need to enter into contracts with Apple. Again, the information on these contracts is difficult to change, so be careful when supplying this information.

Now that you have an iTunes Connect account, you can proceed with the rest of the steps in this hour.

Using the Certificate Utility

As you will see in the next section, applications bound for the Mac App Store must be digitally signed. It might seem like an inconvenience the first few times you go through the process, but it is definitely worth the effort. Signing your code prevents someone else from submitting code to Apple and pretending to be you. This keeps people from being able to submit bogus applications on your behalf.

This security carries forward to the App Store. Users of the App Store can be sure that all of the applications contained within have passed certain quality measures and, more importantly, are the expected applications developed by the expected vendors.

The first step in the certificate utility is creating an App ID. App IDs are identifiers in the reverse domain name format that uniquely identify your application. This unique identifier is the *bundle identifier* for the application you build in Xcode.

Figure 23.1 shows the App ID screen in the developer certificate utility.

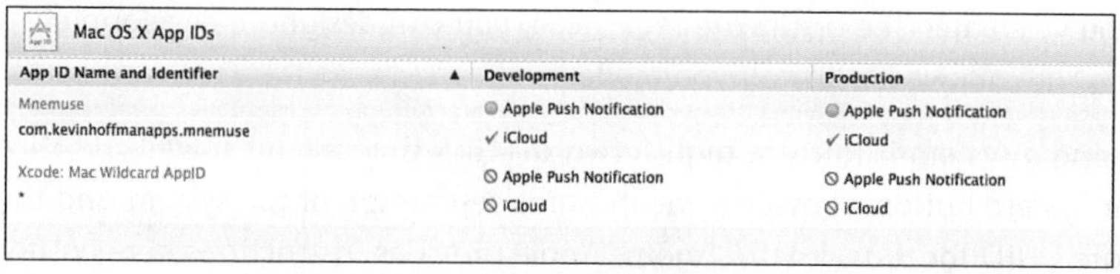

FIGURE 23.1
Viewing App IDs
in the developer
certificate utility.

You can get to the developer certificate utility by logging in to the MacDeveloperCenter and clicking the link on the right side for the certificate utility. You can also reach this utility from a few other places scattered throughout the MacDeveloperCenter.

After you have an App ID, you can move on to creating certificates. The process of creating a certificate involves the following steps:

1. Create a certificate request using Keychain Access on your computer. Don't worry—the certificate utility does a great job of showing you exactly how to create this request.

2. The certificate request contains a newly generated *private key* to which *only you* have access. You then upload this certificate request to the website and Apple will use that request to generate a certificate. Figure 23.2 shows the Create Certificate screen, where you need to choose which type of certificate you'll be creating. At a bare minimum, you must create a development certificate.

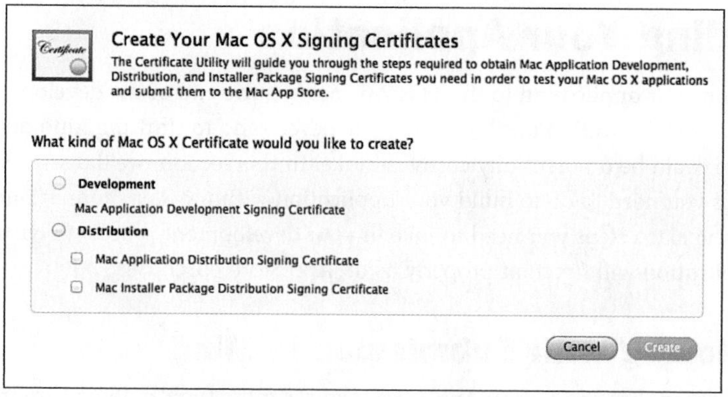

FIGURE 23.2
Creating a
certificate.

3. After the certificate has been created, you must download and install this certificate. You install the certificate into your *login* keychain by double-clicking the file you download.

After you've created the certificates you need, you can designate development systems that are allowed to install your code.

Registering a system is fairly straightforward—click the Systems folder and click the Register System button. Provide a meaningful description of the system and the hardware UUID for that system. Again, Apple provides instructions here on how to find the UUID.

Next, we move to *provisioning profiles*. You can think of a provisioning profile as a statement of permission that says the following:

*For a given **app id**, code signed with a **given certificate** can run on the indicated **systems**.*

The key thing to remember is that a provisioning profile can reference only *one* App ID. When you install a provisioning profile on your Mac, you are telling the App Store and code-signing infrastructure that your Mac has permission to install and execute code signed with that certificate *for that one App ID* and *only on your Mac*.

Building Your Application

Submitting your application to the Mac App Store is the end of the development process. However, waiting until you are done developing to start thinking about the App Store could be a potentially costly mistake. In this section, we'll discuss some of the things you need to do to build your application with the App Store in mind and some of the extra steps you need to take in your development process to ensure that your application will function properly as an App Store purchase.

Developing with Submission in Mind

Building an application for the App Store involves more than making sure that the application does what you expect. Apple enforces quite a few guidelines on applications to ensure that applications in the store meet or exceed Apple's high standards for quality.

Some of these requirements may seem like common sense, but others can be tricky; it's better that you know about these requirements before you start building your application. The last thing anyone wants is for you to spend your valuable time (and possibly money) on a project only to find out after you've finished that it violates Apple's guidelines and won't be accepted.

The *Mac App Store Review Guidelines* provide explicit detail with regard to what your application can and cannot do. If your application violates any of the guidelines in this document, it is likely that Apple will reject your application.

The current guidelines can be found at http://developer.apple.com/appstore/mac/resources/approval/guidelines.html.

The guidelines fall into the following categories:

- ▶ **Functionality**—Specific things that your application should or should not do.

- ▶ **Metadata**—Guidelines for properly describing and annotating your application and its content.

- ▶ **Location**—Guidelines for how your application must handle location services, where applicable.

- ▶ **Trademarks and Trade Dress**—Guidelines for dealing with intellectual property, trademarks, and so on.

- ▶ **User Interface**—Guidelines for your user interface, including one of the most important UI rules regarding following the *Apple Human Interface Guidelines*.

- ▶ **Purchasing and Currencies**—Guidelines for dealing with in-app purchases, subscription content, and particularly hairy issues about using your application to sell things that exist outside the application.

- ▶ **Scraping and Aggregation**—Guidelines regarding the consumption and repurposing of external and third-party content.

- ▶ **Damage to Products**—Guidelines indicating that your application cannot encourage users to damage other products and, more importantly, your application cannot do things that rapidly consume battery life or generate excessive heat.

- ▶ **Personal Attacks**—Guidelines restricting defamatory, offensive, or otherwise inflammatory content in applications.

- ▶ **Violence**—Guidelines prohibiting the encouragement of violent acts within an application, among other things.

- ▶ **Objectionable Content**—Guidelines prohibiting objectionable content. The guidelines here do not explicitly define "objectionable," so be sure you do your homework on what constitutes objectionable before building such an application.

▶ **Privacy**—Very important guidelines regarding what you can and cannot do with protected or otherwise private user information.

▶ **Pornography**—Pornographic applications (using Webster's dictionary definition of pornography) will be rejected.

▶ **Religion, Culture, Ethnicity**—Guidelines concerning defamatory, prejudicial, other otherwise mean-spirited content targeted at specific races, cultures, religions, and so on.

▶ **Contents and Lotteries**—Guidelines concerning the facilitation of contests and lotteries within your application.

▶ **Charitable Contributions**—Guidelines concerning charitable contributions facilitated with applications.

▶ **Legal Requirements**—Guidelines concerning doing or encouraging illegal activities with your application.

▶ **Push Notifications**—Guidelines concerning how your application deals with or participates in push notifications.

It might seem like a daunting list of review requirements, but it is well worth reading (and then rereading!) early in your application design process. As mentioned earlier, the last thing anyone wants is to get all the way through the development process of an application only to find out that you've violated one or more of the review guidelines.

The upside is that, with a few exceptions, if your application complies with Apple's review guidelines for Mac OS X applications, there's a good chance that the same application will also comply with the requirements for iOS, Android, Windows, and Windows Phone 7 marketplaces, giving you a good potential audience for porting your application to other platforms.

Following the Human Interface Guidelines

One of the quickest ways to ensure that your application will *not* get accepted into the Mac App Store is to disregard the *Human Interface Guidelines*. You can find these guidelines at http://developer.apple.com/library/mac/#documentation/UserExperience/Conceptual/AppleHIGuidelines/Intro/Intro.html.

To read through the HIG from start to finish will take you several hours, and you will probably find yourself using that document as a reference many times throughout the development of your application. These guidelines are especially useful if you have not been a Mac OS X user for a long time. Native Mac uses take for granted many styles and conventions that might not be immediately obvious to developers new to the platform.

All told, this is a 276 page document, so you'll need to allocate quite a bit of time to get through the document from start to finish. To read it quickly, I suggest starting with the section titled "Philosophy of UI Design: Fundamental Principles," and from there read the section titled "User Experience Guidelines."

Fortunately, many of the guidelines revolve around some of the things that we've been building throughout this book. Again, you might think that reading a 276 page book before submitting your application is an inordinate amount of work, but it is well worth it, and much of the document is a quick, easy read.

Validating Receipts

Developing applications that you intend to sell in the App Store is, for the most part, just like developing any other Mac OS X application. However, we need to do a few extra things and write some extra code to be good citizens within the App Store.

One such task is *validating receipts*. When a user buys your application from the App Store, a cryptographically signed receipt is placed in the application's bundle. Mac OS X will not validate this receipt for you. It is up to you to write code that verifies that your application was purchased legitimately from the App Store. If you do not do this, someone can buy your application, duplicate the installer package, and share it on file-sharing sites. Without receipt validation in place, this pirated installer package can potentially be used on anyone's computer, whether they bought your application or not.

Apple has documentation on how to validate these receipts to make sure that your application exits appropriately with the right error code when it is launched without a valid receipt. You can find this documentation at

https://developer.apple.com/library/mac/#releasenotes/General/ ValidateAppStoreReceipt/_index.html

Unfortunately, these receipts are not stored in a file format that is readily accessible to developers. It is stored in a file format called ASN.1. There is a code-generation tool available called asn1c that will build data type declarations and C functions for decoding the ASN.1 payload containing the receipt.

You can get this tool from MacPort or from SourceForge, or if you have HomeBrew installed, you can type the following at a Terminal prompt:

```
brew install asn1c
```

There isn't enough time in this hour to go into the details of writing code to validate receipts. Stack Overflow, Google, and the Apple Developer Forums all have several examples of how to accomplish this.

> Homebrew can be found at http://mxcl.github.com/homebrew. If you log in to the Apple Developer Forums, you can search for "validating receipts" to pull up a wealth of information (and frustration) on this topic.

As tedious as it may sound, skipping the step of validating receipts could literally cost you a lot of money, because an application without receipt validation is easily pirated.

Further, as you'll see in the next hour, if you plan to support In-App purchases, you will have to write code that validates receipts for those purchases as well, making receipt validation a necessary evil of writing robust, commercial-ready applications for the Mac App Store.

Preparing Your Application for Submission

When you're satisfied that your application conforms to the *Human Interface Guidelines* and it doesn't violate any of the application review guidelines, you'll need to prepare your application for submission.

Gathering Assets and Information

When you submit your application to the Mac App Store, you need to provide enough information about the application so that your potential users can find the application and so that Apple can properly display, categorize, and surface the application in search results.

The information you need to have *before* you submit the application includes the following:

▶ **Application Name.**

▶ **Application Description.**

▶ **Primary, Secondary, and Subcategories**—Spend some time sifting through the categories in the App Store to make sure you find the right place for your application. Properly categorizing your application is crucial to your users finding it in the store.

▶ **Copyright.**

▶ **Application Rating**—You need to determine the type of content contained within your application and choose an appropriate ESRB rating for it.

▶ **SKU Number**—This number is meaningful only to you or your organization. This SKU is what appears on financial and tax reports and should be unique to your application.

▶ **Keywords**.

▶ **Application URL**—The Internet URL of the application's home page.

▶ **Screenshots**.

▶ **Support URL**—URL of a web page the users of your application can use for information on how to obtain support. Remember that Apple is not responsible for support of your application, only for the plumbing that makes the App Store work.

▶ **Support Email Address**—The email address that your users can use to contact you or your organization for support with the application.

▶ **End User License Agreement**—If there is a license agreement that users must accept upon purchase/use of your application, you'll need that before submission.

▶ **Pricing**—Although you can't simply type random numbers when choosing a price for your application, a large number of pricing tiers are available, and you should give some thought to the price before submitting the application.

▶ **Availability Date and Location**—You'll need to choose when the application is available and whether there are any restrictions on its geographic availability.

Although you might be able to go back to edit this information after your application has already been created, take the time to ensure that everything is *exactly* as you want it to appear in the store before finalizing this metadata.

Assigning Keywords

Assigning keywords for your application is crucial for enabling your application to appear in search results. The iOS App Store has more than 300,000 applications in it, and the Mac App Store is rapidly growing, as well. Making sure your application is easy to find for your target audience is crucial.

As a result, you should put some time and extra thought into which keywords you want to use for your application. You are prompted for a set of keywords when the application is initially submitted, and you can change those keywords after the application has been submitted.

Apple has a document available to give you some guidance with regard to choosing application keywords. You can find this document at http://developer.apple.com/ news/pdf/ASQR_Assigning_Keywords.pdf.

Signing Your Code

Apple needs to know that application submissions come only from those developers authorized to submit applications. As a result, you need to sign your code with a certificate that was issued to you by Apple using the process mentioned earlier in this hour.

To sign your code, open your project in Xcode, select the target in the project navigator, and then click the Build Settings tab. There is a Code Signing group (you can either scroll down to this group or search for it in the search box). Click the drop-down list next to the Code Signing Identity and choose a developer certificate to sign your code with, as shown in Figure 23.3.

FIGURE 23.3
Choosing a
Code-Signing
Identity.

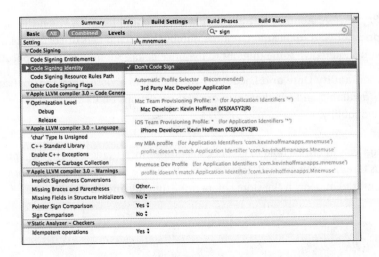

Make sure that you can build the application after having chosen the signing identity. Contained within that signing identity is a *private key* to which only you have access (however, you can use the Xcode organizer to export/import developer identities in case you work on more than one machine). If that private key is not on your machine at the time you build the application with the signing identity, the application will fail to build. You *will not* be able to submit an application to the App Store if you have not first been able to build it with a proper signing identity.

Submitting Your Application

You've written your application, you've tested it, your friends and co-workers have tested it, and you've double and triple-checked that your application doesn't violate any of the review guidelines and adheres to the *Human Interface Guidelines*. Now you're ready to submit your application.

Before you can submit the compiled bundle for your application, you need to go to iTunes Connect and use the website to create an application definition.

At any time, you can go directly to iTunes Connect using the URL http://itunesconnect.apple.com. This way, you don't have to hunt around for links to iTunes Connect from wherever you are in the developer centers.

Did You Know?

Click the Add New App button and you are prompted for which type of application you want to create, as shown in Figure 23.4.

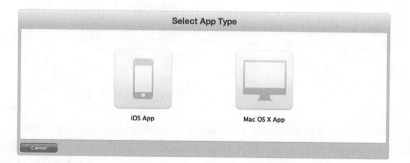

FIGURE 23.4
Choosing which type of application to create.

After selecting the type of application you plan to create (since this book is about Mac OS X Lion, you should be choosing Mac OS X App), you will be asked for the most basic information about your application, as shown in Figure 23.5.

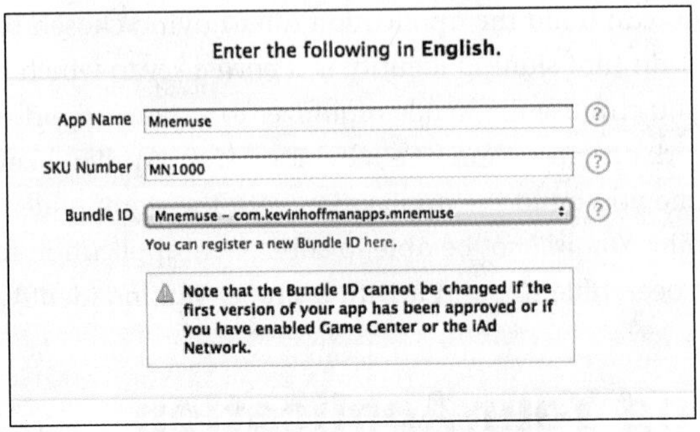

FIGURE 23.5
Supplying an App
Name, Bundle
ID, and SKU.

FIGURE 23.5
Supplying an App
Name, Bundle
ID, and SKU.

Next you will be prompted for your application metadata, including the application description, keywords, URLs, copyright information, contact information, support information, and the like. Figure 23.6 shows the screen prompting for application metadata.

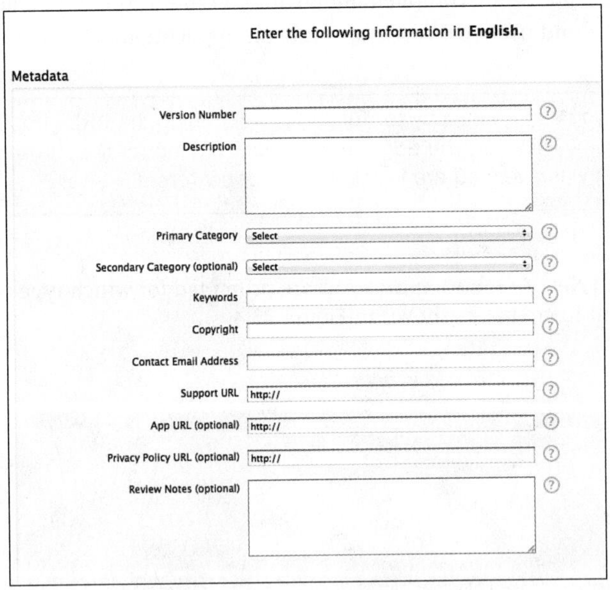

FIGURE 23.6
Supplying
application
metadata.

As mentioned earlier in this hour, you need to provide information about the type of content your application either contains or to which it facilitates access. You might be tempted to give this section very little consideration, but you need to make sure you rate your application accurately. For instance, if your application gives users the ability to access arbitrary Internet content, you cannot select young audience ratings because the *possibility exists* that mature content can be delivered through your application. Figure 23.7 shows the screen where you can supply the ratings for different content available in your application.

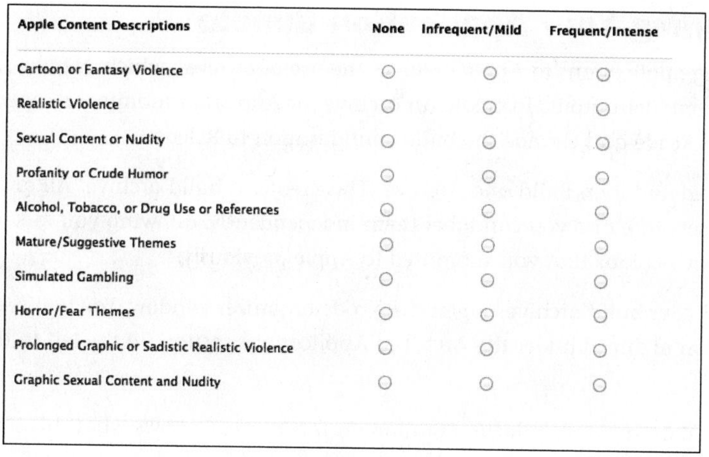

Apple Content Descriptions	None	Infrequent/Mild	Frequent/Intense
Cartoon or Fantasy Violence	○	○	○
Realistic Violence	○	○	○
Sexual Content or Nudity	○	○	○
Profanity or Crude Humor	○	○	○
Alcohol, Tobacco, or Drug Use or References	○	○	○
Mature/Suggestive Themes	○	○	○
Simulated Gambling	○	○	○
Horror/Fear Themes	○	○	○
Prolonged Graphic or Sadistic Realistic Violence	○	○	○
Graphic Sexual Content and Nudity	○	○	○

FIGURE 23.7
Rating your application content.

When you have finished defining your application on iTunes Connect, you can use a couple of different methods for uploading your application binary to Apple. The easiest, and the one we'll cover in this hour, is using Xcode.

Testing the Installation Process

Before you upload your application to the store, you need to know that it will install properly and work as designed when running as a sandboxed application that someone purchased from the store. Just running your application in Debug mode within Xcode doesn't give you enough certainty that your application will work as a purchased application.

To test the installation process, you'll need to do a little extra work. Execute the following from a Terminal window to install your application:

```
sudo installer -store -pkg path-to-package -target /
```

The tricky part here is the path to your application package. This is often a very difficult-to-locate path. The easiest way to find it is to right- (or Ctrl-) click the .app product in your project navigator and select Show in Finder. For testing, you can then copy this file to an easier-to-use location.

The installer tool will install your application in the /Applications directory just like an application that was purchased and downloaded from the Mac App Store. If your application works properly and doesn't have any security issues or bugs when running as a store-bought app, you can move on to uploading it to iTunes Connect.

Uploading Your Application Bundle

Uploading applications to Apple involves the use of *archives*, which are like snap-shots of compiler output. To create an archive for App Store submission, open your project in Xcode and change the build configuration to Release.

Select Build and then Build and Archive. This creates a build archive. All archives are kept separate and you can label them independently, allowing you to keep track of different versions that you submitted to Apple previously.

To see all your build archives, open the Xcode organizer window. You will see your application archived under the Archived Applications section on the left in the navigator.

Figure 23.8 (from Apple's documentation on this process) shows what this screen looks like.

FIGURE 23.8
Apple documentation—submitting apps with Xcode.

Three very important buttons appear when you select an application archive:

- ▶ **Validate**—This will perform some static analysis on your code and make sure that all the things your application bundle needs are included. Many developers make a habit of validating application archives before submitting because the feedback can save a lot of time correcting rejections later.

- ▶ **Share**—If you want other people to beta test your application before you submit it to the App Store, the Share button will enable this.

- ▶ **Submit**—Submits your application to the App Store. It will ask you for a signing identity, where you will need to pick the one that starts with "3rd Party Mac Developer Installer" (you need to have created, downloaded, and installed an installer certificate).

With your application defined, configured, and properly described in iTunes Connect, your contracts signed (assuming your app isn't free), and the application bundle successfully uploaded, your app should be available in the store shortly.

> As always, anything can happen. Many developers, even though they are Cocoa experts, have had iOS and Mac OS X applications rejected upon initial submission for various reasons. Plan for an iterative process where you may need to correct issues with your application and resubmit before it is finally accepted.

Watch Out!

Summary

This hour covered a lot of information about the process of submitting applications to the Mac App Store. We covered everything from the application review guidelines to the *Human Interface Guidelines* to code signing and, finally, the submission of the application code itself.

Throughout this book, many hours have involved a step-by-step walkthrough of building a sample application. There is no step-by-step walkthrough available for submitting an application to the App Store, and for legal (among other) reasons, we can't create artificial applications just to see what the process looks like.

As a result, this hour provided you with the information you need to get started and provided links to detailed documentation on Apple's website. Although it might take you less than an hour to submit your application to iTunes Connect, it will probably take you far more than that to read through the documentation and guidelines.

Being prepared and knowledgeable about the submission process will help you in the long run by making your submission process quicker, and you will have to deal with fewer rejections.

The Mac App Store is a huge opportunity for developers to increase exposure and sell their applications for profit. Developers should not try to rush through the submission process, because getting it done right is crucial to your application's acceptance and ability to make money.

Q&A

Q. *Does it cost money to submit apps to the Mac App Store?*

A. Yes, you must be a paid member of the Mac Developer Program, which costs $99/year, in order to submit applications to the Mac App Store. You must pay an additional $99/year in order to submit applications to the iOS App Store; you cannot re-use one paid membership for both platforms.

Q. *What is it that ensures nobody can submit Apps pretending to be me or my company?*

A. Certificates. Certificates are basically a file on disk that stores a public/private key pair. Your code is signed with your private key and verified by Apple with your public key. Mac App Store security prevents someone from submitting an application who doesn't have your private key, ensuring that no one can pretend to be you or your company and submit bogus applications.

Q. *Do I need to be concerned with user experience when submitting to the App Store?*

A. Absolutely. Apple holds its developers to very high standards in terms of application reliability and user experience. You must read (and adhere to) Apple's Human Interface Guidelines if you want your application to pass the certification process.

HOUR 24

Supporting In-App Purchases

What you'll learn in this hour:

▶ Overview of In-App Purchasing for Mac OS X

▶ How to Create In-App Purchase Products in iTunes Connect

▶ Using StoreKit to Support In-App Purchasing

At the time this book was written, of the top 25 grossing applications in the iOS App Store, 14 of them were *free* applications that made all their money through In-App Purchases.

In-App Purchases allow your application to sell additional functionality, content, or features to your users. In this hour, we'll explore the steps necessary to get your application ready for In-App Purchasing and the code you need to write to facilitate In-App Purchases.

Introducing In-App Purchasing

In-App Purchases provide a way for your application to earn additional money from within the application. Your application can offer the following types of products:

▶ **Consumable**—A consumable purchase is something that can be purchased multiple times and is "consumed" each time it is purchased. You might use a consumable purchase for food for in-game creatures, to buy extra gold or weapons in a game, and so on.

▶ **Nonconsumable**—Nonconsumable purchases are purchased once and never again. These types of purchases are usually linked directly to unlockable content or functionality, such as upgrading to a "premium" version of the application or turning on a specific feature. Nonconsumable purchases carry over to all devices from which the user logs in with the same iTunes account.

You can also create autorenewing purchases, which let you offer things like subscription-based content directly within your application. Be sure that you read the In-App Purchases guidelines because you cannot use these purchases to sell *real* products. You can use In-App Purchases *only* to unlock features, functionality, or content within the application.

Each In-App Purchase is assigned a unique product ID that your code uses to refer to the product when the user completes a purchase. You also supply names and descriptions *in a localized manner* so that the products you offer can appear in English or whatever other languages your application supports.

For this reason, you should *always* use the StoreKit APIs (discussed later in this hour) to retrieve product information based on product IDs rather than hard-coding the product titles and descriptions into your application.

Creating In-App Purchase Products in iTunes Connect

The process of going from an empty starting point to having a product catalog of In-App Purchases configured in iTunes Connect can be daunting, confusing, and can even involve lengthy waits while Apple's website propagates your data to the sandbox environments.

Although this process might get frustrating at times, it is well worth the effort. As mentioned at the beginning of this hour, there is a great deal of money to be made from In-App Purchases, and ignoring their potential could cost you a lot of potential revenue.

Setting Up Contract, Tax, and Bank Information

Although it is possible to go all the way through to the process of submitting and publishing free applications in either the iOS or the Mac App Store without providing any financial information, you *must* provide this financial information for your application to support In-App Purchases.

By their very definition, In-App Purchases require the user to spend money. As such, you can't support them without giving Apple the information it needs. Apple will require you to agree (don't worry, you can do it electronically) to a contract for paid applications.

After you've accepted the terms of the agreement, you can supply the details for your bank, including the routing number, account number, and branch address information. You'll also need to fill out a W-9 tax form because the IRS considers any money you earn from App Store purchases taxable income. This situation gets even more interesting if you do not live in the United States.

To agree to contracts, define legal entity contacts, and set up tax and financial information, you need to log in to iTunes Connect and click the Contracts, Tax, and Banking link.

Until you have accepted all the current agreements and provided bank and tax information, you won't be able to fully support In-App Purchases in your applications, even while testing in your development environment.

Creating Test User Accounts

In-App Purchases involve a financial transaction between the user of your application and Apple. Eventually you will get money, but the basic unit of work for In-App Purchases is a financial transaction between your user and Apple.

This transaction typically requires a person with a credit card. To test your In-App Purchases and not go broke spending money every time you need to perform a test transaction, iTunes Connect gives you the ability to create test users.

Not only is this ability good for keeping you from going broke, but the use of iTunes Connect test users is *mandatory* for development. Applications signed with developer certificates will use a *sandbox* environment for In-App Purchases and App Store receipts. As such, purchases against this sandbox must be done with iTunes Connect test users.

To create test users, log in to iTunes Connect and click the Manage Users link. You will be prompted to choose between managing iTunes Connect users or Test Users, as shown in Figure 24.1.

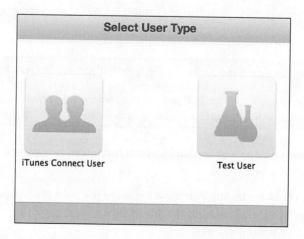

Select User Type

iTunes Connect User

Test User

FIGURE 24.1
Choosing users to manage in iTunes Connect.

Select Test User and you will go to a screen titled Manage Test Users. Click the Add New User button at the top-left corner of the page and follow the directions and fill in the prompts to create a new test user.

The email address associated with the Mac Developer account you used when you were logged in to iTunes Connect will receive an email verification request. You'll need to follow through the verification process for this test user (although you can stop without supplying credit card information).

Figure 24.2 shows what this screen looks like after having created a single test user.

FIGURE 24.2
Managing test users in iTunes Connect.

After you've created your test users, you can move on to creating a catalog of In-App Purchase products.

Configuring a Product Catalog

Before you can configure your product catalog, you need to have a product. For this, you need to create an application in the App Store using the information provided in the previous hour coupled with Apple's copious documentation on the subject.

The product need not be published and available for download, but the metadata *and application binary* must be in iTunes Connect for you to manage your IAP products.

By the Way

> If you have a fully configured product but you do not see the Manage In-App Purchases button on the right, make sure that you have agreed to the latest version of all the contracts in iTunes Connect. This, among other missing metadata, is often a cause for In-App Purchases being unavailable for a given app.

Figure 24.3 shows an application that has been configured to the point where it can have a product catalog defined.

If you click the Manage In-App Purchases button to the right of an application, you will see a page that looks similar to the one in Figure 24.4.

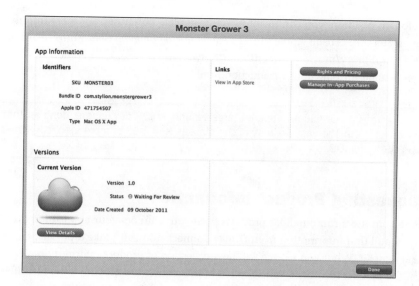

FIGURE 24.3
An App Store application, awaiting review.

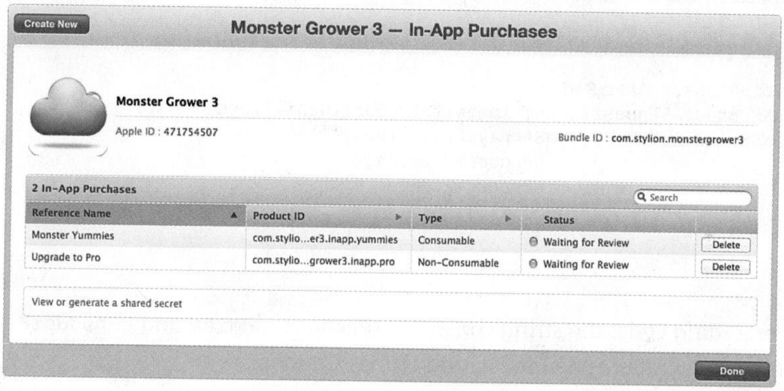

FIGURE 24.4
In-App Purchase product catalog.

From this page you can add, remove, and edit individual products. These products can be consumable or nonconsumable. You provide languages for these products, and for each language, you provide a title and description. This localized metadata is what the users will see when purchasing your products, depending on the language configuration of their Mac at the time of purchase.

Using StoreKit to Support In-App Purchases

StoreKit is a collection of classes and API methods that give your application the ability to interact with iTunes Connect product catalogs. Using StoreKit, your application can query pricing, availability, and localized metadata from the product

catalog. In addition, you can facilitate and complete purchases. For more information on StoreKit, consult Apple's *In-App Purchase Programming Guide*, http://developer.
apple.com/library/mac/#documentation/NetworkingInternet/Conceptual/
StoreKitGuide/Introduction/Introduction.html

Did You Know?

> Although this guide initially appears targeted only at iOS developers, don't let that discourage you. The vast majority of the classes and methods are identical across Mac OS X and iOS.

Requesting Product Information

Before your users can purchase products from your catalog, your application must be able to pull that information from iTunes Connect. You can make a product request using StoreKit. What you receive will be a collection of product information objects or, if the product identifiers you supplied to the request are invalid, those identifiers will appear in an `invalidProductIdentifiers` property of the response.

To make a product request, you use code similar to the following:

```
SKProductsRequest *request =
    [[SKProductsRequestalloc] initWithProductIdentifiers:
     [NSSetsetWithArray:[NSArrayarrayWithObjects:
                         kProductYummies,
                         kProductPremium,
                         nil]]];
request.delegate = self;
[request start];
```

In the preceding code, the string constants `kProductYummies` and `kProductPremium` represent product IDs as defined within iTunes Connect.

The delegate class (in the preceding code, `self`) needs to implement the `SKProductsRequestDelegate` protocol. This protocol defines methods for handling the responses that come from the store.

A delegate method for handling the product request response might look something like this:

```
- (void)productsRequest:(SKProductsRequest *)request
     didReceiveResponse:(SKProductsResponse *)response
{
    NSLog(@"got product request response: %@", response);
    NSLog(@"products: %@ %ld", response.products, [response.productscount]);
    for (SKProduct *prod in response.products) {
        [_productssetValue:prod forKey:prod.productIdentifier];
        NSLog(@"products:%@ %@", prod.localizedTitle, prod.price);
    }
    NSLog(@"invalid IDs: %@", response.invalidProductIdentifiers);
}
```

The response contains an array of SKProduct objects. These objects contain properties like localizedTitle and localizedDescription as well as a property containing the product's price.

In the preceding code, I'm adding the SKProduct objects to an NSMutableDictionary where the key is the product identifier. This makes the SKProduct objects easy to fetch later in case the user wants to make a purchase (we'll need the SKProductreference to make a purchase).

Purchasing Products

Now that your application has references to the products in your iTunes Connect product catalog, you can facilitate purchases. Before you start a purchase, your application needs to designate an observer for when changes are made to the StoreKit payment queue. This queue changes when transactions are added because of user action in your application or when transactions are restored from purchases made on other devices.

A purchase transaction is started by your application and then, when a transaction is added to the payment queue with a transaction state of SKPaymentTransactionStatePurchased, it is your application's responsibility to complete the transaction by calling finishTransaction: on the payment queue.

To get started, you can add your application delegate as an observer in the applicationDidFinishLaunching: method:

```
- (void)applicationDidFinishLaunching:(NSNotification *)aNotification
{
    // Insert code here to initialize your application
    if (![SKPaymentQueuecanMakePayments]) {
        NSLog(
@"Store isn't available for this user... disable in-app purchases!");
    }
    [[SKPaymentQueuedefaultQueue] addTransactionObserver:self];
}
```

Payment transaction observer classes must implement the SKPaymentTransactionObserver protocol. It is completely up to you how your application provides a UI that enables product purchases, but you will need to use StoreKit to give the user the ability to complete a purchase:

```
- (IBAction)buyYummies:(id)sender {
    if ([SKPaymentQueuecanMakePayments]) {
        SKProduct *yummiesProduct = [_productsvalueForKey:kProductYummies];
        SKPayment *payment = [SKPaymentpaymentWithProduct:yummiesProduct];
        [[SKPaymentQueuedefaultQueue] addPayment:payment];
    }
}
```

At this point, the user will be prompted to log in to the iTunes Store. In the case of a developer-signed application, you will be prompted to sign in to the sandbox version, as shown in Figure 24.5.

FIGURE 24.5
Signing in to the
iTunes Store
sandbox.

Assuming you have created an iTunes Connect Test User, you should be able to log in with that account and complete the purchase (you'll see how to test this in the next section).

Figure 24.6 shows the Mac App Store prompt for an In-App Purchase. This user interface is completely supplied by Apple and uses the localized strings for product title and description. Note that the dialog box clearly indicates that you are working against the sandbox.

FIGURE 24.6
Mac App Store
In-App Purchase
prompt.

When the user completes an In-App Purchase, your application will be notified via the SKPaymentTransactionObserver protocol and can implement the following method to react to this new purchase:

```
- (void)paymentQueue:(SKPaymentQueue *)queue
updatedTransactions:(NSArray *)transactions {

    for (SKPaymentTransaction *transaction in transactions)
    {
        switch (transaction.transactionState)
        {
            caseSKPaymentTransactionStatePurchased:
                [selfcompleteTransaction:transaction];
                break;
            caseSKPaymentTransactionStateFailed:
                [selffailedTransaction:transaction];
```

```
            break;
        caseSKPaymentTransactionStateRestored:
            [selfrestoreTransaction:transaction];
        default:
            break;
        }
    }
}
```

The code for the `completeTransaction:` method is as follows:

```
- (void) completeTransaction: (SKPaymentTransaction *)transaction
{
    [selfrecordTransaction: transaction];
    [selfprovideContent: transaction.payment.productIdentifier];
    // Remove the transaction from the payment queue.
    [[SKPaymentQueuedefaultQueue] finishTransaction: transaction];
}
```

The `recordTransaction:` method is a placeholder method we can use to allow our application to record that a purchase took place, potentially unlocking functionality or features in the UI.

The `provideContent:` method, also written by us, gives us a chance to display information to the user indicating that we have received an acknowledgement from the App Store that a purchase took place, as shown in Figure 24.7.

FIGURE 24.7
Displaying content to indicate a completed purchase.

The `finishTransaction:` method on the payment queue is *mandatory*. If your application does not call this method, the transaction will continue to reappear in the queue until you do, and the Mac App Store will not consider the transaction complete.

Testing the Application Installation

Before you can test the features and functionality of StoreKit and In-App Purchases, you will need to test the application installation. This is because your application needs a valid receipt before your users can make purchases, and your application *cannot* get a valid receipt unless it is running in a context as if it was a legitimately installed App Store package.

Before you test the application installation, you need to make sure that you are using a developer code signing identity associated with a valid provisioning profile.

Thankfully, we can install applications locally without going through the App Store in order to test them. The first thing we need to do is build the application for archiving. To do this, open your project in Xcode and select Product and then Build for Archiving. Then select Product, Archive. This will produce a product archive that you can see inside the Xcode Organizer window.

Open the Xcode Organizer window and select the archive you just created. Click the Share button and choose Mac OS X App Store package. Save the resulting file in an easily accessible location, such as your desktop.

Watch Out!

> This process will create a .pkg installer package. No matter how tempting it may be, do *not* double-click this package. You must install this package using the command-line tool mentioned in this hour, not the standard installer.

Now you will need to clean your application by selecting Product, Clean. This will remove the compiled binaries and bundles for your application from the disk. This step is *absolutely necessary* for the command-line application installer to work properly.

With a clean application project (nothing compiled on disk) and the installer package in an easy-to-access location, enter the following command at a Terminal prompt:

```
sudo installer -store -pkg (path to pkg including filename) -target /
```

You will see output that looks similar to the following text:

```
installer: monstergrowerpackage.pkg has valid signature for submission:
 3rd Party Mac Developer Installer: Kevin Hoffman
installer: Installation Check: Passed
installer: Volume Check: Passed
installer: Bundle com.stylion.monstergrower3 will be installed
➥to /Applications/monstergrower.app
installer: Starting install
installer: Install 0.0% complete
```

```
installer: Install 10.9% complete
installer: Install 100.0% complete
installer: Finished install
```

At this point, your application will appear in Launchpad, and you can click it to launch it. Because it was signed with a developer certificate, an App Store Receipt will be added to your application bundle, validating the application and enabling In-App Purchases.

You should now be able to test In-App Purchases in your application using your iTunes Connect Test Users to buy consumable and nonconsumable products.

Validating Product Receipts

As mentioned previously, your application will be granted a receipt when you are running it with a developer certificate and installed locally. To make sure that your application isn't easily pirated, your application should certify the presence and validity of that receipt.

The first step is to make sure your application has a receipt. If it does not, you need to exit the application with a specific exit code (173). This exit code value indicates to the operating system that there was a problem validating the application's receipt.

To check for the presence of the receipt, you can use the following code:

```
- (void)applicationWillFinishLaunching:(NSNotification *)notification
{
    NSURL *receiptUrl = [[NSBundlemainBundle] appStoreReceiptURL];
    if (![[NSFileManagerdefaultManager] fileExistsAtPath:[receiptUrl path]])
    {
        NSLog(@"did not have an app store receipt, exiting w/code 173.");
        exit(173);
    }
}
```

This checks only for the *presence* of the application receipt, not whether the receipt is legitimate.

By the Way

Note that this code will prevent your application from executing in standard Xcode debug mode. Applications running under Xcode are not granted receipts, ever. You will need to comment out or conditionally define that code while you are testing to allow the application to start normally. Alternatively, you can attach to an existing process (an installed App) to debug it with the receipt environment intact.

Early in the first days of the Mac App Store, many applications were released without checking for the legitimacy of the receipt. As a result, pirates were able to replace the receipt from a free application with the receipt in paid applications' bundles and enabled them to be shared without the intervention of the App Store.

Validating the legitimacy of the receipt granted by the Mac App Store is a complex and lengthy topic, involving the manipulation of encrypted files and low-level C code. This topic is outside the scope of this hour, but when you are ready, you can research this topic at the following URL: https://developer.apple.com/library/mac/#releasenotes/General/ValidateAppStoreReceipt/_index.html.

When you do look up the procedure for validating receipts, make sure you are not reading the iOS documentation. Although the StoreKit APIs are nearly identical between platforms, the method by which those platforms store and validate receipts are different.

Summary

In this hour, you saw the culmination of the skills and techniques that you have been learning throughout the book. With the fundamentals of application development under your belt, and with the knowledge of how to create and upload an application to the Mac App Store, this hour covered one of the most profitable aspects of the App Store: In-App Purchases.

We discussed how to use iTunes Connect to create a product catalog and expose that catalog to your applications via StoreKit. With that product catalog exposed, we discussed how to start and finish payment transactions and use that information to dynamically enable on-demand, purchased content or features.

Q&A

Q. *What can you sell within the In-App Purchase system?*

A. You are allowed to sell additional functionality, features, or virtual in-application items. You cannot sell actual physical goods, nor can you sell things like audio tracks (unless the audio accompanies a purchased feature, etc.). A good rule of thumb is this: If an In-App purchase only changes the way in which your application behaves or what it displays, then you should be OK.

Q. *How do you configure In-App Purchases?*

A. In-App Purchase items are configured through iTunes Connect. You will first have to create a new application within iTunes Connect in order to support these purchases. Additionally, In-App Purchase menu items will NOT appear unless all of your contracts, tax, and financial information is up to date.

Q. *How can you be certain that a user has purchased something via In-App Purchases in the past?*

A. Your application must validate receipts. It is a tedious development task, but validating receipts is the only way in which your app can be sure that a user has purchased the application and has legitimately purchased the In-App items they claim.

Index

336

events

How can we make this index more useful? Email us at indexes@samspublishing.com

Sams Teach Yourself

When you only have time
for the answers™

Whatever your need and whatever your time frame, there's a Sams **Teach Yourself** book for you. With a Sams **Teach Yourself** book as your guide, you can quickly get up to speed on just about any new product or technology—in the absolute shortest period of time possible. Guaranteed.

Learning how to do new things with your computer shouldn't be tedious or time-consuming. Sams **Teach Yourself** makes learning anything quick, easy, and even a little bit fun.

iOS 5 Application Development in 24 Hours

John Ray
ISBN-13: 978-0-672-33576-1

Java in 24 Hours

Rogers Cadenhead

ISBN-13: 978-0-672-33575-4

Android Application Development in 24 Hours

Lauren Darcey
Shane Conder

ISBN-13: 978-0-672-33569-3

HTML, CSS, and JavaScript All in One

Julie C. Meloni

ISBN-13: 978-0-672-33332-3

Windows Phone 7 Game Programming in 24 Hours

Jonathan Harbour

ISBN-13: 978-0-672-33554-9

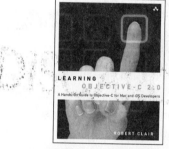

**FREE
Online Edition**

Safari
Books Online

Your purchase of *Sams Teach Yourself Mac OS® X Lion™ App Development in
24 Hours* includes access to a free online edition for 45 days through the **Safari Books
Online** subscription service. Nearly every Sams book is available online through **Safari
Books Online**, along with thousands of books and videos from publishers such as Addison-
Wesley Professional, Cisco Press, Exam Cram, IBM Press, O'Reilly Media, Prentice Hall, Que,
and VMware Press.

Safari Books Online is a digital library providing searchable, on-demand access to
thousands of technology, digital media, and professional development books and videos from
leading publishers. With one monthly or yearly subscription price, you get unlimited access to
learning tools and information on topics including mobile app and software development, tips
and tricks on using your favorite gadgets, networking, project management, graphic design, and
much more.

Activate your FREE Online Edition at
informit.com/safarifree

STEP 1:   Enter the coupon code: ZAXGHFH.

STEP 2:   New Safari users, complete the brief registration form.
Safari subscribers, just log in.

If you have difficulty registering on Safari or accessing the online edition,
please e-mail customer-service@safaribooksonline.com